Town and country
in England:
frameworks for
archaeological research

Cirencester College, GL7 1XA
Telephone: 01285 640994

Town and country in England: frameworks for archaeological research

DOMINIC PERRING

with contributions by
MARK WHYMAN,
FRANCES CONDRON,
JONATHAN FINCH,
AND REBECCA ROSEFF

CBA RESEARCH REPORT 134
COUNCIL FOR BRITISH ARCHAEOLOGY 2002

First published in 2002 by The Council for British Archaeology
Bowes Morrell House, 111 Walmgate, York, YO1 9WA

Copyright © 2002 Authors and Council For British Archæology

British Library Cataloguing in Publication Data
A catalogue for this book is available from the British Library

ISBN 1-902771-32-X

The CBA acknowledges with gratitiude a grant from English Heritage
towards the publication of this volume

Cover and text designed in Monotype Sabon
by Geoff Green Book Design, Cambridge
Printed by Pennine Printing Services Ltd, Ripponden, West Yorkshire

Front cover: St Augustine reading the City of God,
Dutch miniature of 1445, Albert Ier, MS 9015, folio 1.
(Royal Library of Belgium, Brussels)

Contents

List of figures

List of tables

Acknowledgements

The research summarised here was conducted by the principal authors of this report (Condron, Perring, Roseff, and Whyman) and funded by English Heritage.

The research team was supported by an advisory group that included Martin Carver, David Mattingly, Deirdre O'Sullivan, Henry Owen-John, James Rackham, Steve Roskams, Chris Scull, and Tim Williams. All involved read and commented on a series of position papers from which this report has been assembled. David Mattingly, Chris Scull and Deirdre O'Sullivan made very extensive contributions to the papers brought together here in chapter 2, whilst James Rackham's contribution to chapter 3 was equally substantial. Martin Carver and Steve Roskams gave important impetus to the definition of objectives and their contribution is particularly evident in the introduction and conclusions. We are particularly grateful to Tim Williams and Chris Scull of English Heritage for their support and enthusiasm for the project.

A series of project seminars extended the research range of the project team, and papers were presented by Derek Keene, Christopher Dyer, David Hill, John Newman, Henrik Thrane, Dan Carlsson, Ian Douglas, and Herbert Girardet. We are also grateful to Neil Christie, Julian Richards, and Tania Dickinson for their contributions to project meetings and seminars.

We are also indebted to the many people who contributed ideas and information about specific aspects of the study. In particular we would like to thank Umberto Albarella, Nat Alcock, Steve Atkinson, Richard Brickstock, Don Brothwell, David Buckley, Bob Carr, John Creighton, John Davies, Gerald Dawe, Keith Dobney, Chris Dyer, Myk Flitcroft, Helen Geake, Kate Giles, Jeremy Goldberg, Damian Goodburn, Frank Green, James Greig, Jane Grenville, Peter Guest, Richard Havis, Gill Hey, Mike Hodder, Della Hooke, David Hopkins, John Hunt, Tom James, Evan Johns, Sarah Rees Jones, Emma Jones, Keith Lilley, Chris Loveluck, Helen MacLagan, Hilary Major, John Maloney, Edward Martin, Maria Medlycott, Maureen Mellor, Peter Murphy, Lisa Moffett, John Newman, Clive Orton, Nick Palmer, Martin Pitts, Judith Plouviez, Dominic Powlesland, Ken Qualman, Stephanie Rátkai, Richard Reece, Helen Rees, Felicity Riddy, Ben Robinson, Andrew Rogerson, Mark Samuels, John Schofield, Graham Scobie, Paul Sealey, David Shotter, Jane Siddell, David Stocker, Jennie Stopford, Susanna Stymne, Alan Vince, Keith Wade, and Stuart Wrathmell. The help offered by many County and District Archaeologists and Sites and Monuments Records Officers, in providing information and comment on England's archaeological landscapes, is also gratefully acknowledged.

Terry O'Connor and Martin Millett read the first draft of the text and suggested a series of important improvements. These influenced the final editing of the report for publication (by Dominic Perring), at which point Jon Finch kindly stepped in to prepare chapter 4.5 (based in part on a draft by Rebecca Roseff).

Notwithstanding such extensive and generous help from so many sources the views expressed remain those of the authors alone, who take full responsibility for any errors of omission or commission that may be found here.

Summary

This report describes the results of a research project, the Urban Hinterlands Project, undertaken at the Universities of York and Leicester in 1997–8.

Archaeologists have long been interested in the study of urbanism, and in particular in the genesis, function, and morphology of ancient and medieval towns. It has also long been argued that one particular aspect of this research, the study of the relationship between town and country, needs more detailed attention. It has, however, been difficult to establish useful and affordable programmes of study within this field. This is in part because of the complexity of the subject and the intractability of some of the archaeological sources. The Urban Hinterlands Project was established to see how best such problems might be overcome.

In describing the results of this research exercise our first purpose is to draw attention to ways in which archaeology might contribute to the study of the dialogue between town and country in England. This report therefore proposes research directions and explains how archaeological data can be structured to facilitate future work. It is primarily aimed at the archaeological profession, and in particular at those involved in preparing and implementing programmes of investigation. It is also structured to inform scholars in cognate fields who wish to know what archaeological research in this area of study has achieved and where it is heading. The description of how archaeological finds are used to support research should also be useful to students with an advanced interest in the interpretation of such materials.

The introduction, chapter 1, describes why the report was written, introduces some of the research themes that lie at the heart of the study, and explains how the site specific nature of much archaeological fieldwork has made it difficult to study the settlement landscapes within which towns were located. The subject of study is defined as the urban process rather than the urban artefact. The report is consequently concerned with the networks of social and economic relationships that sustained, and were sustained by, complex hierarchies of settlement. It is argued that towns were born as architectural and social impositions, inscribed onto pre-urban landscapes to serve the interests of people in power. As such they served as but one locus for the exercise of authority within vastly more complicated landscapes. The report argues that these networks of relationships are best represented in the archaeological record by patterns of consumption and discard, as witnessed by artefacts and ecofacts. Pottery and animal bone are often the most useful. This emphasis on the material record places the study of urban strategies firmly in the context of the non-urban alternatives.

After briefly looking at some problems of definition, chapter 2 reviews theoretical models and recent studies in order to inform a research agenda. The focus of attention is on periods and regions where systems changed: from the late pre-Roman Iron Age down to the later medieval period. The object is to better describe and understand such change through the archaeological evidence. Here we consider how the development of settlement hierarchies can be understood in the context of changing socio-economic strategies. The main phases of urban development are separately discussed. These include Iron Age *oppida*, early Roman colonies, Romano-British *civitas* capitals, late antique cities, early medieval *emporia*, Saxon *burhs*, and medieval market towns. The conclusions are summarised as a series of research questions that can be used in the construction of future programmes of research.

Chapter 3 describes the characteristics of those archaeological assemblages that deserve closest study. This chapter reviews methodological developments in the study of the main classes of archaeological find, and suggests ways in which samples can be improved. Our more important conclusions about the ways in which archaeological finds testify to changes in how surplus was produced, redistributed, and consumed are illustrated in a series of tables. These describe the 'life cycles' involved in the production, utilisation and discard of animal bone, botanical remains, pottery, coin, and human bone.

A series of case studies are proposed in chapter 4. These illustrate ways in which the ideas described in the earlier chapters might be explored through further applied research. An exploration of contrasting social and economic strategies adopted in response to late Iron Age and early Roman urbanisation in the Colchester area (chapter 4.2) is followed by a survey of how closer studies of coin-use in late Roman Britain might illuminate our understanding of the role of such towns in regional patterns of exchange (chapter 4.3). The early medieval settlement hierarchy is the subject of a further study, and explores the role of *emporia* (*wics*), using *Hamwic* and Ipswich as examples. The contrast between nucleated and dispersed areas of settlement in the medieval period, and the ways in which this might relate to domestic arrangements and urban change are considered in the context of Warwickshire and Norfolk. The final case study considers the environmental and ecological impact of London in the context of studies of urban sustainability.

A concluding chapter (chapter 5) summarises the recommendations that emerge from this review, with reference to the management of the resource, experimental methodology, and future directions of research.

Zusammenfassung

Diese Abhandlung beschreibt die Ergebnisse eines Forschungsprojekts, das „Städtische Umland Projekt", dass von den Universitäten York und Leicester in den Jahren 1997 bis 1998 durchgeführt wurde. Archäologen haben seit langem ein besonderes Interesse an dem Prozess der Verstädterung, insbesondere die Entstehung, Funktion und Morphologie von altertümlichen und mittelalterlichen Städten. Ein besonderer Aspekt dieser Forschung, nämlich die Frage der Beziehung zwischen Stadt und Land, steht schon lange in der Diskussion und soll deshalb genauer untersucht werden. Es hat sich allerdings als schwierig erwiesen in diesem Bereich sowohl nützliche als auch erschwingliche Studienprogramme zu entwerfen. Das hängt zum Teil mit der Komplexität des Forschungsthemas zusammen, aber auch mit der schweren Zugänglichkeit des Beweismaterials aus archäologischen Quellen. Ein Hauptziel des „Städtischen Umland Projekts" war es Lösungen zu dieser Problembewältigung aufzuzeigen.

Bei der Beschreibung dieser Forschungsresultate ist unserer Hauptzweck darauf hinzuweisen wie die Archäologie zu der Untersuchung der Wechselbeziehung von Stadt und Land in England beitragen kann. Somit werden in diesem Bericht zukünftige Forschungsrichtungen vorgeschlagen und es wird erklärt wie archäologische Daten so strukturiert werden können, damit zukünftige Forschungsprojekte ermöglicht werden können. Dieser Bericht wendet sich vor allem an Berufsarchäologen, besonders solche, die an der Vorbereitung und Durchführung von Forschungsprogrammen aktiv beteiligt sind. Es sollen damit gezielt Wissenschaftler verwandter Bereiche informiert werden, die wissen möchten was die archäologische Forschung bisher erreicht hat, und wohin die Zukunft führt. Eine Beschreibung der Art wie archäologische Funde die Forschung unterstützen, soll auch Studenten die ein fortgeschrittenes Interesse an der Interpretation solcher Materialien haben, helfen.

In der Einleitung (1. Kapitel) wird der Zweck dieser Abhandlung erläutert, es werden zentrale Forschungsthemen vorgestellt, und es wird verständlich gemacht, weshalb das Wesen der archäologischen Geländearbeit es schwierig macht, die Siedlungslandschaft in denen die Städte gegründet wurden, zu verstehen. Das Studienthema wird vor allem als Urbanisierungsprozess definiert, die Stadt wird also nicht als Artefakt gesehen. Dieser Bericht beschäftigt sich daher in erster Linie mit dem Netzwerk der sozialen und ökonomischen Beziehungen, welche die vielschichtigen Hierarchien unterstützten und unterstützt wurden. Es wird argumentiert, das Städte als architektonische und soziale Auferlegung entstanden, und in der prä-urbanen Landschaft gegründet worden sind, um den Interessen der Führungsklasse zu dienen. Somit dienten sie als ein Lokus um Autorität im Rahmen einer weitaus komplizierteren Landschaft geltend zu machen. Es wird in diesem Bericht argumentiert, dass diese Netzwerke von Beziehungen in archäologischen Datensätzen als Verteilungsmuster von Konsum und Abfall überliefert werden, also durch Artefakte und ökofakte. Tongefässe und Tierknochen sind für solche Studien am besten geeignet.

Im 2. Kapitel werden einige Definitionsprobleme diskutiert, danach werden im 2. Kapitel theoretische Modelle und aktuelle Studien besprochen, um über Forschungsziele zu informieren. Der Schwerpunkt liegt bei Zeitabschnitten und Regionen in denen Systemveränderungen stattfanden: die Zeit von der späten prä-römischen Eisenzeit bis zum späten Mittelalter. Es ist hier beabsichtigt die Veränderungen durch archäologische Beweismaterialien zu beschreiben und zu verstehen. Hier wird erwogen wie die Entwicklung von Siedlungshierarchien im Zusammenhang mit sich verändernden sozio-ökonomischen Strategien verstanden werden kann. Die Hauptphasen der Verstädterung werden separat diskutiert, anhand von oppida aus der Eisenzeit, frühen römischen Siedlungen und Romano-Britischen civitas Hauptstädte, spätantiken Städte, frühmittelalterlichen emporia, sächsischen burhs, und mittelalterlichen Marktstädtchen. Als Abschluss werden eine Reihe von Forschungsfragen zusammengefasst, die der Gestaltung von zukünftigen Forschungsprogrammen zugute kommen können.

Im 3. Kapitel werden die charakteristischen Merkmale von archäologischen Funden, die eine detailliertere Untersuchung verdienen, beschrieben. Dieses Kapitel bespricht die Entwicklung von Studienmethoden die für die Hauptkategorien von archäologischen Fundstücken angewandt werden, und es werden Vorschläge zur Verbesserung von Stichprobenentnahmen gemacht. Unsere wichtigsten Schlussfolgerungen über die Art wie archäologische Funde Entwicklungen in der Produktion von überschuss, dessen Umverteilung und Konsum widerspiegeln, werden in einer Reihe von Tabellen veranschaulicht. Sie beschreiben den Lebenszyklus von Tierknochen, botanischen überresten, Tongefässen, Münzen, und menschlichen Knochenüberresten, von der Produktion und Nutzung bis zu deren Entsorgung.

Im 4. Kapitel werden eine Reihe von Fallstudien vorgestellt. Hier wird veranschaulicht wie die Konzepte, die in den vorhergehenden Kapiteln erläutert wurden, anhand von angewandter Forschung weiter entwickelt werden können. Eine Fallstudie aus dem Umland von Colchester (Kapitel 4.2) untersucht die diversen sozialen und ökonomischen Strategien die im Zuge der Verstädterung während in der späten Eisenzeit und frühen Römerzeit übernommen wurden. Eine detaillierte Studie des Gebrauchs von Münzen im Spätrömischen Britannien (Kapitel 4.3) kann unser Verständnis über die Rolle von Städten in der regionalen Handelsstruktur erläutern. Eine weitere Studie widmet sich der Siedlungshierarchie im frühen Mittelalter und untersucht die Rolle von emporia (wics) anhand von Beispielen aus Hamwic und Ipswich. Der Kontrast zwischen mittelalterlichen Haufendörfern und offenen Siedlungsformen und deren Verhältnis zu häuslicher Gliederung und urbanen Veränderungen wird Anhand von Beispielen aus Warwickshire und Norfolk besprochen. Die letzte Fallstudie behandelt die ökologischen Auswirkungen der Stadt London im Zusammenhang mit Studien die sich mit der Städteerhaltung beschäftigen.

Das Schlusskapitel (5. Kapitel) fasst die Empfehlungen zusammen, die sich aus diesem überblick herausgebildet haben, besonders was Denkmalpflege, Methoden zur experimentellen Archäologie und zukünftige Forschungsrichtungen betrifft.

Résumé

La ville et la campagne en Angleterre: cadres pour la
recherche archéologique, de Dominic Perring

Ce rapport décrit les résultats d'un projet de
recherche, le Projet de l'arrière-pays urbain [Urban
Hinterlands Project]. entrepris aux universités de
York et de Leicester en 1997–8.

Cela fait longtemps que les archéologues s'intéressent à l'urbanisme, et tout particulièrement à la
genèse, la fonction et la morphologie des villes pré-
antiques à celles du moyen-âge. On a longtemps
soutenu qu'il faudrait étudier de plus près un aspect
particulier de cette recherche, l'étude des rapports
entre la ville et la campagne. Il a néanmoins été difficile de mettre en place des programmes d'étude
utiles et abordables dans ce domaine. C'est en partie
dû à la complexité du sujet et à la difficulté de cer-
taines sources archéologiques. Le Projet de l'arrière-
pays urbain a été établi pour découvrir la meilleure
manière de surmonter ce genre de problème.

En décrivant les résultats de cet exercice de
recherche, notre premier but est d'attirer l'attention
sur les manières dont l'archéologie pourrait con-
tribuer à l'étude du dialogue entre la ville et la campagne en Angleterre. Ce rapport propose donc des
directions de recherche et explique comment les
données archéologiques peuvent être structurées
pour faciliter le travail futur. Il cible principalement
les archéologues professionnels, et tout particulièrement les archéologues impliqués dans la préparation
et la mise en œuvre de programmes d'enquête. Il est
également construit de manière à informer les spé-
cialistes dans les domaines apparentés désireux de
connaître les résultats obtenus par la recherche
archéologique dans ce domaine d'étude ainsi que ses
orientations. La description de l'utilisation des
découvertes archéologiques pour soutenir la

recherche devrait également être utile aux étudiants
qui s'intéressent à l'interprétation de ce genre de
matériel.

L'introduction, chapitre 1, décrit les raisons de
l'écriture de ce rapport a été écrit, introduit certains
thèmes de la recherche qui se trouvent au cœur de
cette étude, et explique comment la nature 'spéci-
fique au site' d'une grande partie du travail
archéologique sur le terrain a rendu difficile l'étude
des paysages de peuplement dans lesquels se trou-
vaient les villes. Le sujet de l'étude est défini comme
le processus urbain plutôt que comme l'objet fab-
riqué urbain. Par conséquent, le rapport concerne
les réseaux de relations sociales et économiques qui
soutenaient, ou qui étaient soutenues par, les hiérarchies complexes de peuplement. On soutient que les
villes s'étaient développées en tant qu'impositions
architecturales et sociales, inscrites sur les paysages
pré-urbains, afin de servir les intérêts de ceux qui
étaient au pouvoir. En tant que telles, elles étaient
l'un des lieux d'exercice de l'autorité au sein de
paysages beaucoup plus compliqués. Le rapport
soutient que ces réseaux de relations sont mieux
représentés dans le document archéologique par les
modèles de consommation et de mise au rebut,
comme en témoignent les objets fabriqués et les
indices écologiques. La céramique et les ossements
d'animaux sont souvent les plus utiles. Cette
emphase sur le document matériel localise ferme-
ment l'étude des stratégies urbaines dans le contexte
des alternatives non urbaines.

Après avoir brièvement examiné certains prob-
lèmes de définition, le chapitre 2 met en revue des
modèles théoriques et des études récentes afin de
définir un programme de recherche. Ce chapitre se
concentre sur les périodes et les régions où les sys-

tèmes ont changé: de la fin de l'âge de fer pré-romain à la fin de la période médiévale. Il a pour but de mieux décrire et de mieux comprendre de tels changements à travers les indices archéologiques. Ici, nous considérons comment peut être compris le développement des hiérarchies d'habitation dans le contexte de l'évolution des stratégies socio-économiques. Les principales phases de développement urbain sont traitées séparément. Elles englobent les oppida de l'âge de fer, les premières colonies romaines, et les capitales civitas britanno-romains les cités anciennes les plus récentes, les premiers emporia médiévaux, les burhs saxons et les villes de marché médiévales. Les conclusions sont résumées sous la forme d'une série de questions de recherche, lesquelles peuvent être utilisées pour édifier de futurs programmes de recherche.

Le chapitre 3 décrit les caractéristiques des ensembles archéologiques qui méritent d'être étudiés de plus près. Le chapitre met en revue les développements méthodologiques dans l'étude des principales classes de découvertes archéologiques, et il suggère des manières d'améliorer les échantillons. Nos conclusions plus importantes sur les manières dont les découvertes archéologiques attestent des changements dans la production, la redistribution et la consommation du surplus sont illustrées dans une série de tableaux. Ceux-ci décrivent les 'cycles de vie' impliqués dans la production, l'utilisation et la mise au rebut d'ossements d'animaux, de restes botaniques, de céramique, de pièces de monnaie et d'ossements humains.

Le chapitre 4 propose une série d'études de cas. Elles illustrent les manières dont les idées décrites dans les chapitres précédents pourraient être explorées par le biais d'autres recherches appliquées. Une exploration des stratégies sociales et économiques très différentes adoptées dans la région de Colchester à la suite de l'urbanisation de la fin de l'âge de fer et du début de la période romaine (chapitre 4.2) est suivie d'une étude indiquant comment des études plus poussées de l'utilisation des pièces de monnaie à la fin de la période romaine pourrait nous aider à comprendre le rôle de telles villes dans les modèles d'échange régionaux (chapitre 4.3). La hiérarchie des premiers peuplements médiévaux fait l'objet d'une autre étude, et le rôle des emporia (wics) est exploré, en utilisant Hamwic et Ipswich comme exemples. Le contraste entre les zones nucléées et les zones dispersées de peuplement pendant la période médiévale, et les manières dont ceci pourrait être lié aux agencements ménagers et au changement urbain, sont considérés dans le contexte du Warwickshire et du Norfolk. La dernière étude de cas considère l'impact environnemental et écologique de Londres dans le contexte des études de pérennité urbaine.

Un chapitre en conclusion (chapitre 5) résume les recommandations qui émergent de ce bilan, et fait référence à la gestion des ressources, à la méthodologie expérimentale, et aux directions futures de la recherche.

CHAPTER ONE

Introduction

1.1 Town and country in England

p England's modern landscape is an urban one. Cities so thoroughly dominate contemporary life that it is hard to conceive of any part of the country that has not been touched by the urban process. This is as true of our institutions and social practices as it is of the environment that we inhabit; both country and countryside have been shaped against urban desires. Many characteristics of our urban identity are of comparatively recent origin, formed in the wake of industrial revolution and empire. Cities have, however, played a commanding role in the making of England for most of the past 2000 years. The longer-term history of the relationship between town and country is necessarily a complicated one and it can not be studied properly without the aid of archaeological sources.

The purpose of this report is to review the different ways in which these archaeological sources can contribute to the study of this important theme. Our aim is to focus attention on research directions open to archaeologists interested in the dialogue between city and country, and to highlight some of the ways in which archaeological data can be structured to facilitate future research. Although our main audience is a professional one, our ambitions are closely relevant to all those interested in the history of urban society.

Most towns were born as architectural and social impositions, inscribed onto pre-urban landscapes to serve the interests of people in power. But urbanisation has not been a one-way process, not simply a brute march of brick and mortar across the supine face of a ravaged countryside. Towns have thrived because they have served needs and aspirations. And once brought into being, urban communities have been swift to elaborate their own creative dynamic, in which new identities and new realities were forged. Such communities have usually prospered because of their ability to serve or accommodate the interests of an elite that also drew power from the countryside. The command of rural surplus has always been a critical component in the construction of social power. Towns therefore stand as but one locus for the exercise of authority within vastly more complicated landscapes.

Since power has been differently structured and articulated by different communities, so towns have been differently conceived through the ages (Castells 1977). The distinctions that can be drawn between towns, cities, and other nucleated settlements are not constant but a product of changing perceptions and legal distinctions. These perceptions and distinctions in turn reflect on the contrasting political and economic structures used to sustain social authority. We are consequently bedevilled by problems of definition when we try to describe such places. This is a major problem in a study such as this, where our interests range from Britain's pre-Roman *oppida* to the market towns of late medieval England, by way of Roman cities and Saxon *burhs*. These were very different kinds of communities, sustained by different values and ambitions, and no all-embracing terminology will be entirely satisfactory. As has often been observed, towns defy universal definition (Mumford 1961). In this situation the more neutral expression 'urban settlement' often serves archaeology better than the specifics of historic title. Indeed at some places in this report we are really concerned with 'central places' in general, rather than just the metropolitan centres. But the monotonous use of these clumsily correct indifferent terms would make for dull reading, and so we continue to refer to towns and cities where it seems more comfortable to do so.

In this report our subject is urbanism as a process and system, rather than the urban artefact. This is consequently a study of the networks of social and economic relationships that sustained, and were sustained by, complex hierarchies of settlement. It is our view (as elaborated further in chapter 2.1) that these networks of relationships are best represented in the archaeological record by the patterns of consumption and discard that are witnessed by finds (artefacts and ecofacts). Our emphasis on the material record, which is the principal product of archaeological excavation, places the study of urban strategies firmly in the context of the non-urban alternatives. By concentrating on the evidence of hierarchies of settlement, rather than first establishing sample parameters which exclude certain classes of site, it also becomes less important to establish a priori definitions of what is or is not a 'town' or 'city'.

1.2 Some general models of relationships between town and country

Most studies of the relationship between town and country have concentrated on the role played by urban central places in promoting, articulating, and mediating economic and social change. The contribution of archaeology to this subject is framed by a substantial history of research built on the work of historians, economists, geographers, and sociologists. These different fields of study have inspired a range of different approaches. This is not the place for a full review of such work, but a few general observations can be made by way of general introduction.

A critical theme has been the study of the contribution that urban communities may have made to the development of ancient, feudal, and capitalist economies (Childe 1956, see also chapter 2.3.1 below). Towns have often been credited with a crucial role in driving forward the pace of economic development, subordinating all else to their needs (as Braudel 1972, 278).

Following Pirenne (1925), medieval historians have engaged in a protracted debate about whether or not towns could be characterised as 'non-feudal islands in a feudal sea': places of comparative economic liberty amidst a world of tied social relations. The dichotomy is an exaggerated one, and recent scholarship has instead emphasised the ways in which urban populations and privileges were embedded within the feudal discourse (Abrams and Wrigley 1978; Hilton 1992). For some the main impetus for the development of capitalism should now be sought in the countryside (see below p 107), although few would deny that urban markets contributed significantly to the commercialisation of English society (see Britnell 1996). These are issues that we will return to in chapter 2.4.5.

Inspired largely by the arguments of Weber (1921), ancient historians have instead debated whether towns in antiquity contributed to economic growth or were essentially 'consumer cities', where profits from rural estates were used to support the social competition of a town-based elite society (see also chapter 2.4.2 below). The most complete and compelling description of the 'consumer city' argument remains that of Finley (1985). Several different models have subsequently been developed to show how the administrative and social functions of the Roman town also contributed to the urban dynamic (as surveyed by Whittaker 1990; 1995; Wallace-Hadrill 1991). Although some studies have been described in terms that challenge the 'consumer city' ideal type (eg Engels 1990, but see Whittaker 1995, 12–14), the main consequence of this work has been to demonstrate that the social circumstances described by Weber and Finley were not a bar to urban economic development. Terminological inexactitude over the scale and significance of economic growth has, however, complicated study (Saller 2001).

Towns certainly played an important role in tax administration, as points through which cash economies were sometimes structured, and as ports through which long-distance exchange and supply could be directed (Hopkins 1978; 1980). These activities witness the contribution that towns made to the economic affairs of empire, and promoted circumstances in which some urban economies developed beyond the bounds and needs of a territorial aristocracy. This does not, however, contradict the premise of a society in which civic power was buttressed by land ownership and sustained through urban display. Urban economies can therefore be seen as generally incidental, but far from irrelevant, to these relations of power built on the command of rural surplus.

This concern with the economic function of the ancient city can be criticised for projecting modern interests in the development of capitalism onto the past (as Laurence 1994, 133; Mattingly 1997a, 212). Cities were the outcome of social as well as economic forces and this has been the subject of growing attention in recent research (see also chapter 2.3.2). Sjoberg's (1960) exploration of the contribution made to urban trajectories by changes in the formation and organisation of social power has been influential. Recent work has consequently given increased emphasis to the city as a product of social surplus and to the complexity of the urban communities generated by the dynamics of urban power (eg Harvey 1988, 238–40).

A somewhat different tradition of academic research has focused on the genesis and morphology of settlement patterns and urban landscapes. Archaeologists have been much influenced by central place theory, building on the work of geographers and economists such as Christaller (1966) and von Thünen (Hall 1966). This has involved the mapping of settlement hierarchies and spheres of urban influence, although work in this field has been taken towards the limits of its usefulness (see Grant 1986). Rules have also been sought to explain the history of urban form, based on a range of spatial analysis (eg Carter 1972; Hillier and Hanson 1984; Morris 1979). These deterministic models have not been able to address the full complexity of the relationship between town and country and are somewhat peripheral to the interests of this survey (for similar conclusions reached in the field of urban sociology see Saunders 1986).

A further research topic that has generated a substantial literature is that of the ecological and environmental impact of urbanisation. The Chicago School of Urban Ecology pioneered work in this field and was responsible for generating a substantial body of empirical research, although the detailed modelling involved has proved difficult to adapt to the incomplete and biased sources usually obtained from archaeological investigation. These ideas have therefore had only a limited impact on archaeological research in England but will none the less be explored further below (see chapter 2.3.3).

Most studies that have progressed beyond empirical description have recognised, in one way or another, that 'urban histories are inseparable from the histories of the economic, social and political systems of which they are a part' (Hohenberg and Lees 1985, 2). This recognition that urban processes are historically contingent makes it difficult to define research questions aimed at the generality of the urban experience. In order, however, to set the rest of this report in context it is perhaps worth trying to summarise some broadly defined research themes that must influence our study, whilst recognising the limitations of any such exercise. Tentatively, therefore, we can suggest that the following questions remain central to the archaeological study of most urban landscapes:

- How and why did settlement hierarchies based around towns come into being and evolve?
- How were urban settlements fed and supplied and what impact did this have on economic and social development within surrounding territories?
- What contribution did urban settlements make to the development of market economies or to the reinforcement of socially embedded ones?
- How significant were such places as centres for the manufacture and distribution of goods and services, and how do they compare with non-urban alternatives?
- How important were urban settlements in mediating social change, and how influential was urban society in framing identities, fashions, and ideas?

These questions are essentially concerned with the different ways in which towns have contributed to the construction and replication of power, as fabricated from social and economic ties, mediated by ideologies, and expressed in identities. In chapter 2 we will look at how such generally framed questions might inform the analysis of specific settlement landscapes.

1.3 The contribution of archaeology to the study of urban hinterlands

The potential of archaeology to contribute to the study of the relationship between town and country is more frequently stated than realised. This is a matter of concern, given that over the last half century British archaeology has been dominated, at least in terms of resource allocation, by the study of towns (*cf* Carver 1987, 103–11). Most urban excavation has been reactive to the needs of redevelopment, and the wealth of archaeological data obtained has been under-utilised in the development of interpretative models. Often the principal stated objective of such work is to establish an archive: a hoarding of data against dimly understood future demands, although this is not to deny that the presence of such archives can suggest exciting avenues of research (Schofield 1987). Where research objectives have been articulated, these generally reflect the site-specific nature of urban investigations. Particular towns have been described and their trajectory of change charted, but attempts to understand their place in broader patterns of settlement, society, and economy have been uninspired. The emphasis given to the detailed analysis of individual sites has not been matched by attempts to understand systems of sites, except in studies of individual classes of finds (as Maltby 1989), or at the theoretical level (as Hodder and Millett 1980). Consequently 'one is left with the feeling that many archaeologists are content to examine the city as an artefact when what they should be doing is using their particular skills to study it as the material manifestation of socio-economic and socio-political systems' (Cunliffe 1985, 1).

Equally, the study of rural settlement pattern has often depended on mapping exercises, in which details of artefactual and ecofactual signatures and socio-economic character have received little attention. Although rural survey has had a particularly important effect on archaeological research over the past twenty years (Millett 1991; Taylor 2001), the results of such research have not yet been fully brought to bear on the urban question. The recent survey of the hinterland of Roman Wroxeter remains something of an exception (Gaffney *et al* forthcoming). It is in any case evident that: 'survey on its own is insufficient. There must also be sample excavation to provide windows on the hinterland's chronology and assemblages, so as to compare with those windows opened in the town itself ... production in the hinterland can be compared with rubbish disposed of in the towns to show how interdependent towns and the hinterland were at different periods' (Carver 1993a).

1.4 Frameworks for archaeological research

The subject of urban hinterlands has been discussed as a coming area of archaeological research with some regularity over the last quarter century. The need to 'investigate more fully the relationship between the town and its wider context' was given particular emphasis in a paper drafted by Derek Keene and endorsed by the Ancient Monuments Board (the body that then took the lead in strategic planning in English archaeology) as long ago as 1978. That paper recommended a programme of coordinated research, designed to allow valid comparison between different periods and different types of site. It noted that: 'such studies would necessarily be regionally based and the choice of areas would depend on a careful assessment of the range of questions that could be asked ... this choice would be a major academic exercise in its own right' (Thomas 1983, 41).

The importance of the study of urban hinterlands has also been described in a series of more recent regional reviews of research directions. The five counties of East Anglia presently boast one of the better examples of this kind of document (Glazebrook 1997). In its consideration of priorities for the study of Roman period remains this study argues that: 'settlements of all kinds need to be examined, not as isolated entities but in relation to their hinterlands and ... future projects should consider both town and countryside in conjunction as far as possible' (Going 1997, 37). This view is expressed even more forcefully with respect to the post-Roman period for which: 'archaeological evidence has much to offer any study of the urban economy and the inter-relationship between urban activity and the produce of the countryside ... . Fundamental problems of the change from a subsistence economy to one of surplus need to be investigated so that the preconditions for urban growth within post-Roman society are more fully understood' (Ayers 1997, 61).

Similar observations are widespread in the literature now being generated to provide regional and local guidance to archaeological contractors. These interests have been reflected in several national surveys (notably those of the Council for British Archaeology: *Themes for Urban Research, c 100BC to AD 200*; *Urban Themes, AD 1000–1600*). Notwithstanding this widespread agreement in principle about the potential importance of such research, comparatively little work has been undertaken and the subject has come to be seen as a difficult one to tackle. Significant results have been obtained from several specialist studies, especially in the analysis of urban animal bone assemblages and regional pottery distributions, but few more broadly based works of synthesis have been attempted.

There are several good reasons why, with a few important exceptions, this area of research is little advanced. Problems of definition and classification make it difficult to establish parameters and objectives, and there is a natural tendency to postpone the study of relationships between settlements until we have achieved better descriptions of the settlements themselves (Millett 2001, 66). Archaeology is most comfortable with individual excavation sites, and specialist studies of single classes of artefact. It is much harder to draw together data of different types from different excavations. Divergent sampling policies and systems of classification limit comparison. This is in part the consequence of a healthy variety of approaches within the archaeological profession, but also reflects the circumstances in which work is undertaken. Most fieldwork in England takes place when archaeological remains are threatened by development. Such investigations are not guided by research objectives but by the need to acquire information against determining conservation strategies. In most cases the archaeological data can not be exploited to their full potential because the samples are small and commercial funding can not usually stretch to broader studies of synthesis. Only by combining the descriptions obtained from networks of interrelated sites can the value of such information be realised: a deceptively simple objective that is difficult to achieve because of the volume and diversity of the evidence generated by the urban process.

1.5 The Urban Hinterlands Project

This report is one of a series of strategic reviews of research directions commissioned by English Heritage (eg Fulford and Huddlestone 1991; Mellor 1994; James and Millett 2001). The emphasis that has been given to the construction of research frameworks (eg Olivier 1996; Buckley 1997) is in part a response to changes in archaeological practice crystallised by the publication of Planning Policy Guidance Note 16 (DoE 1990). The prominence that government policy has given to the conservation of archaeological remains is seen by some to discourage research, and concerns have been expressed about a perceived lack of academic focus to current archaeological work (as summarised in Olivier 1996). Field archaeologists have developed impressive skills in data collection, the practice of which has sometimes been seen as an end in itself, with the consequence that data is sometimes poorly structured for subsequent use.

The Urban Hinterlands Project was established in response to such concerns, with the following objectives:

- To develop national and regional research frameworks for hinterland studies, thereby informing curatorial decisions and promoting the more purposive management of the archaeological resource,

- To draw on archaeological data obtained from rural survey and urban excavation to enhance understanding of pre-modern relationships between town and country,

- To encourage improved methods of data recovery and analysis, allowing for the better use of available and forthcoming data in constructing and testing models,

- To promote dialogue between academic and field archaeologists and researchers from related disciplines, and to disseminate the results of the research.

There are two useful ways in which a study such as this might contribute to the development of research frameworks. At one level we can attempt to describe the quantity and quality of the information available for study. Such descriptions (essentially a form of metadata), provide a necessary basis for establishing the potential of a subject. They allow us to establish whether or not the information that we have is conducive to the research that we desire. Secondly we can describe our research ambitions within the context of current research paradigms, placing emphasis on the questions that might be asked of the evidence.

Ideally our research agendas should be structured both by what is known and by what is thought to be knowable, and should be developed within the context of current lines of intellectual inquiry. A distinction can be drawn between knowledge-claims in setting up our models of past town/country relations and the role of metadata in enabling us to plan means of testing those models. Both issues were addressed in the research that led to the writing of this report, but in the text presented here we have given greater emphasis to the ideas that might merit testing rather than to the data that are available.

In attempting to develop a suitable methodology for advancing the research, three classes of information were reviewed:

- *Models* – different ways of thinking about and studying the relationship between town and country,
- *Variables* – different classes of archaeological information which, when appropriately described, should make it possible to test the models,
- *Samples* – investigations of the archaeological landscape that may have produced information that will let us compare variability within the settlement hierarchy.

Our aim was to describe which models might be tested through the measurement of which variables on which samples. Archaeological finds (artefacts and ecofacts) are the most abundant source of information in the study of pre-modern inter-site relationships. Such information includes:

- Stratified urban assemblages which chart changing patterns of supply and consumption (animal bone is of particular value because of the information that it provides about changing agricultural practice within the urban catchment area);
- Distributions of finds from territories surrounding towns (in particular pottery). These illustrate patterns of exchange within the sphere of urban influence but often lack the chronological precision of stratified urban sequences.

Although other sources of archaeological information are closely relevant to this study, such as architecture and landscapes, the evidence of finds assemblages is key to the study of the extractive and redistributive processes at work. The information derived from these assemblages also offers the best basis for comparative analysis. This is therefore essentially a study of the research potential of the differences between collections of archaeological finds. It is underpinned by the following assumptions:

- Archaeological research into urban hinterlands is best furthered by the comparative study of dated assemblages. Our improved ability to quantify and describe finds and to analyse patterns of distribution adds to the potential of such studies,
- There is no single type-site, or typical settlement landscape, which allows for valid generalisation, and research should address the evidence of different regions and periods,
- The criteria for selecting which areas to study, and which sites and finds to draw on in detailed studies, should be based on considered research questions and goals (with pragmatic regard to the availability of suitable data),
- Much effort has been invested in the recovery and measurement of stratified assemblages, especially in programmes of urban excavation and post-excavation analysis. Where possible better use should be made of this information in preference to further data recovery,
- Evaluations and small-scale excavations commissioned in the context of proposed redevelopment have produced information from areas that previously might not have received attention. The data obtained from such work can combine with that from urban excavation and rural survey to permit a more detailed approach to hinterland studies than has hitherto been possible.

The emphasis placed here on material culture sets limits to the scope of study. The urban process is easier to study where it is well represented in the archaeological record by closely dated finds. The proposals explored in most detail here are those that exploit artefactual information, and there is consequently a bias towards areas of research which offer easier rewards because of the abundance of available data. Some areas and periods are inherently ill suited for such study because of the paucity of appropriate material. It remains the case, however, that critical processes of change occurred in such places. An important research objective is therefore to find ways of better describing paucity and developing sampling strategies that will compensate for some of the imbalances found in this survey.

Because of this bias towards finds assemblages, research based on topographic, geographic, and field survey is not covered in equivalent detail here. This report is also addressed exclusively to the archaeology of pre-modern England, although the research structure could usefully be extended to other settlement landscapes and many of our themes would benefit from broader spatial and temporal range. Within these parameters, a wide review of problems and issues is attempted. In order to combat the drift towards superficiality inherent in a work of this nature, a series of case studies is included to concentrate attention on the less

abstract research practicalities that these suggest.

It is important to stress that we do not pretend to provide an exhaustive treatment of all themes that warrant attention. This report does not describe a prescriptive programme, and is intended to present a platform from which competing and complementary proposals can be developed. There are many other research projects addressing town/country relationships that could be taken forward on the basis of the agenda for study that is summarised here. Others still may be the fruit of completely different approaches to the subject. Here we have identified only some of the ways in which the subject can be tackled. We hope that a greater awareness of the research opportunities will encourage more ambitious approaches to the use of the wealth of information routinely recovered from archaeological fieldwork in England.

1.6 Organisation of this report

The main focus of our attention is on periods and regions where systems changed: from the late pre-Roman Iron Age (LPRIA) down to the developed market economies of the later medieval period. We hope to better describe and understand such change through the archaeological evidence. The study of processes of change requires some form of contextual distance, and in order to understand systems in which central places were important these need to be compared with neighbouring systems where such things did not exist, or carried different weight. This report therefore gives considerable attention to places and times where the things that might be called towns lay close to some spatial or temporal horizon, but where they were not yet securely established.

We first review theoretical models and recent studies into town/country relationships, in order to inform a research agenda (chapter 2). In this review we start by considering how the development of settlement hierarchies might be understood in the context of changing socio-economic strategies, and then summarise the current state of research into Roman and medieval towns in England. Our conclusions are summarised as a series of research questions that can be used in the construction of future programmes of research. These questions are used as the starting point for the case studies described in chapter 4 of this report, but are also intended to offer a point of reference in the

construction of local and regional research frameworks.

In chapter 3 we survey the potential of archaeological information (mainly artefacts and ecofacts) in order to establish which characteristics of archaeological assemblages might deserve closest study in the pursuit of our research objectives. Since the quality of the archaeological sample is not always adequate for more ambitious programmes of research, we suggest some ways in which better samples can be obtained in the future and in which the limitations of existing collections of archaeological finds might be overcome.

Although some of the research we discuss here requires new programmes of fieldwork, we believe that much can also be achieved from the better use of the results of past excavations and surveys. A scoping survey was therefore undertaken in order to assess the potential of such material. Information on sites and landscapes was canvassed from a wide range of sources, and a series of archives consulted. We wished to find out what information was available from the settlement hierarchies that might become the subject of further study. This was a rapid exercise drawing on available databases and informed by fairly extensive consultations (above p ix). Although the results were extremely useful, and have been drawn on in the case studies presented in chapter 4 of this report, the survey was too partial to be wholly reliable. It would be misleading to publish provisional and incomplete findings, and so this aspect of our research is not presented here.

These three surveys – of research frameworks (chapter 2); of the potential of archaeological assemblages (chapter 3); and of the availability of databases and excavated material – were used to define a series of studies that might be undertaken (chapter 4). The proposed studies concentrate attention on periods of change when urban strategies were more actively promoted and when modes of production and exploitation may have changed most radically (the late Iron Age and early Roman period; the 7th–9th centuries; and in the later medieval spread of urbanism). Each proposal is made specific to key landscapes and outlines some of the ways in which research could be advanced.

An exploration of contrasting social and economic strategies adopted in response to late Iron Age and early Roman urbanisation in the Colchester area (chapter 4.2) is followed by a study of the ways in which increasing coin use in late Roman Britain affected the relationship between town and country

(chapter 4.3). The early medieval settlement hierarchy is the subject of a further study, and explores the role of *emporia* (*wics*), using both *Hamwic* and Ipswich as examples (chapter 4.4). The contrast between nucleated and dispersed areas of settlement in the medieval period, and the ways in which this might relate to domestic arrangements and urban change are considered in the context of Warwickshire and Norfolk (in chapter 4.5). The final case study (chapter 4.6) considers the environmental and ecological impact of London in the context of studies of urban sustainability. Two other research topics are identified, but are not explored in further detail in our case studies: the economic and social character of the late Saxon *burh*, and the place of the town in later medieval specialisation and innovation.

A concluding chapter summarises the recommendations that emerge from this review, with reference to the management of the resource, experimental methodology, and future directions of research.

The research environment

Frances Condron, Dominic Perring, and Mark Whyman

2.1 Introduction

In this chapter we summarise recent archæological research into the relationship between town and country in England. Since the subject of our study is not self-evident we begin by addressing problems of definition. How, if at all, can we decide what is a town or how its hinterland might be described? We then consider ways in which archaeological finds illustrate economic and social relationships. We approach this theme from three directions. Firstly we review economic models that describe how wealth was obtained and distributed. This is followed by a consideration of the social and ideological forces that shaped relationships between town and country. Finally we take account of some of the work that has been undertaken on the environmental impact of urbanism.

This brief survey of some of the theoretical issues sets the scene for a review of current thinking about how English settlement landscapes have evolved, which we take from the late Iron Age to around AD 1500. In this review we focus on eras of transition and consolidation. Thus we start by describing *oppida* (pre-Roman central places) and the impact of Roman conquest and administration. This is followed by a discussion of the transition from the Roman to early medieval period. Towns did not survive in early Saxon England, and thus the 7th-century emergence of nucleated settlements (*emporia*) forms the basis of the next section. This is followed by a review of the late Saxon reorganisation of the settlement landscape, where our concern is in the foundation of *burhs*. In a more summary treatment of the later medieval period we look at the 'long 13th century' in terms of the expansion of urban networks and population growth. The impact of the epidemics in the late 14th century on town/country relations, and the slow recovery through the 15th century form the final part of the review.

In this survey we identify some common threads in the study of town/country relations and these are drawn on in the final discussion. The chapter ends with a series of research questions that act both as a summary of the chapter and as a source of reference throughout this book.

2.2 Definitions

2.2.1 Towns

The main problem that we have had to confront in this survey is that towns carry different meanings to different people at different times. An illustration of this is found in the polyfocal landscape of 7th-century London. One putative town, the place that later became the City of London, can be described from its Roman legacy, its town walls and its bishop's see. These are urban features. This was, however, but an empty shell: a once and future metropolis that lived on rank alone. It was a symbol of urban status that lacked an urban population.

A very different settlement sprawled busily along

the Thames at Aldwich. This was *Lundenwic*, a site that had both the people and industry to rank as an important middle Saxon emporium (as p 96). But this sometimes squalid place lacked the very symbols of status and power that were attached to the derelict Roman City downstream. This contrast draws our attention to the fact that urban signifiers operate in different spheres. Towns may or may not serve social, legal, administrative, ritual, symbolic, military, distributive, economic, and industrial functions. The relative weight that we give to these different attributes is a product of the nature of our interest in urbanism. Cities are conceptual not merely material, and when we describe a town we are usually describing an idea rather than an artefact.

Another problem follows from this confusion over the nature of urban function. Almost all of the things that towns appear to do can also be done elsewhere in the landscape. Palaces, monasteries, forts, temples, villas, castles, and industrial sites all carry something of the urban. These different classes of settlement are closely relevant to the relationship between town and country and merit our attention in this review. In order to describe the relationship between city and country we therefore need to explore the role of all nucleated settlements that had high population levels or housed diverse specialist activities.

In trying to define the elusive subject of their interest, urban archaeologists have been much influenced by the available documentary evidence. The testimony of chartered status has been given privileged attention in studies of both Roman Britain and medieval England (eg Wacher 1995, 424, Introduction n3; Holt and Rosser 1990, 3). Although it is instructive to contrast the archaeological character of places of differing legal status – and the matter of status could have an important bearing on urban fabric and function – this approach lends attention to but one aspect of urban function. Places of similar status may in fact have operated very differently one from the other, and classifications built from the evidence of urban title are sometimes more misleading than helpful. It is also easy to lose sight of the fact that these legal distinctions, which were in some instances little more than a badge of status rather then a significant feature of urban identity, may soon have lost relevance. For instance the different constitutions of the Roman *municipium* at Verulamium, *colonia* at Colchester, and *civitas* capital at Silchester reflected differences in the ways in which

these places were politically conceived *c* AD 50, but tell us little about how these places functioned thereafter.

Towns have alternatively been classified by 'shopping lists' or *kriterien-bundel* of vital components (as reviewed by Biddle 1976, 100). The presence of walls, specialist buildings, complex street layouts, and other physical markers are used alongside evidence for specialist production and consumption of goods to construct a settlement hierarchy, in which sites can be ranked by the scale and range of features evident. Millett, in responding to the excessive reliance placed on the evidence of legal status, has suggested (2001, 64) that the study of Romano-British towns stands most to benefit from classifications built on architectural variables such as size, settlement density, planning, public space, house types and spatial zoning. These approaches to site description are undeniably more instructive than those based uniquely on the documentary sources. But architecture, like legal status, tends to be the product of ideological and political choices. These are important subjects of study but can misrepresent underlying economic and social realities (see Horden and Purcell 2000, 92–6 for a more extended discussion of this issue). Such classifications make only limited use of the evidence available to archaeology.

Material culture permits a more sensitive exploration of settlement diversity than one based uniquely on architecture or civic status. Urban lifestyles were qualitatively different to rural ones, and this is reflected in the archaeological record. Critically a significant proportion of urban populations was not engaged in subsistence agricultural production. Diversity was a fundamental characteristic of towns, which relied on immigration to sustain population levels, and this encouraged the creation of new social relationships and ties. Notions of urban freedoms were also associated with the evolution of urban identity, and the changing influence of landlords over town populations is a major theme. Town life could relieve ties of tenure and patronage, and urban populations often enjoyed a greater degree of self-determination. Not only was it normal for urban settlements to support a wide range of specialist activities, but these were also places which witnessed unusually high levels of consumption.

This emphasis on variation in patterns of consumption offers a convenient escape from the 'what is a town?' debate. Archaeological finds describe peaks of consumption within the landscape. We are interested in places that had obtained a disproportionate proportion of the available social surplus, and where the consumption of such surplus has left its mark in the archaeological record in the form of both architectural remains and assemblages of finds. The character of consumption and the means by which it was supported allow us to characterise different classes of site (for an example of the utility of this approach see Loveluck 2001). The study of the landscape of consumption encompasses all settlements with features that merit description in a study of urbanism. An emphasis on 'peaks of consumption' accommodates the fact that urbanism is not a single phenomenon but is differently conceived by different communities. Since we cannot usefully agree on all-embracing definitions of what constitutes a town, the object here is instead to redirect attention to ways in which archaeology can usefully describe differences in the settlement landscapes within which towns occurred.

We are not suggesting that towns do not exist and cannot be studied, but believe that future study will benefit from changing the focus of our attention in such a way that we do not founder on these problems of definition. In this we find ourselves in a similar position to that advocated by Abrams (1978, 2–3), who treats cities as a 'fields of action integral to some larger world' (see also Horden and Purcell 2000, 99).

2.2.2 Hinterlands

It is no easier to achieve a satisfactory definition of an archaeological 'hinterland'. The term is borrowed from the German, where it is used to describe the broader market reach of a settlement, as distinct from the immediate surroundings (*umland*) from which towns drew their food (see further below p 108). In the study of human geography a hinterland has come to be defined as the zone around the town incorporated into and reliant upon its economic system (through its market, range of services, labour, finance, etc). The emphasis on economic indicators limits the utility to archaeology of models borrowed from geography, although the emphasis on spatial relationships has attracted considerable

attention (eg in the application of central place theory to archaeological data, see p 3). With the use of computer-driven Geographical Information Systems such trends can only increase and we must be all the more cautious in the ways in which they are applied to the past.

The impact of urban settlement on the landscape is usually explored through the study of functional spheres of influence: legal, judicial, administrative, economic, religious, cultural, and defensive. A 'Theory of Urban Fields', drawn from Set Theory, has been developed for the later medieval period, where documentary evidence is used to map zones of urban influence against specific criteria (eg the residences of people in debt to townsfolk). Archaeology can similarly identify urban fields through the distribution patterns of goods, where these were mediated by urban central places. As documentary evidence makes clear, the movement of objects was not primarily dictated by the shortest route nor obviously constrained by modern notions of transport costs. Rather, such movement was influenced by invisible controls such as tribute to lords, links between dispersed estate holdings, and networks of patronage, obligation, and tradition. These have important implications for this study, as it is manifestly wrong to assume that urban sites influenced all settlements in the surrounding landscape.

By adopting an 'Urban Fields' approach, models of complex, overlapping zones of influence acting diversely across the landscape can be built. The spatial organisation of landscapes in most periods was not based on large, coherent blocks, but, rather, was a patchwork of settlements linked into overlapping exchange networks at various levels, ranging from major towns and specialist production for long-distance markets, to subsistence settlements with little interaction in local or regional networks. This patchwork is as true of the ties of kinship and patronage that link rural populations to urban central places, as it is of economic relationships. Hinterlands cannot be viewed as continuous, homogenous regions or uncontested spaces, and their study is the study of variation in settlement interaction within and between differently defined urban fields.

2.3 The study of settlement hierarchies

2.3.1 Economic models

As we have already observed (above p 3), many current models of settlement interaction focus on economic function. This reflects a concern with the genesis of modern free-market economies and has been particularly influenced by Marxist models. According to these 'the analysis of the city and its relation to the countryside is ... premised on the analysis of class relations inscribed within specific modes of production' (Saunders 1986, 22). This argument offers a useful starting point for this review.

The effective mobilisation of labour, itself a feature of increasing social complexity (Earle 1991), has almost always been linked with the evolution of central places and towns. For such resources to be mobilised a surplus must be obtained. The study of different approaches to the use of surplus is therefore central to the study of how settlement hierarchies have evolved. These different approaches to the command of surplus can be described in terms of domestic, tributary, tax-based, seigniorial, and market modes of production. These economic structures can coexist, although there is still a tendency to describe change ('evolutions' and 'transformations'), through reference to shifts from one mode of production to another (as, rather unsatisfactorily, Southall 1998).

Domestic production

Domestic production is supposedly typified by a subsistence economy. It is actually improbable that many societies have ever aimed simply to subsist, since the accumulation of a healthy amount of transferable surplus is a necessary insurance against the risks of famine and need. As Horden and Purcell have observed (2000, 273) 'overproduction is the only safe plan'. In any case few, if any, settlements in our period of study were uninfluenced by broader economic ties: as is shown in the distribution of coins and ceramics. The characteristics of domestic production therefore identify communities that were poorly integrated into broader systems rather than wholly outside them. The most obvious feature of these poorly integrated communities is that the artefacts and ecofacts that they produced and consumed would reflect independence rather than interdependence. What is at issue is economic self-reliance, rather than subsistence. The archaeological evidence for this might include some of the following:

- Archaeobotanical data would show little reliance on 'cash crops' and a comparatively unspecialised production,
- Food processing would have taken place near the occupation site,
- Animals of all ages would be represented in bone assemblages, with little stock specialisation,
- The exploitation of wild species would vary, but exotic species would not be widely represented,
- Local products using basic methods of production and a narrow range of forms would dominate ceramic assemblages,
- The presence of other artefact types would be restricted, with few exotic imports. Coin would be rare or absent.

There are difficulties inherent in such a characterisation and its archaeological recognition:

- Production sites leave few traces of the surplus they rendered where this was in kind or mediated through high-value coinage. It is therefore difficult to distinguish between a subservient site within a tributary or taxation network, and one that stood outside it. Small discrepancies between otherwise comparable sites, such as the presence/absence of small volumes of coinage, non-local pottery, or other artefacts, may be decisive. This imposes considerable demands on the quality of the archaeological sampling;
- The notion of a subsistence site within a domestic context of production assumes the concept of discrete and persistent habitation sites. Communities may, however, have been mobile. Transhumant agriculture was commonplace in the Iron Age, and the movement of early Saxon settlements (5th–6th centuries) is much commented on. Mobility and seasonality amongst agriculturists can itself be an indicator of the degree of integration into hierarchical settlement systems, which are characterised by a tendency towards more static and permanent habitation sites;
- Self–sufficient agriculturists also made things, and some sites will have evidence for ore smelt-

ing, metalworking and other forms of production. The degree to which this can be seen as specialisation depends on the scale of production and its context (eg the degree to which industrial production was separate from other aspects of agrarian production);

- Datable artefacts are usually characteristic of developed systems of production and distribution. Such artefacts are therefore scarce or absent on sites that were not integrated into these broader systems. There is, therefore, a problem in establishing the contemporaneity of such sites with contemporary consumer sites.

Tributary production

Tribute can be exacted in the form of labour and services, but also taken in kind. Once obtained it can be consumed or redistributed. The introduction of a tributary system might result in the development of specialist craft production or in the redistribution of agricultural surplus, and be evident in the distribution of high-status goods between and within settlements. Useful comparisons can be drawn between high-status or nucleated settlements supported by tribute and those that provided the goods. Tributary extraction is usually more visible on those sites that received the tribute, rather than on those which produced the surplus.

The location of artisans is particularly crucial to our understanding of changing controls over access to prestige goods. Ceramics offer insight into craft specialisation, and their study provides models for activities poorly represented in the archaeological record (eg metalworking, textiles, glass making, minting).

Tributary production may also be revealed in changes in agricultural regimes. The critical feature to trace is the introduction of trends in consumption that suggest a degree of perversity in resource use. Features that are economically non-rational within the parameters of subsistence production require alternative explanation. The lordly command of surplus is evident when animals were no longer being slaughtered at what would appear to be the most sensible point in the production cycle, either because of the needs of specialist production (eg hides for leather) or to supply the table (evident in breeding strategies). Further to this, crops may reach sites processed, or different proportions of cereals may be consumed on some sites (eg more bread wheat as opposed to rye or barley: Astill and Grant 1988).

Ceramics and other portable objects should show a greater range of forms, some of which may be indicative of high status. Coinage may also reflect settlement status (see p 51). Another relevant feature is the introduction of mechanisms to measure and store surplus, as for instance in the use of standardised containers (Saunders 1992, 240).

Tax and rent-based production

Power can be structured directly through the control of people or indirectly through the control of property, and the changing emphasis placed on these sources of power has been critical to the success of towns. Most urban societies depend on taxes and rents obtained from property, and the perceived need to raise such taxes and rents has often been one of the reasons that towns were first founded.

Systems dependent on the extraction of surplus through taxation can be difficult to distinguish from tributary systems. Taxation played a key role in the Roman Empire, which operated a complex network of social, political, and institutional structures (eg the army, networks of friends, the census, etc) to exploit people and land. The redistributive processes involved, and the use of coin to levy tax may have stimulated market exchange, with a consequent impact on the progress of urbanisation (Hopkins 1980). Howgego (1994, 16–20) has, however, questioned the importance of taxation to the monetisation of the Roman economy. Furthermore the contribution of Roman taxation to the emergence of market economies in Britain may have been limited by reliance on taxation in kind, and in many instances liability devolved to local estate owners or *civitas* officials. The extent to which rural populations in Roman Britain were involved in monetised exchange remains uncertain. This is an important area of research where archaeological evidence is critical (below p 87).

The creation of large estates may have been encouraged by the availability of slave labour. In the longer term such establishments are more likely to have relied on the exaction of 'rents' in kind paid by tenant farmers (processed crops, animal products, livestock, etc). It is possible to suggest an increasingly feudal society in the later Roman period. The social ties of patron/client relationships, on which Rome had long depended, were translated into more rigidly imposed economic obligations. Peasant-tenants owed services and goods to a landlord-baron. Surplus was taken from household units tied to rented plots, and where labour was used to pay rent the lord could control the ways in which land was exploited.

This issue of the feudal control of people and land is central to the discussion of the transition from antiquity to the Middle Ages (eg Wickham 1994; Barnish 1989 reviewing Hodges and White-house 1983 and Ward-Perkins 1984; Bintliffe and Hamerow 1995). It is uncertain, however, that medieval Britain followed the traditional feudal model. For instance Reynolds (1994) argues that barons did not effectively control local populations. Moreover the place of towns within the medieval feudal system is being questioned; particularly the concept that royal boroughs occupied a privileged position as free islands floating above a feudal sea (Palliser 1997, see also p 107). There is scope to further question the centrality of feudal relationships to Britain's medieval economy.

Market production

In a free market, labour and goods become mobile commodities. In pre-modern economies the laws of supply and demand were not allowed free rein. Market production will, however, have reduced social constraint over exchange (with consequent disruption to the ways in which social hierarchies were maintained), and is likely to have involved a greater proportion of the population than the tributary mode. The use of cash is a feature of effective markets. It is not easy to identify the point at which exchange developed to incorporate commodities. The issues involved are complicated and this is a current area of debate. The market was undoubtedly an important feature in villa economies in the Roman period (as attested in the wine and olive oil production of Roman Italy, Spain, and North Africa), although even here production is likely to have been influenced by other factors. Despite the growth of town-based markets, the relatively high value of coins until the later 3rd century may have hindered cash transactions. Hodges (1996) suggests coinage again became a medium for commodity exchange in southern and eastern England around the late 8th century, in response to developments in Carolingian Europe. The transition was neither sudden nor universal. Britnell (1996, 228–237) argues for the importance of non-monetised exchange through the later medieval period, alongside increases in coin use up to 1300. The market was never absolute.

These different models of economic organisation are not mutually exclusive. For example, research on late medieval estate provisioning (Galloway *et al* 1996) illustrates the complex overlapping of different 'modes of production'. Further research into the relationship between town and country can build from the study of such overlapping economies (see, in particular, chapter 4.2).

2.3.2 The social context

Patterns of economic relationships do not translate directly into the archaeological record, and urbanism is as much a social as an economic phenomenon. Central places – palaces, religious, administrative, and defensive sites – are concerned with the demonstration and practice of social control. Towns were ideological constructs designed to represent, reproduce, and reward power. As Carver has argued (1993a), this involved political choice. Urban strategies could be differently conceived and, indeed, rejected. The relationship between town and country influenced decisions about where power should be located in the settlement landscape, and was in turn a product of such strategic choices. Wealth and status can be expressed in radically different ways – through monuments, rituals, burials, hoarding, or consumption – even where the economic basis of power may have been similar. The question of why power was exercised through towns is central to the study of cultural change. This is a particularly important theme in the study of the Romanisation of Britain, where urban values (although not necessarily the towns themselves) may have held paramount importance in defining Roman identity.

Different expressions of identity shaped urban communities: for instance 'foreign', 'religious', or 'ethnic' quarters were a feature of medieval towns. The construction of identity is witnessed in patterns of display, and is therefore evident in different approaches to the consumption of surplus. Much has been made of a distinction that might be drawn between Roman and native in the Roman provinces (eg Mattingly 1997b). Hingley (1997), amongst others, has usefully challenged established models which assume an unquestioning acceptance of Roman values by native societies, although there is a risk that the distinction he draws is an artificial one. There is disagreement over whether Romanisation was essentially a product of internal forces, an indigenous impulse to copy and adapt by local elites who wished to secure their status within the new social order (as Millett 1990), or was actively promoted by the imperial administration (Woolf 1995; Whittaker 1997, 152; Hanson 1997). This is perhaps a false dichotomy, since the evidence suggests that both forces were at work. There was a complicated dialogue, engaged in differently by the individuals involved, resulting in the creative adaptation of some aspects of Roman culture, as well as the rejection of others. No two urban communities in the Roman world presented an identical interpretation of the Roman ideal: regional and local identities were clearly expressed (eg Woolf 1998; Perring 2002). Global 'Roman' culture (more Hellenistic than *Latin* in its origins) was arguably as diversely constructed and interpreted as 'Western' culture is today.

The ways in which 'Roman' items were assimilated is poorly understood. The uses to which individuals put goods to promote their identity and status may have signalled affiliations based on lineage, tribe, age, and gender, not simply a universal 'high status' (see also Jones 1997 on the problems of reading ethnicity from the evidence of material culture). It is also possible that the values attached to the use of some goods were so differently constructed that they involved the rejection of the values usually associated with Romanisation.

The issues that underpin the debate over the Romanisation of British society are relevant to other periods and other cultural transforms. Indeed the role played by material culture in the construction of identity has become a favourite subject in recent literature on archaeological theory (as Barrett 1997). Cultural identity was negotiated through place as much as through class or ethnic affiliation. The relationship between town and country is critical to our understanding of these processes of cultural interaction. There is a tension between urban (cosmopolitan) sophistication and rustic (pagan) simplicity. The study of the role of towns in constructing regional identities is another important research theme in the agenda we propose (see, in particular, case study 4.5).

The importance of understanding how culture shapes and is shaped by expressions of identity, how it constitutes part of the process by which social affiliations and distinctions are formed, should not detract from the fact that these processes operate within and not independently of dialogues of power based on the social control of resources.

2.3.3 Environmental impacts

Towns have exaggerated appetites that make extensive demands of the productive capacity of the supporting landscape. Modern concerns over population growth, resource depletion, and environmental degradation have encouraged research into the past ecological impact of urbanisation, although there has been a tendency to create pseudo ecologies by projecting modern ideas onto the ancient world (O Rackham 1996). Research frameworks for the study of this aspect of the relationship between town and country can usefully be informed by the debate over sustainable development (see Mather and Chapman 1995 and Barrow 1995 for summaries of the arguments involved).

Unfortunately sustainability is a rather vaguely defined term. The concept works best when applied to the use of renewable resources, where sustainable use can be achieved when projected rates of depletion do not exceed projected rates of renewal or replacement. Arguments about sustainability tend to underestimate the importance of cultural factors in determining productive capacity and place too great an emphasis on basics such as food and fuel (Davis 1991, 238). Resource availability is not fixed, and stress can encourage innovation in the creation of new resources or redirection of supply mechanisms (Simon 1981). Towns engender sophisticated supply mechanisms to support patterns of consumption and these can be highly responsive to changing demand.

A related theme is that of 'carrying capacity'. It has been argued, following Malthus, that any given habitat can only support a certain population level (the 'carrying capacity' of that habitat) and that this will periodically be exceeded resulting in overload ('ecological overshoot') and collapse. This concept has been applied in archaeological explanation. A widely quoted example is that of the Easter Islands, where the extensive deforestation attached to the demands of transporting stone statues has been proposed as a cause of environmental degradation and population decline (Bahn and Flenley 1992).

Postan (1975) and Braudel (1977) have suggested that medieval Europe fluctuated between periods of sustainable population growth and episodes of overload. In particular the Black Death of 1348 has been described as a Malthusian check to rising population levels (eg Abel 1980). This analysis involves over-simplified modelling. Boserup (1983) has argued that population pressures were successfully addressed by innovation in the replacement of pastoralism and long-fallow agriculture by short-fallow systems, and contends that periods of stress could be coped with by changes in diet. Medieval Europe had supported rising population levels by extending agriculture onto marginal lands, through better regimes of land tenure and sustainable intensification. The problems of the 14th century cannot, therefore, be reduced to those of over-population (see Southgate *et al* 1990). Indeed the sharp increase in population levels after the mid-16th century shows that productive capacity could be increased. At the end of this period of massive population growth, food prices were under less pressure and the population less vulnerable to poor harvests (Wrigley, quoted in Mather and Chapman 1995, 240). But as Horden and Purcell have observed (2000, 295) there is no inevitability to such a response. There are many documented instances of population growth failing to spark improvements in productivity. Indeed it can be argued that 'it was economic opportunity that attracted new people rather than the other way around' (van Andel and Runnels 1988). It is not really possible to establish generalised models based on the concept of carrying capacity, given the spatial and temporal specificity of ecological circumstance (Horden and Purcell 2000, 49).

It remains the case, however, that little archaeological research has addressed the issue of how much land was needed to support specific settlements at particular points in their history, and what techniques (technical, social, and cultural) were adopted in response to population growth and urban specialisation. The Feeding and Fuelling the City projects based on the study of London's medieval supply (Campbell *et al* 1993; Galloway *et al* 1996), although historical rather than archaeological in their emphasis, are valuable illustrations of the directions that research might take.

The land's ability to support high population levels is as much (if not more) a product of cultural factors as it is of ecological productivity, and will depend on variables such as the level of technology, material expectations, and systems of distribution. Some variables can be modelled. For instance ecological accounting builds from the assumption that every category of energy, material consumption, and waste discharge requires the productive or absorptive capacity of a finite area of land or water and that this can be measured. If the area required for consumption and waste by a defined population are added up, the total area represents the land requirements (or 'ecological footprint') of that population (Wackernagel and Rees 1996; Jopling and Girardet 1996). Several reasons for being suspicious of such simplified models have already been alluded to in this study, but such accounting does offer a useful shorthand comparison of the scale of impact of different settlement types. We return to these issues in chapter 4.6 of this report, where we outline a programme of research into the economic and ecological impact of England's biggest city: London (see also p 63).

2.4 A review of recent research

Several principal phases of urban development are commonly recognised in the archaeological literature. Differences can be described between the worlds of the Iron Age *oppidum*, classical city, late antique town, early medieval emporium, and medieval *burh* (as Dark 1994, 22). Central places were undoubtedly differently conceived in these different periods, and our ability to draw instructive contrasts between these approaches to urbanism is a test of the contribution that archaeological research can make to the study of towns. For this reason this chapter treats settlement development as a dynamic process.

After briefly considering the issues of how towns were first formed, the emergence of settlement hierarchies in the late Iron Age and early Roman periods is discussed. This is followed by a separate consideration of the late and sub-Roman periods. The emergence of *emporia* and the nature of early medieval settlement interaction are then discussed. *Burh* formation and the complex evidence for continuity and change around the time of the Norman Conquest form the focus for a further section. The late medieval period is split into sub-phases defined by fluctuations in urban fortunes. The choice of 1500 as an end-date for this study follows the common if questionable use of this date as marking the transition from medieval to post-medieval (see Gaimster and Stamper 1997 for a review of the issues). This is not because archaeology is unable to cast light on the transition into the early modern period, but the range of sources for the study of the modern period within which the archaeological evidence should be contextualised is a somewhat different one.

2.4.1 Models for primary urbanisation

Organised settlements with centralised functions are a feature from the Neolithic onwards. A general trend leading to primary urbanisation is increasing complexity (see Renfrew 1974). Key developments are visible social differentiation (revealed through burial practices, organic and portable finds, and architecture), emerging settlement hierarchy (defined by size, building style, layout and organisation, and longevity), intensification of production and, more importantly, the exercise of centralised control over production and distribution (both of agricultural and craft production). This is coupled with an intensification of exchange, tribute, and warfare both within and between social groups. These trends can be used to identify social stratification, agricultural labourers forming the lowest rank with higher social status awarded to artisans, priests, warriors, and aristocrats. The emergence of 'central places' is seen as a late stage, at least in the European west. This basic model has been adapted to explain the emergence of 'palaces' in Minoan and Mycenaean Greece (Cherry 1984); late 3rd/early 2nd millennium BC changes in Britain (Renfrew and Shennan 1982); the emergence of hillforts and *oppida* in lowland Britain and Europe (Bradley 1984); and the appearance of post-Roman *emporia* in north-west Europe (Cunliffe 1988).

The universality with which this model can be applied suggests that it is no more than a banal descriptive tool. Even when couched in the historical and geographic context of the culture being studied, it does not address crucial problems such as identifying how change came about. Nor does it account for the very different ways in which these early central places were designed and experienced.

2.4.2 Late Iron Age and Roman

Most narratives have described the transition from British to Romano-British as a uniform process, if played out at different speeds and intensities. They describe a phase of state formation on the borders of the Roman world preceding military and political conquest, which is then followed by the foundation of cities and the development of an economy based on villa estates in which the market is supposed to

have played a significant role. Research has concentrated on describing the ways in which Britain became a Roman province. Attention has shifted from using the evidence of forts, towns, and texts to construct political and military histories (Frere 1987), to the elucidation of the cultural choices that contributed to the Romanisation of Britain (Millett 1990). The study of the ways in which Britain's diverse communities responded to Roman power and interpreted Romano-Hellenistic culture have increasingly focused on the issue of how identities were formed and made manifest, and in particular on the way in which material culture mediated such processes. Hill (2001) offers a useful summary of current thinking in this area. Interest in the ways in which material culture described and describes the relationship between Rome and Britain has encouraged a greater awareness of regional variation within the province. Different communities responded to the imposition of a Roman administration in different ways, and consequently the transition from British to Romano-British now seems anything but uniform. Some broad trends can, however, be described.

State formation

Archaeological evidence describes a centralisation of power in south-east Britain in the half century or so prior to Roman conquest. This has been viewed as a response to the Roman presence in Gaul (Haselgrove 1982; 1987, although see Woolf 1990 for cautionary observations on the utility of core/periphery theory in describing this process). Tribal leaders reinforced power through access to a limited supply of continental luxuries, the exchange and consumption of which conferred status. This supply, greater opportunities to acquire wealth through raiding and trading, and the potency of Roman political imagery promoted the changes evident on the borders of the Roman world.

Oppida are a key feature in the changes of this period (Armit *et al* 2000, 130). Excavations at Silchester suggest that this particular settlement was a planned foundation of the Augustan period, colonised by members of the Gallic Atrebates who sustained Romanised patterns of consumption through the import of continental goods and luxuries (Fulford and Timby 2000). Other complex sites of this period were associated with adjacent aristocratic estates but do not seem to have incorporated a planned core (eg Verulamium/Gorhambury and Camulodunum/Gosbecks). These heterogeneous and polyfocal sites appear to have been multifunctional settlements, acting as places of specialist production, exchange, and as mints. British kings named these places on their coinage and they were associated with the exercise of power (Foster 1986). It seems likely, however, that they were not always places of elite residence; authority is more likely to have attached to important people rather than important places. One possibility is that some *oppida* developed from clan meeting places that came to symbolise tribal identity, and only in an advanced phase were they also developed as elite sites (Millett 1990, 25–6). Whatever the case, changing political strategies and elite fashion were critical to their establishment.

The importance of trade to their existence is debated (Wells 1986; Haselgrove 1987). Continental evidence shows that trade could survive where *oppida* did not (Roymans 1996). In any case most goods supplied to Britain were likely to have been the product of gift exchange within kinship groups and related networks of patronage. There is little evidence for unregulated trade. Questions remain as to how *oppida* were founded, populated, and supplied.

Oppida were not the only settlements associated with growing social complexity. In regions devoid of *oppida* other forms of nucleated settlements may have served as focal points (eg Dragonby in Lincolnshire). In the west and midlands hillforts remained in occupation up to the period of conquest, though this is not to suggest that society here remained static. The analysis of settlement change needs to be approached at a regional level, such that *oppida* can be studied in the context of networks of settlements. Few areas, however, have been studied in sufficient detail for this to take place.

Comparisons need to be made between the material culture of *oppida* and other contemporary settlements. Networks of power can be reconstructed from the evidence of differential access to prestige items, the location of specialist production and patterns of architectural display. The study of the distribution and iconography of Iron Age coinage has been particularly rewarding (eg Haselgrove 1987; Creighton 2000). Patterns suggested by this evidence can be compared with access to imported luxury goods, such as pottery and metalwork. Studies have revealed Gallo-Roman influence in patterns of consumption at *oppida* (Evans 2001, 32), and it is possible to describe the extent to which

other sites in the settlement hierarchy deviated from such patterns. The reconstruction of these networks of power and cultural affiliation, and of those associated with the command of rural produce, will illustrate tensions between tribute-based and market modes of production and distribution (as discussed in chapter 2.3 above).

Military conquest

The conquest of Britain was protracted, and followed a period of contact and negotiation between British and Roman aristocracies. Military progress is illustrated by an infrastructure of roads, forts, and supply bases (Webster 1980; Jones and Mattingly 1990). The provisioning of the Roman forces relied on complex patterns of supply that defied economic rationality: for instance grain was imported into Britain from the further reaches of the Mediterranean (Straker 1987), whilst military requisitioning involved the wasteful slaughter of working and pregnant livestock (Berg 1999).

Aspects of the direct economic impact of forts can be described from the predictability of garrison appetites. The amount of land required to feed soldiers in the fortress at Longthorpe (near Peterborough) has been estimated, and compared with the archaeological evidence for diet (Dannell and Wild 1987). Shirley (2000) has similarly estimated quantities of labour and materials involved in building the Roman fort at Inchtuthil. Such modelling of inputs and outputs is supplemented by the anecdotal information concerning the supply of Rome's northern frontier forts (Bowman and Thomas 1994).

Notwithstanding our ability to describe such aspects of the material impact of the Roman army, the nature of the relations between Rome's forts and the surrounding populations remains poorly understood (James 2001, 82). Comparative study has been hampered by sampling bias, in which low-status 'native' sites have received less attention than the military installations, and by the limited distribution of Roman goods outside the forts and towns. The failure of Roman goods to penetrate more widely suggests a poor level of integration between forts and surrounding territories (Clarke 1999).

The long-term military presence in the north and west of Britain may have inhibited the progress of rural Romanisation. The use of Iron Age coin and the presence of *oppida* generally presaged the dissemination of Roman material culture (Perring 2002, fig 71). These features suggest the pre-conquest centralisation of political power within the hands of a landowning elite. Civilian administrations and villa estates were soon established in territories that boasted these pre-Roman characteristics. The army, however, came to be stationed in areas where such trends were not evident, and where pre-existing social arrangements may have militated against the adoption of Roman values. The presence of the Roman administration, and the social hierarchies that it engendered, may have contributed to the fossilisation of these divergent pre-Roman approaches to the command of rural surplus, and thereby influenced the extent to which rural communities were drawn into Roman patterns of consumption and exchange.

The foundation of towns

Throughout most of lowland Britain the imperial administration secured the participation of a Romanising elite in a restructured settlement hierarchy, in which towns were necessary for the exercise of power. Much attention has been given to why towns were established at some sites but not others. Military *vici*, the settlements found at the gates of the Roman forts, have been viewed as precursors to some towns. Army spending might arguably have stimulated markets in such places, and these might have become sufficiently well established to survive the passing of the troops (Grew and Hobley 1985; Webster 1988), but it is unlikely that *vicani* could have dictated where towns were placed. Urban foundations must have been politically determined, and involved the co-option of elite classes in local administration (Millett 1990, 75). The new settlement pattern reflected a complex range of choices. Those who invested in towns preferred to build on the plains rather than on hilltops, and urban outcomes were influenced by the enhanced role played by the Roman communication system (Woolf 1998, 114–16).

The reordering of social ties consequent on conquest generated opportunities for individual advancement. This may have been a factor in the progress of early urban growth and a cause of social tension (Trow 1990). The revolt of Boudicca in AD 60 reflects such stresses, and the havoc wrought on the nascent towns at London, Colchester, and Verulamium suggests an anti-urban dimension to this episode (Webster 1978).

It is generally assumed, however, that pre-conquest tribes were transformed into the *civitates*

of Roman Britain with little change (eg Branigan 1987), and in the process formal territories and boundaries were established or confirmed. A tendency to stress cultural differences between native and Roman, based on outmoded assumptions about the monolithic nature of ethnic identity, has limited our ability to study how Roman-style material culture contributed to the reproduction and transformation of identity at this juncture (Jones 1997, 29–39). The complex sequence of negotiation and conquest, and the abiding influence of pre-conquest social arrangements, resulted in a variety of imperial landscapes. An awareness of these differences is crucial to our understanding of the ways in which Roman urban models were adopted (Mattingly 1997b).

We have already mentioned (p 10) that significant legal distinctions were drawn between the towns founded after the conquest. The first *coloniae* were established through veteran settlement and would have involved some displacement of local populations and redistribution of land in the surrounding territories (Hurst 1999). Colonial settlement brought with it the seeds of an urban economy, based on lands attached to the city but perhaps also benefiting from military contracts and other ties of patronage established in military service. The *coloniae* may therefore have had privileged access to long-distance trade networks. These advantages, and the accumulated capital represented by an infrastructure inherited from the military occupation and the savings of veteran colonists, facilitated urban development. Less is known of the way in which other urban sites were supported in their earliest phases. Work at Verulamium and surrounding villa estates (eg Niblett and Thompson forthcoming; Neal *et al* 1990), indicates that although these communities may have been differently conceived, they were in no way inferior to the colonial foundations in their ability to direct surplus into towns and villas. Our understanding of the processes involved is likely to be furthered by the contrasts that can be drawn with patterns of consumption at the different classes of site. Such studies have been facilitated by the publication of early Roman assemblages from London, Colchester, and Silchester.

We still know comparatively little about where the first townspeople came from and how swiftly new urban identities were forged. Different communities can sometimes be recognised through distinct styles of material culture and these suggest some interesting contrasts in urban and suburban lifestyles (eg Milne and Wardle 1995). Tombstones and inscriptions also identify individual immigrants, but the epigraphic habit was too unevenly distributed for it to describe patterns of immigration. Recent work on oxygen isotope signatures in bone and tooth mineral promises to better discriminate between populations, but remains a crude tool (below p 58). The evidence of Roman Britain's early cemeteries has yet to be properly exploited, and this is an important area for future research (Millett 2001).

Economies

We have already described (above p 2) how the study of the ancient economy has been dominated by the debate over the extent to which the city was essentially a consumer of rural surplus, where manufacture and trade were subordinate to the interests of property (Parkins 1997). That this was generally the case is not in question here, although there was greater variation in the nature and significance of the commerce directed through towns than is sometimes recognised. It has been argued that 'the interesting economic questions ... are unrelated to the internal divisions between town and country' (Whittaker 1990, 117). This represents a reaction to a concern with urban consumption, in which other aspects of the relationship between social power and economic activity have not been adequately explored. But the uneven distribution of power is a critical feature in the study of past economies, and there are important differences in the relationship between town and country that demand attention. Many current models present a static picture of urban economies, but archaeological sources witness major fluctuations that need explanation. The wealth of archaeological data recovered from Romano-British towns has been under-exploited in this debate (Fulford 1982 is an exception).

Supply to towns is generally held to have been through the urban market, with additional goods produced locally. The widespread use of coin, supported by the written sources, leaves little doubt that markets played a useful part in moving goods from producers to consumers. Such models understate, however, the importance of other systems of supply (eg estate provisioning, gift exchange, army supply, etc). Britain also had one of the lowest densities of towns in the Empire (Bekker-Nielsen 1989) and town-based markets could not have met most

needs. Transactions took place elsewhere. Villa estates and temples offered a range of services, and may have served as occasional markets or fairs (*cf* Frayn 1993). Other exchange probably took place within the context of extended family and clientage networks (including assistance in bad years, payment to confirm alliances such as marriage, inheritance, blood money, etc).

Romano-British marketing strategies can be reconstructed from the evidence of ceramic assemblages (eg Griffiths 1989; Allen and Fulford 1996), but the evidence of pottery is partial. The impact of markets on low-status sites deserves more attention, but the potential for detailed analysis is limited by difficulties encountered in dating assemblages of locally produced items, particularly in those regions that made little use of pottery. The low-level, local exchange of mundane objects can be difficult to identify from archaeological evidence. A survey of the hinterlands of Roman Wroxeter indicates that the territory surrounding the town was virtually aceramic (White and Van Leusen 1997). The survey consequently focused on the importance of faunal remains as indicators of local value systems, although it is difficult to achieve a fine chronology in the absence of diagnostic finds. The lack of portable luxuries has been taken to indicate bailiff-run establishments, with the elite remaining in the town. This model contradicts that proposed for the southern parts of Britain, where elite residence was more likely to be rural than urban. Work around Chester suggests that the limited distribution of coins and ceramics in the area may instead have been because of a continued reliance placed on cattle to store wealth and represent power. This practice might represent a rejection or restriction of Roman elite culture as a means of describing status.

Imperial supply networks helped sustain long-distance trade (Middleton 1979; Wickham 1988). In Britain the distribution of 1st-century AD imported pottery confirms that the army had privileged access to such supplies, but shows that there is no simple distinction between military and civilian (Willis 1996). The needs and directions of supply were not static, and were driven by political and strategic considerations. For instance Britain was both an importer and exporter of grain according to the shifting focus of military campaigns. The importance of towns and forts in the organisation of such supply also showed considerable variation. The economies of London and York, like those of the forts on the northern frontier, appear to have owed more to the changing requirements of the imperial administration than to local or regional factors.

Some areas of surplus production were intensified within the context of command economies structured around imperial estates, the needs of the army, and in support of municipal expenditure. This was most obviously the case in the extraction of mineral wealth (Cleere 1974; Condron 1997), and perhaps influenced the location and character of pottery production in later Roman Britain (Swan 1984; Jones and Mattingly 1990). Cattle ranching may also have been favoured as a means of mobilising surplus within urban economies in Rome's northern provinces. Parallels can be drawn with the emphasis placed on viticulture and oil production in the Mediterranean. The particular importance of ranching is suggested by several sources of evidence. Animal bone assemblages from towns, villas, and forts in the north-west provinces show an unusual bias towards cattle (King 1984). This may reflect the dietary preferences of these communities, but might equally derive from the economic strategies adopted in such places. Although livestock had been used to represent wealth in Iron Age society, the Roman period witnessed a greater determination to maximise the transferable value of the animal carcass. Particular emphasis was given to the post-mortem products that could be preserved, stored, and transported. Butchers' waste, tanneries, and the detritus of salt works suggest the large-scale extraction of smoked and salt beef, leather, and marrow fat and salt (eg Dobney 2001, 40–1; Perring 1991a, 51). The importance of cattle ranching appears to have increased through time, and there is some evidence for investment in both stock improvement (Lauwerier 1988; Dobney 2001, 38–9) and the construction of new stock enclosures and droveways (eg Clarke 1998).

The countryside

Notwithstanding an early investment in urban fabric, elaborate Roman-style houses first appeared in the countryside, especially in the context of late pre-Roman Iron Age aristocratic estates (Millett 1990, 96–7; Perring 2002). These houses served as symbols of power and the estates that they commanded were central to both the generation and representation of surplus (Purcell 1995). Rivet's (1964) model of town/country relations, in which villas were rural residences of an urban elite and their estates supplied urban populations *via* town markets, is still widely accepted (eg Branigan and Miles 1989). More recent work suggests that most Romano-British towns served the interests of an elite class that remained resolutely rural, and it is far from certain that they played a significant role in marketing rural produce. Studies from other provinces illustrate the involvement of villa estates in specialised production for long-distance trade (eg Carandini 1980; Calvo 1995; Mattingly 1988), and towns may have been more important to such trade.

Multiple estate holdings were common in the ancient world. Whilst some villas produced an agricultural or industrial surplus, others were elite residences where lavish consumption drew on resources extracted from holdings elsewhere. Thus a luxurious villa need not be the product of local wealth. Furthermore the strategy of investing surplus in villas, although a common feature, was far from universal. Regional variation in villa types is therefore a product of social choice, and not a barometer of prosperity.

The presence of dependant villas has been taken as an index of a town's importance. Hodder and Millett (1980) have used a distance/decay model to illustrate that towns with an administrative role attracted more villas to their territories than lesser centres. Gregson (1989) developed this argument by exploring the distribution of villas around Cirencester. He showed that larger villas were generally situated at a middle distance from the town: early villas were more likely to be near towns, but a more dispersed distribution pattern rapidly evolved. A more recent study, of villas in the Severn valley, suggests that the distance/decay model may be flawed by a lack of knowledge about villa development around towns (Meheux 1994). These studies are in any case over-reliant on the evidence of masonry villa architecture. The adoption of Roman architectural forms was influenced by the presence of towns, but many of the estates on which masonry houses were built are likely to have been formed before the Roman conquest. In other words the towns were the later feature within the settlement hierarchy, and were located to provide a central forum to a pre-existing network of rural sites.

Villa distributions have also been used to chart the spread of Roman ideas. The Ordnance Survey *Map of Roman Britain* (1991) shows the north and west devoid of elaborate rural settlement. There are also few villas in areas of industrial extraction, such as lead mining Derbyshire and the ironworking Weald (Dearn 1991 suggests that mining rights were held by absentee owners), and in the territory of the Iceni (possibly because of confiscation following Boudicca's rebellion). However, Scott's survey (1993), shows more sites and a different pattern emerges. In particular, the territory of the Iceni no longer seems depopulated. This raises a crucial point to be considered when using arbitrarily defined site types, such as villas, to identify contrasting patterns of regional development: we are not usually comparing like with like. In the first place the descriptive terms are not systematically applied. Building types considered 'native' in the south-east might be thought 'Roman' in the north-west. Sites without high-status imports are often described as prehistoric, but may also have been occupied in the early Roman period. Site recognition is influenced by the terrain within which sites were located and by changing fashions in building design. Such differences in visibility add to the problems of describing landscapes from distributions of classes of sites. The Roman Rural Settlement Project undertaken at Durham University has addressed some of these problems (Taylor 2001), although the main conclusion to be drawn is that broadly based mapping projects can give no more than a crude picture of the complexity of settlement landscapes.

The term 'small town' is applied to a host of different settlements, ranging from specialist production and religious sites to possible *civitas* capitals (Burnham and Wacher 1990; Brown 1995). The clumsier but more apt description of such sites as 'secondary agglomerations' has now been promoted (Millett 2001 from Petit *et al* 1994). Some may have been integrated with rural production and exchange networks, under the control of wealthy landowners. Parallels are found in Roman North Africa and Spain (Calvo 1995), where the villa *fundus* included agricultural and other production (eg metalworking and pottery manufacture) in an integrated system of land and labour exploitation.

The rural population may have had restricted access to the specialist products of the workshops found in towns, villas, and roadside settlements. Assemblages can be used to build up a picture of access to simple luxuries such as iron tools, imported tableware and exotic foodstuffs. These need to be compared with the evidence of architectural complexity and rural productivity (see Jones 1989), to explore the extent to which rural populations were able to benefit from their labours.

The classification of Romano-British settlements into military sites, major and small towns, villas, villages, religious sites, and farmsteads understates the complexity of the changing archaeological landscape. The investment in the built environment described by such classifications was only one form of wealth display. Rich hoards have been found in regions of impoverished architecture (Hingley 1989; Brooks and Bedwin 1989), although the comparative chronologies of these different forms of surplus disposal need study.

2.4.3 Late Roman and sub-Roman

The nature of Romano-British urbanism in late antiquity has been much debated since Reece argued that towns effectively ceased to exist in Britain by the middle of the 3rd century (Reece 1980). This exaggerated hypothesis has justly been criticised (eg Evans 1990). Nevertheless, it has prompted discussion as to what constitutes a town and drawn attention to the fundamental changes that took place at this time. More recently, the term 'post-classical urbanism' (Faulkner 1994) has been coined, emphasising the differences between later Romano-British towns and their 2nd-century predecessors, whilst asserting their 'urban' character.

The Roman Empire suffered a series of setbacks, both economic and military, in the course of the 3rd century and this had an adverse impact on the urban dynamic. Some problems had roots in the 2nd century, and there is evidence of urban contraction at some sites from as early as the middle of that century. London was particularly affected by population decline in this period (Perring 1991a, 76–89). The 2nd century also witnessed changes in the way in which elite status was displayed, with an increased emphasis on houses rather than public buildings as spheres for social interaction.

A decline in urban economic activity may have been offset by changes in the countryside, where the spread of goods and coinage suggests a growing cash economy. Several processes may have been at work. The needs of military supply and the transport of booty had sustained long-distance trade directed through forts and towns, but such commerce declined as limits were drawn to Roman expansion. At the same time a more concerted effort was made to increase the profitability of rural production. Surpluses were needed to support competition for status amongst the propertied classes, where networks of political patronage relied on resource-hungry patterns of ostentatious hospitality and architecture. Income was also needed to meet a growing tax burden, as imperial and civic bureaucracies recovered from the loss of the profits of imperial expansion. Rural economies may also have benefited from the opportunity to replace imported luxuries with local produce. Constraints imposed on urban markets by taxes, more easily regulated after the construction of town walls, may have further encouraged a shift in economic activity from town to country.

Economic change does not, however, seem to have been effected at the cost of social control. Most elaborate rural settlements in Britain date to the 3rd and 4th centuries, and architectural changes appear to illustrate a consolidation of elite power over rural populations (Scott 1994). Investment in improvements in agricultural practices (Jones 1989) marked a shift to tighter controls over production and exchange. The alienation and commodification of land were essential precursors to these developments. A lack of information on the size or organisation of villa estates limits our ability to study these processes in detail, although developments in this direction had almost certainly taken place prior to the Roman conquest. Few working areas of villas have been excavated, although there are notable exceptions (eg Gorhambury and Stanwick in Northamptonshire).

Changes in the rural economy have implications for the status of small town and village populations. It is possible that such communities were formed of sharecropping *coloni* and artisans dependent on villa owners (as Todd 1970). A transition from 'antique' to 'feudal' modes of production can perhaps be seen within the Roman period (contra Wickham 1984), and this is an important area for investigation. It is unfortunate that little attention has been paid to rural settlement other than villas (Hingley 1989 although useful is essentially a study of settlement morphology). There is a growing body of evidence from recent fieldwork (Taylor 2001), but only a small proportion of this information has yet been put to use in the construction of interpretative models.

Changes in the structure of late Romano-British society can be interpreted as a social consolidation in response to threats represented by destabilising, market-based, monetised exchange, its attendant supply and demand-led price fluctuations, and consequent social fragmentation. This picture, which differs in major respects from that portrayed by Esmonde-Cleary (1989) and Higham (1992), emphasises the role of market exchange in transforming and ultimately destabilising 4th-century Britain. Coinage is clearly a central concern here, and the theme is consequently explored in greater detail in one of the case studies found in chapter 4 of this book.

Many commentators propose that Britain witnessed something of a late antique 'golden age', witnessed by the flourishing of decorative arts found in the mosaics and silver hoards of the early to mid 4th century. Many other parts of the Roman world witnessed prosperity at this tine, attributed to the political and economic reforms effected by the Tetrarchs and under Constantine. Britain's towns were comparatively unaffected by this process, although an increase in the number of farms operating within town walls (eg Cirencester: McWhirr 1986) can be presented as evidence for the changing nature of urban lifestyles. 'Dark earth', a product of reworked urban deposits, is a feature of this changing urban environment and suggests the presence of a considerable amount of open space. Biological evidence (insect populations and animal bone supply) suggests, however, that some towns retained urban environments and sophisticated supply mechanisms well into the 4th century (Dobney *et al* 1998). It is also possible that the evidence for 'squatter occupation' found over the cleared remains of urban public buildings (Mackreth 1987), reflected public investment in key areas of industrial production.

Elsewhere in the Roman world the church had a profound influence on the relationship between town and country (eg Harries 1992), but we are woefully ignorant about the status and character of municipal Christianity in late Roman Britain (Frend 1992). Our models for this period should recognise the important distinctions that should now be drawn between the imperial administration and its agents, a largely rural landowning aristocracy, and the organised church.

The early 5th-century collapse of the Roman administration accompanied the demise of Romano-British urban society (in so far as such society had survived the changes of the previous century). This is most evident in changed patterns of consumption, as Roman culture lost its central role in the display of status. There are consequently problems in dating late-Roman levels, because the diagnostic finds are absent. It has sometimes been possible to suggest chronologies from sequences of building alteration and deposit formation (Frere 1983; Hurst and Roskams 1984; Cunliffe and Davenport 1985). But such approaches are difficult to apply systematically and permit alternative readings. Along with the decline of town life, there were shifting notions of what a town was, as a consequence of which archaeological and historical sources can seem strangely divergent. Settlement continuity into the 5th century is both difficult to identify and to place within historical narratives.

2.4.4 Early medieval

The archaeological record shows evidence for developing social differentiation and political centralisation from the late 5th century, culminating in the establishment of the regional Anglo-Saxon kingdoms by the early 7th century (Bassett 1989). This may be attributed to peer competition between the emergent elite, the development of internal social inequalities within local polities, and an increasing territorialisation of authority (Arnold 1988; Scull 1993).

Models for early medieval social development are largely derived from documentary sources, but can be refined and tested by archaeological evidence. Critical markers, as suggested for the area around Sutton Hoo (Carver 1989), include increasingly complex burial practices, a developing settlement hierarchy with evidence for planned layout (eg Hines 1984), changing land use, and a social hierarchy reflected in access to goods. Significant parallels can be seen with the narrative framework developed for the late pre-Roman period.

The emergence of emporia (wics) in eastern and southern England is a late development. The study of these nucleated settlements provides a test of the nature of relations between those in power and the arrangement of production, labour, and supply across the landscape. Critical to this is the relationship between the emporia and other settlements (which issue is explored in detail in case study 4.4, below).

Settlement hierarchies

Many 5th to 6th-century settlements did not survive in the 7th and 8th centuries. This was probably a consequence of landscape reorganisation, involving the creation of new estates, following the centralisation of political authority. A chronology of development can be suggested, placing these changes within the framework of kingdom formation (Bassett 1989). The church also emerged as a major power and landlord (early minster sites remain an important focus for research). The bishoprics established by the Roman church in the 7th century followed the continental metropolitan model, and were placed within or immediately outside the walls of relict Roman towns under the direction of kings and church leaders. The old town might be a suitable place for a bishop's see even if otherwise lacking urban features.

The period AD 600–800 saw the emergence of a new system with several components, showing parallels with north-European settlements. Five broad classes of site can be recognised (albeit indistinctly, see below p 93):

- Large scale high-status sites that can be described as 'palaces' (eg Yeavering),
- Other high-status sites which are usually interpreted as manors, estate centres, or monastic communities (Morris 1989; Cambridge and Rollason 1995),
- Emporia (including Ipswich, Hamwic, Lundenwic, and perhaps York/Eoforwic),
- 'Productive sites' known from surface concentrations of finds, but which cannot be better described for the want of excavated evidence,
- Low-status settlements such as subsistence farms (eg Maxey).

Documentary evidence portrays a landscape organised into large estates, each looking to a caput or estate centre (as perhaps Wicken Bonhunt). Peripatetic kingship allowed the royal household to move from estate to estate living off the king's food rents. Palace sites and estate centres to which rent/tax/tribute was rendered, would have been an integral part of such a system. Part of this redistribution could have fed the population of the emporia (O'Connor 1989b). According to this model, the 'manorial' unit need not have come into being until the 9th century when large estates were alienated piecemeal into smaller holdings. The important point, however, is that a settlement hierarchy had emerged, with all that this implies for social organisation: involving territorial authority, political centralisation and complex interaction between sites (Scull 1993, drawing on Charles-Edwards 1972).

Structures of power were given greater permanence, represented by increased investment in buildings and boundaries (Hall 1988). Estate charters survive from the 8th century (in small numbers), and indicate greater organisation of the landscape (Hooke 1988a; Hooke and Burnell 1995). This is likely to have been accompanied by the consolidation of elite control over labour and goods. As society became more hierarchical (with an emerging middle layer of *cnichts*), estates become increasingly self sufficient, land being granted to *thegns* and individuals from royal lands. The processes behind the creation of monastic estates are consistent with this, although minster and royal estates were generally larger than average (Blair 1988). Great estates such as those of the church were still being built into the post-Conquest period.

Although subsequent rural developments are typified by the evolution of the manor and associated nucleated village, this was by no means universal. Settlement pattern was influenced both by the landscape and by past agricultural practices (Hooke 1996). Thus large tracts of the west, south-west, and parts of eastern England were populated by dispersed hamlets and farmsteads well into the post-conquest period.

In western Britain the changes of the period AD 600–800 were reflected in a shift in overseas trade, from Mediterranean to continental sources (Alcock 1992; Cunliffe 1993). High-status sites (eg Dumbarton, Whithorn, Dinas Powys, Tintagel, and Bantham), are revealed by the range of imported glass and ceramic vessels (notably wine *amphorae* and drinking vessels) and finely worked metal.

Emporia

Our main interest here is in the *emporia*. Recent syntheses include Hodges and Hobley (1988), Clarke and Ambrosiani (1995), and Scull (1997). The study of this subject has been profoundly influenced by the work of Richard Hodges (1989; 1996) who relied, perhaps excessively, on the results of excavations at Southampton. These he set in the context of continental developments (eg Heidinga 1987). Hodges saw the first *emporia* as seasonal ports-of-trade at the periphery of political territories and largely excluded from elite control (his type A *emporia*). *Emporia* avoided the sites of Roman administrative power but might, as Biddle has observed, have been subordinate to higher status sites (as suggested by the relationship of Hamtun to *Hamwic* and Lundenburh to *Lundenwic*). Hodges argues that from the 670s *emporia* were better integrated into regional exchange networks, and overseas trade was consolidated (his type B *emporia*). These later *emporia* were in estates under the control of monastic and/or royal overlords, were

developed into regional market centres around the end of the 8th century, and were precursor to the *burhs*.

Recent approaches instead suggest that the origins of *emporia* lie in the formation and consolidation of estates, and that royal or monastic lords controlled them. The separation between the elite and the artisan traders of *emporia* assumed in Hodges' model has not been demonstrated: on the contrary high-status burials at Ipswich and London illustrate the presence of an elite in these 7th-century settlements (Hodges and Hobley 1988; Scull 1997). An early phase of seasonal occupation can not be identified at Ipswich, and this makes it harder to argue that the site began as an administered centre populated by continental trader agents. The early involvement of *emporia* in craft production also suggests that they were integrated into local economic systems from the start.

Having argued that *emporia* were integrated into regional settlement hierarchies, we now need to develop more detailed models of the effect that this had on social and economic relationships. The spatial and social locus of craft production is a significant area of research. Hodges (1989) stresses the importance of workshops in *emporia*, and describes how they had their origins in earlier village/estate production. Bayley's (1991) study of early medieval metalworking also describes extensive production outside *emporia*. It is evident that industrial production had no great need of the town but benefited from the factors that gave impetus to urban growth.

Emporia housed a mixed population of artisans and traders, but it is not clear how these communities were formed and interacted. It would be rewarding to identify the origins of traders – for instance were they of a particular social group? (eg Frisians: see Scull 1997; Heidinga 1987). These are issues that can be explored through the study of culturally embedded patterns of consumption within the *emporia*: imported finds could represent items introduced by traders for their own use as much as exchange.

The study of the supply of *emporia*, and the impact that this had on regional economies, is an important area of current study. There is some evidence for agricultural production on the borders of London and Ipswich, in contrast with the suggested controlled provision of *Hamwic's* population from surrounding rural settlements (Bourdillon 1988). Animals brought in on the hoof would have provided food and raw materials for the artisans (handle makers using horn and bone; leather preparation and working; textile production). Crabtree (1996) has demonstrated that Ipswich was provided with meat from a limited range of domestic animals, and that the creation of the *emporium* preceded, and presumably contributed to, the development of specialised production in the surrounding countryside (eg pork at Wicken Bonunt and wool at Brandon – see Table 13). Distributions of Ipswich ware and *sceatta* coins in East Anglia illustrate links between the *emporia* and rural settlement (not only high-status sites), and testify to the importance of local and regional exchange networks.

The burden of supplying the *emporia* could be presented as evidence of an administered economy, integrating rural production on estates with the 'proto-urban' artisans. The planned and specialist nature of these settlements also suggests controlled origins. Hodges (1989; 1996) sees this as evidence of a controlling royal monopoly. However, the large tenements demarcated by streets could represent blocks owned by different aristocrats (Scull 1997). Hence Clarke and Ambrosiani (1995) suggest that *emporia* were held by several aristocratic families under the jurisdiction of a king.

Although their coastal or estuarine position appears peripheral, current knowledge of contemporary political territories shows that *emporia* were situated within kingdoms. They were not the gateway communities described by Hodges. Production involved the conversion of rural produce into items for bulk exchange (including slaves) alongside imported pottery and metalwork (Scull 1997, contra Hodges 1989, 129). Layout and activities suggest that they were very much part of these polities, and ongoing projects highlight the potential of the material culture to reveal these connections (Bourdillon 1989; O'Connor 1989b).

There is currently a lively academic interest in how regional political and economic networks were formed and the ways in which surplus was extracted and distributed. The study of the links between *emporia* and other sites in the settlement hierarchy is essential. In particular further work is needed to establish the nature of 'productive sites', since these cannot be assumed to be lesser centres of exchange (see p 94).

Emporia were in decline early in the 9th century. The failure of these settlements can in part be attributed to a period of insecurity in the face of Viking raids, but when towns were revived towards the end of the century different sites were usually preferred.

This suggests a complex pattern of redundancy, influenced by changing political strategies.

Burhs

The late 9th century was a period of forceful urban foundation. A network of planned, defended settlements was established in Alfred's Wessex (as described in the Burghal Hidage), and similar developments took place in the Danelaw. The old Roman towns, some of which had already been developed as seats of ecclesiastical or royal power (like London, York, Canterbury, and Winchester), were preferred. The promotion of such sites as administrative units took inspiration from developments on the continent. Winchester illustrates the radical changes that took place (Biddle and Hill 1971; Kipling 1994). The Old Minster had been established within the Roman site (probably in the 7th century), and the pre-Alfredan settlement also included a royal palace and attendant service population. In late 9th-century re-planning, city walls were built, a street grid established, and new properties created. This re-planned town housed royal, ecclesiastic, mercantile, and artisan communities.

Hodges describes two basic types of Alfredan *burh*: larger foundations (over 16 acres) with a range of administrative and economic functions, and smaller sites that were essentially forts (Hodges 1989, 164–77). His analysis almost certainly places too much emphasis on the role of the market. First and foremost the new urban system established controls over population and land: these were defended strongholds associated with the collection of rents and tribute. *Burhs* reinforced the position of the royal and ecclesiastic elite that sponsored their foundation. They emerged as complex settlements housing a wide range of activities: defensive, administrative, royal, monastic, ecclesiastic, industrial, and mercantile (Vince 1994). Aston (1986) sees this as a policy of bringing together various functions that had previously been dispersed through the landscape.

Burhs inhabited a complex settlement landscape, and were not necessarily at its apex. Royal *vills*, such as the port at Langport and the palace at Somerton, were also established (Cunliffe 1993). *Tuns* continued, along with estate centres, minster churches, and hundred meeting places (important gathering points even to the 17th century). Some bishoprics were not moved to towns until after the Conquest, and rural fairs continued.

We do not know how much use rural populations made of town markets and services. When first established, the *burhs* may have relied on provisioning from royal estates, but market-based exchange networks developed in which urban goods and services could be exchanged for rural produce and from which the landlords could extract profit (Vince 1994; Carver 1993a).

The subsequent history of these towns shows great variation: Canterbury had a specialist market centre by 932 (in cattle), and the monastery and see continued as important foci of the town. London, York, and Norwich prospered. But Exeter grew only slowly from the late 10th century, and at Cricklade the defended interior was unsettled. It is possible to view the creation of *burhs* as an experiment that sometimes went wrong. New *burhs* were also founded in the 11th century, to provide extra revenue for estates, and their development remained in the control of aristocratic and monastic landowners.

Aristocratic control over land and people is also revealed in the rise of the manor and attendant village (eg Beresford 1987 on Goltho). The late Saxon period saw increasing nucleation of rural settlements, particularly in the Midlands (Roberts 1985, see also p 108), although there is considerable regional variation. Another feature of the period is the growth of monastic estates. Documentary evidence (especially for the south and east, Faull 1984) shows the consolidation of estates (through marriage alliances and inheritance) and the consolidation of close ties between gentry and local settlements. This might represent the development of feudal ties prior to the Norman Conquest (Saunders 1992).

Viking and Danish settlement was both a disruptive force and a stimulus, encouraging new patterns of social relationships and defining new regional identities. The Viking contribution to town life has been emphasised by discoveries in York and Dublin (Clarke and Ambrosiani 1995; Wallace 1985). Constitutional history shows that the Danish settlement also exercised a lasting influence on regional administration (Hart 1992). Excavations have been most intensive at York and Lincoln (some work has also been undertaken at Stamford and Thetford; little is known of Derby and Nottingham). Planned settlements, with evidence for functional zoning, were established within the old Roman walled towns, much in the fashion of the *burhs* further south (Roskams 1996). These towns show a complex layout with both British and Scandinavian influences evident.

Excavated urban assemblages witness complex models of provisioning and land management in the areas of Danish and Scandinavian settlement, although little is known of the impact that this had on the countryside. Little rural survey has been undertaken (although see Cramp and Miket 1982; West Yorks Metropolitan County Council 1981), and the settlement pattern is known chiefly through place-name evidence. The economic environment can, however, be studied through the distribution of the products of the major ceramic industries at Stamford, Thetford, and Stafford. Little is also understood of changes in estates; church records, normally the most complete for this period, are scarce in the Danelaw because the first settlers were pagan and few 7th to 8th-century monastic sites survived.

Key issues include:

- The influence of minsters and *villae regales* on *burh* formation (Blair 1988),
- The topographic and economic relationship of *burhs* to the estates from which they were formed,
- Changes to the ways in which *burhs* were supplied (the respective importance of estate provisioning and the market), and their comparative importance as markets or as administered distribution centres,
- The significance of estates and boroughs in the development of specialist production,
- Comparison between *burhs* and monasteries (which were also fixed communities with relatively stable land holdings and an increasing involvement in production),
- The impact of Danish and Scandinavian settlement on settlement dynamics.

2.4.5 Later medieval

The population of England grew between the 11th and 13th centuries, reaching levels at the end of this period that were not equalled until the 16th century. Towns grew in number, and this was accompanied by developments in rural settlement and agricultural practice (Britnell and Campbell 1995). In a period rich in documentary sources archaeology nevertheless has much to contribute. It offers a measure of settlement character to contrast with the evidence of documented status, and a test of the models built on such evidence. In particular pottery allows the study of local and regional production and exchange at a fine level of detail and is a critical source for charting the growth of markets.

The consolidation of settlement frameworks, 1000–1190

Although social and tenurial arrangements survived the Norman Conquest, they were not unchanged. Land ownership was soon concentrated in the hands of a small Norman aristocracy that implemented its control through the trappings of Anglo-Saxon society. Domesday records only 8% of land remaining with old English families, the rest now held by the conquerors and church. The king and his family were the largest landowners with 17% of the available land (Miller and Hatcher 1978, 15). The impact of these changes on settlement character is an important area of research.

This was a period of conspicuous consumption and display, most elaborately revealed by the construction of castles, manors, and churches/cathedrals, but also evident in the consumption of luxury commodities which became necessary symbols of status. Income was needed to support social competition, and the main source of income was rent. Rent demands on agrarian producers encouraged the production of cash crops for market sale. Town markets gave peasant cultivators the opportunity to convert surplus into cash and the organisation of such markets became another source of revenue for landowners.

New urban foundations saw lords converting existing holdings into burgage plots, and several studies have used the evidence of urban morphology to trace such processes (eg Lilley 1994a). Research on Coventry suggests a gradual evolution, with new burgage plots added as the town expanded. This approach relies on the secure identification of plots, although recent work suggests that these were not as regular as is sometimes assumed. Land ownership was divided amongst the church, seigneury, and monarchy. Estates were complex and changing, dividing the landscape and cutting through towns (eg Coventry was split between two landlords, John 1981).

Distinctions can be drawn between royal boroughs (free towns) and towns owned by ecclesiastic or lay landowners, but the importance of these differences to the study of urban economies has probably been exaggerated (Beresford 1988). It can be argued that crown estates were not as closely man-

aged as other holdings and that tenants here could participate more freely in a market economy, allowing the development of more complex social and economic relationships (eg McIntosh 1986). But it has also been shown that seigniorial boroughs could avoid restrictions nominally placed on their autonomy (eg Rigby 1993; Palliser 1997). Hilton suggests (1984; 1992) that seigniorial towns, although tied to feudal manors and the fief system, were more complex than other settlements.

English landlords consolidated their control of the landscape in the late 12th and 13th centuries (via demesne farming). This contrasts with contemporary developments on the continent (Verhulst 1997). Changes in settlement pattern were usually the consequence of changes in tenure, as in the formation of aristocratic alliances through marriage. Economic factors were less important. The long process of village formation continued, and was intimately linked to town formation. Documentary evidence illustrates the importance of both landlords and peasants in effecting such change (eg Courtney forthcoming). Records are generally poor for this period and archaeology can add to our understanding of the evolution of markets and variation in the character of seigniorial control. The ability of poor households to purchase goods through markets is an important area for research, especially in the study of the evolution of different regional economies.

Few surveys have attempted an integrated description of the settlement landscape: for instance see Aston and Lewis (1994) on Wessex where the church, rural settlement, towns, and field systems are dealt with in separate chapters. We need to contrast the patterns of supply and consumption found on church, castle, and town sites. These different communities drew on different livestock pools, reflecting varied land management strategies. Cattle bone from the Bedern in York suggests that the college had a source of beef independent of the general urban market: it was drawing calves and older beasts from dairy herds at a time when the rest of York obtained meat from draught animals and beef herds (Bond and O'Connor 1999). The comparison of castle baileys and adjacent town burgage plots has particular potential. The rubbish found in town ditches and waterfront reclamations is a valuable source of evidence, the potential of which is illustrated by work undertaken in York. Church and castle building is assumed to have been associated with prestige rather than a reflection of local economic development. Did different supply mechanisms (as in the use of building stone, timber, and lead) apply to the construction of these monuments?

Late 12th–14th centuries – the growth of markets

The 13th century witnessed rapid population growth (Gillingham 1984, 65), although the percentage of the population living in towns may not have increased significantly. The period was critical in the development of markets, a development that was facilitated by a marked increase in the use of cash in the economy (Britnell 1995; 1996). Rents were generally paid in coin rather than kind, a development stemming from the early post-Conquest period. Between 1200 and 1500, about 2800 market grants were awarded to lay and ecclesiastic landowners (Beresford and Finberg 1973; Beresford 1981), half of these between 1200 and 1275. These grants were not always exercised, and some new markets failed. The archaeological study of this process is complicated by problems of definition and the ambiguity of the evidence (the problem of Portchester is illustrative, see Cunliffe and Munby 1985, 270–95). Markets were also held in villages and fairs and were not necessarily urban. The pattern that emerged was a complex one with significant regional variation (see Hilton 1992), but to a large extent the distribution of markets reflected aristocratic petitioning and regal patronage.

More things were bought and sold as a matter of course, and documentary sources show that peasants were more likely to have used markets in the later medieval period (Dyer 1989). Objects from archaeological excavations show that even small villages had access to a wide range of goods (Britnell 1995; Snooks 1995; Gimpel 1976; Hallam in MacFarlane 1978, 60). We do not know what range of markets poor households used in the late medieval period. This is an area where archaeology can supplement documentary sources. In particular, studies of regional pottery production and trade can make a significant contribution to our understanding of changing approaches to local markets (Davey and Hodges 1983; Mellor 1994; McCarthy and Brooks 1988). There is increasing evidence for emerging regional economies from this period, although differences were not as marked as they were to become in the 15th century and beyond. The early development of different regional patterns is an area for further research (below p 107).

Post-Conquest politics had dispossessed the English aristocracy of much of their urban holdings, and subsequent developments saw the grip of major landowners reduce on towns. In the 13th century there seems to have been a growing civic consciousness, and it seems likely that control of the urban environment passed from the lords (secular and religious) to groups of citizens. The growth of markets and of mercantile institutions (through guilds) strengthened towns as political entities, and many were declared independent incorporations by their civic leaders (starting with Bristol in 1373). This was reflected in municipal investment in the urban fabric: public buildings, guildhalls, weigh-houses, conduits, lavatories, and quays were built and improved.

Long-distance trade was encouraged and this was facilitated by improvements in ship design. Control of such trade may have lain in the hands of foreigners, in particular Flemings, Gascons, and Italians who had easier access to credit than their English counterparts. This contributed to the development of distinctive urban communities.

Research issues for this period include the following:

- Can an increase in consumerism be traced through the 12th to mid 14th centuries?
- How reliable is evidence for craft specialisation as a means of characterising settlement hierarchy?
- How important were town-based markets as opposed to rural ones?
- To what extent did rural households have access to market-based exchange?
- How influential were regional differences (as characterised by farming regimes) in shaping trade? Phythian-Adams (1987) argues that many small towns were involved in the exchange of rural produce at the interface between different farming regimes (pastoral vs. arable for example);
- How did changes in communication networks affect settlement development?

Late 14th century – c 1500

Urban decline in this period has been blamed on the mid 14th-century plagues; improvements in rural living conditions, in a market where labour was scarce, may have exacerbated urban depopulation. But change was protracted and complicated. Social tensions and economic strains were evident before the end of the 13th century whilst decline was not widely apparent until the later 14th century (Schofield and Vince 1994). Goldberg's (1992) work on York likewise places the 14th-century decline of the town, revealed in the abandonment of tenements, in the context of changing regional economies. Decline need not have resulted in poorer living standards or a reduction in the range of urban activities (Dyer 1989). Further research needs to focus on the regional patterning of change, and could usefully review assumptions about the relationship between prosperity, production, and urbanism.

Urban production and processing was generally aimed at urban consumption, whilst village markets served most rural needs. The main function of towns was as local markets. Even in the largest 14th-century ports (London and Bristol), more income was generated through regional marketing than long-distance trade. However, coastal ports began to outstrip inland and riverine ones in the course of the 14th century. For example, York lost out to Hull, and likewise Norwich and Lincoln saw their role as luxury markets overtaken by King's Lynn and Boston respectively.

Urban hierarchies can be constructed from the documentary sources, in particular the 14th-century Lay Subsidies (eg Glasscock 1975; Slater 1985). This information also charts the distribution of wealth. The richer families and groups (merchants and aristocrats) were most likely to be found in the boroughs, and the south was more prosperous. There is more evidence for competitive consumption and display from the late 14th century onwards. Social differentiation was increasingly defined by fashion, and Courtney (1997b) suggests that the emulation of aristocrats by lower-status individuals encouraged greater elaboration. This competition is also reflected in the built environment – through

public and private buildings as well as processions and displays. The sense of the town as socially and culturally distinct from the countryside is likely to have sharpened

Little is known of the impact of rising consumption on poor households, nor the degree to which they had access to market goods. Archaeological study of the subject is hampered by the scarcity of good urban assemblages of this date. A shift to organised municipal rubbish disposal in this period has left us with a small and biased sample, although more carefully targeted sampling programmes can probably correct this.

Further research could concentrate on regional variations in patterns of urban development (particularly small towns), which subject needs to be studied within the context of contrasting farming regimes (a theme developed further below p 114). Particular attention should be given to the role of peasant 'buying power' and consumption, and to the progress towards specialisation in both production and service industries. The complex relationship between purchasing and estate holdings needs to be acknowledged in describing the importance of market exchange. Contrasts between the material culture and economic fortunes of individual households are needed. In the urban context more can be made of the differences between market places and surrounding plots.

The close of our period is marked by two significant trends: the growth of the English nation as a political and ideological construct, and the reorganisation of regions in particular shaped by specialist cloth production. This 'becoming English' was a slow process and merits close archaeological attention (see Hines 1994 on the construction of identity in 8th-century Britain).

2.5 Some research questions

Our review of current issues in the archaeological study of the relationship between town and country can be summarised as a series of research questions. These reflect the concerns of this report, and are inevitably partial. They are intended to provoke thought on what might be achieved in future study and to set out lines of enquiry that can be adapted to local research strategies. We start with a list of general questions on the definition of urban and other settlements and their visibility in the archaeo-

logical record. Most of these can be redirected to address specific landscapes. The remainder of the chapter is set out following the periods of change described above, from the late pre-Roman Iron Age down to the end of the 15th century. As elsewhere in this report the term 'urban' is sometimes used broadly, to include other nucleated settlements such as *oppida* and *emporia*. Most of these questions are subsequently developed to form the basis of the research frameworks detailed in chapter 4.

2.5.1 General themes

*Descriptions and methodologies
(Research Frameworks 4.2–4.5)*

Q1   How are contrasting economic systems and cultural identities manifest in artefactual and structural signatures?

Q2   Which artefactual correlates provide the most legible and useful characterisations of different classes of site?

Q3   How should sampling be conducted in order to achieve comparable experimental conditions? When are such conditions to be desired?

Power and identity (Research Frameworks 4.2–4.5)

Q4   How were power relations articulated within society and expressed in different settlement hierarchies?

Q5   How distinctive was urban culture? Were towns innovative, and a force behind the definition of regional identities? If so, how did ideas spread into the countryside?

*Production and exchange
(Research Frameworks 4.2–4.5)*

Q6   How did urban household production differ from its rural equivalent?

Q7   Were towns supplied in different ways to other nucleated settlements (eg forts, temples, and monasteries)?

Q8   How important were towns in exchange systems and distributive networks?

Q9   What contribution did towns make to the evolution of new economic systems – including market economies – or to the reinforcement of socially embedded ones?

Environmental impact (Research Framework 4.6)

Q10 How did urban transformations – the creation, modification, and failure of urban centres – affect rural settlement trajectories?

Q11 How has the English countryside been transformed by the presence of towns? To what extent have urban demands depleted natural resources or stimulated improved agricultural productivity?

2.5.2 Iron Age and Roman

Briton into Roman (Research Framework 4.2)

Q12 How were *oppida* integrated into the settlement hierarchy, supplied, and populated? How important were they in social display and in the mediation of exchange? Can differences between sites of seasonal and permanent occupation be identified?

Q13 How significant were the influences of pre-Conquest settlement hierarchies, the experiences of conquest, and the subsequent military and administrative presence in the evolution of regional settlement landscapes in Roman Britain?

Q14 Did different foundations (*colonia*, civitas capitals, etc) show different patterns of relationships with their territories? How durable were any such differences?

Q15 How were forts, villas, small towns, villages, etc integrated into the landscape? Where were production centres and markets located and how did they relate to urban sites?

Q16 Is there evidence of resistance to, as well as penetration of, Roman urban values beyond towns? Which models best account for different patterns of integration?

Late antique change (Research Framework 4.3)

Q17 How were towns and associated settlement patterns in late Roman Britain different from their pre 3rd-century predecessors? Did strategies for supplying urban populations change in the 3rd/4th centuries?

Q18 Was the late Romano-British economy more market based? If so, how did this affect the relationship between town and country?

Q19 Is there evidence for the expansion and intensification of estate production, with the development of 'feudal-type' obligations, services and rents?

2.5.3 Early medieval

*Settlement patterns and emporia
(Research Framework 4.4)*

Q20 What is the range and diversity of settlement in the 7th-9th centuries? When, if at all, does it become possible to distinguish between different 'classes' of site?

Q21 Whose interests did the *emporia* serve? Were they royal foundations, or did kings regulate something that was happening anyway?

Q22 To what extent were *emporia* places of trade or manufacture and how different were they in this regard to other settlements? Can distinctions be drawn between goods obtained by elite provisioning and through exchange?

Q23 Who was involved in exchange at *emporia*? Were *emporia* populations different to contemporary rural populations?

Burh *formation and function*

Q24 Were *burhs* established as military bases provisioned by royal estates, which only subsequently became centres for local exchange and specialist services?

Q25 How important were the *burhs* as markets in local and long-distance exchange systems? Comparison can be drawn with the market functions of ports and fairs?;

Q26 Can different supply mechanisms for royal sites, monasteries, manors, and *burhs* be identified?

Q27 What contributions did estates and *burhs* make to the emergence of specialist production centres?

Q28 What impact did Danish and Scandinavian settlement have on town formation and settlement dynamics?

Q29 What impact did the Norman Conquest have on the economic basis of English towns, both through changes in ownership/estate management and in terms of a putative decline in *burhs*?

2.5.4 Later medieval

Growth of towns (Research Framework 4.5)

Q30 How were high-status sites integrated into exchange networks? In what ways were supply mechanisms developed for monasteries and castles different to those exploited to support low-status sites?

Q31 How important were markets in the exchange of local produce? What economic role can be ascribed to peasant 'buying' power and consumption? How did this reflect access to markets, and regional variation?

Q32 Did towns in regions of dispersed settlement have different functions to those in areas of nucleated settlement? Were fairs, peddlers, and village-based markets of more importance in regions of dispersed settlement?

Q33 How did urban identities develop, and how important were they in the construction of regional identities and style?

The transformation of medieval England

Q34 What explains variation in the development of towns in the late 14th to 16th century, particularly small towns? How did urban decline in this period influence the distributions of economic power through the settlement landscape?

Q35 How did the rise of specialist manufacturing centres influence regional exchange? Changes in pottery style marking a late medieval to early modern transition occur at different dates in different regions. Do other archaeological indicators show the same pattern and are such differences a reflection of differing urban functions?

Q36 What role did towns play in the creation of English identities in the late 15th century?

2.6 Summary

In this chapter we have tackled some of the problems of definition that make it difficult to agree on the subject of our study. From an archaeological point of view architectural and legal definitions of the town are unsatisfactory. Since we are chiefly interested in systems of sites, rather than towns as things, we consider it more instructive to concentrate on the evidence of patterns of consumption

(chapter 2.2.1). This evidence permits the study of how resources were used and transformed in the support of settlement hierarchies. Urban appetites, conceits, and identities are expressed in consumer culture, and this culture can be read in rubbish.

Towns imposed on the landscape in myriad ways. Since different needs promote different relationships, hinterlands are not neatly defined spatial entities (chapter 2.2.2). The fields of urban influence belong in the realm of human behaviour. Geography is only one factor amongst many and spatial modelling has been given disproportionate emphasis in the study of urban hinterlands.

Different societies have adopted different approaches to the ways in which wealth could be created and translated into power (chapter 2.3.1). There is still considerable utility in Marxist descriptive systems, which allow us to identify alternative 'modes of production' (domestic production; systems based on tribute, tax, and rent; and market economies). It is deeply misleading, however, to represent history as a simple evolution through these stages of economic life. Different approaches to the command of surplus coexist. We suggest, therefore, that research should explore ways in which different economic and social strategies were articulated across the settlement landscape. This is not simply a matter of describing how settlement hierarchies were supported. We are also interested in the ways towns contributed to the shaping of regional and cultural identities (chapter 2.3.2), and the impact that urbanism has had on the environment (chapter 2.3.3).

These themes are traced through a series of phases of urban development in the first 1500 years of the Christian era. We have offered some observations on the differences that can be described between the central-place functions of the Iron Age *oppidum*, classical city, late antique town, early medieval *emporium*, late Saxon *burh,* and the high medieval town (chapter 2.4). The research questions deriving from this review have been summarised above (chapter 2.5), and need not be repeated here.

Two general conclusions can be drawn from this chapter. Firstly we wish to promote the study of systems of sites, in which towns can be described within the broader settlement landscape. Secondly the archaeological study of such systems relies on certain classes of find, which can be used to contrast the ways in which different communities were integrated into regional economies. This issue is taken up in more detail in the next chapter (chapter 3) where we also place emphasis on the need for studies that better integrate different types of archaeological information.

CHAPTER THREE

Classes of evidence and their potential

Mark Whyman and Dominic Perring

Archaeological finds are the main sources of new information in the areas of research identified in the previous chapter. In this chapter our attention now turns to the ways in which this archaeological evidence might be used. We have already suggested that central places within settlement hierarchies can be characterised as peaks of consumption. The description of hierarchies of consumption relies on indices of the scale and diversity of production, distribution, and discard. Many classes of archaeological data can be used to measure diversity. However, certain finds have particular value because of their abundance on archaeological sites and because of their power to illuminate the processes we wish to study. Paramount are:

- *Ecofacts*: the animal bone and archaeobotanical assemblages that witness rural production (livestock and crop regimes) and the management of surplus production to supply consumer sites including towns;
- *Ceramics*: the most abundant of archaeological finds on account of the high survival rate of pottery sherds. Pots were used in the storage, transportation, and consumption of food, and pottery distributions illustrate the movement of resources across a landscape;
- *Coinage*: a medium through which exchange could be mediated and surplus negotiated, offering the potential to identify closely datable patterns of such activity at a variety of scales.

These classes of material are given most detailed attention here. Other types of find can be equally illuminating within specific areas of research, but are less universally useful. Skeletal evidence deserves attention because of its contribution to demographic studies, whilst small finds (eg dress accessories) and building materials were deployed to make statements about status and identity. This chapter summarises the ways in which such information can contribute to our understanding of town/country relations, and is concluded by a brief review of the benefits of integrating the different types of information in more ambitious characterisations of patterns of social consumption.

3.1 Animal bone

Animal remains offer many clues about changing farming strategies. Animals were not just a source of food. Indeed they were usually far too valuable to be eaten. As beasts of burden they provided the main source of traction and transport. Herds also converted perishable surplus into energy and transferable wealth. The control of such resources demonstrated status and built social stability. Decisions about animal husbandry were therefore inextricably linked to choices made about cereal production, the management of the landscape, and the display of social rank. The intensified production of surplus for the urban market has an impact on all aspects of the agrarian regime, for which animal bone is just one source of information amongst many.

Animal husbandry normally exploits a full range of both live products (energy, manure, wool, dairy produce, eggs, etc) as well as post-mortem ones (meat, hides, bones, fat, tallow, etc). In the self-sufficient 'domestic mode' of production such products were normally consumed locally. The creation of a surplus (eg wool, dairy products, hides, or meat) for dedicated consumers represents a variation from such domestic production, and introduces a bias to resource use. This might involve:

- The transfer of animals to consumers when they have been replaced by younger equivalents or otherwise reached the end of their working lives,
- The seasonal abundance of certain species (eg pigs and cattle) according to husbandry practices (dependent on the availability of overwintering facilities, limitations on grazing, and other such factors),
- The transfer of animals to consumers when the value of meat is maximised, but where the full potential of the animal in agricultural production has not been utilised (ie shorter lifespans),
- A concentration on rearing particular species, and the modification of herd structure to permit transfer of a live product for consumption.

Differences between mainly-producer and mainly-consumer settlements may be evident in the relative number of different species exploited, the sex and age profiles of the animals present, and possibly in the breeds or types of animals represented (Maltby 1994). These features can be studied from archaeological assemblages, on the basis of:

- Different species present and their relative frequency/abundance,
- Frequency of individual skeletal elements of each species,
- Size and sex of the individual animals,
- Age at death of the animals and therefore the gross slaughter pattern,
- Pathologies deriving from diseases, husbandry practices, and nutrition,
- Genetic and morphological characters that can represent different stocks or populations,
- Post-mortem and pre-depositional impacts (especially butchery),
- Depositional and post-depositional impacts (taphonomy).

3.1.1 The 'life cycle' of animal bone

Bone assemblages represent both the living community from which they derived and the processes that lead to death and deposition (O'Connor 1996). Table 1 illustrates some of the inferences about the exploitation of animal resources that can be drawn from archaeozoological data (for analytical methods see Chaplin 1971; Davis 1986; Grayson 1984; Hesse and Wapnish 1985; Klein and Cruz-Uribe 1984; Rackham 1994a; Schmid 1972). Critical variables are presented here in the context of six key stages in the 'life cycle' of animal bone. These are traced from livestock procurement - through rearing, selection for slaughter, butchery, and consumption - to the eventual discard and reworking of bone waste. These variables characterise different approaches to the command of surplus.

Stage 1 Resource availability

The range and variety of animals represented is a useful discriminant between settlements. Subsistence production can result in a narrow range of domestic animals being exploited (as has been suggested for the British Iron Age: D Rackham, pers comm), although hunting and fishing can add compensatory variety. Species variety has successfully been used to explore differences between town and country (Groenman-van Waateringe 1994).

Although most bone found on archaeological sites comes from domesticated species slaughtered for consumption, other species sometimes give better information on settlement status and drawing power. Falconry and hunting have been aristocratic pursuits (eg Fox 1996), and the presence of hunting animals and game may describe social importance. The archaeology of hunting merits further attention (and might usefully extend to the study of hunt-related injury pathologies in prey species). Wild animals, especially birds and fish, can also be used to study environmental change and ecological niche diversity (Eastham 1997). For instance the disappearance of white-tailed eagles from medieval deposits in York suggests that breeding habitats were being lost in the process of woodland clearance (Bond and O'Connor 1999, 395). Similarly a decline in the exploitation of certain kinds of fish in York has been attributed to water pollution (A. Jones 1988; O'Connor 1991). The impact of urbanisation is evident in the changing character of the local flora and fauna (eg de Moulins 1990). Urban environmental conditions can also be measured from animal populations. The corpses of cats, dogs, rodents, and amphibians are comparatively worthless, and likely to enter the archaeological record near where the animals lived and died. Common trends in the pathology and morbidity of these different species (including, for instance, lead

Table 1 Animal bone: a flow chart indicating the nature of the resource available at the different stages in the cycle of husbandry and use

Research topic	Resource			Character	Interpretation, references	Criteria
1 Sources						
Where animals were obtained	Remote/wild			'Exotic' mammals, marine fish, shellfish	Luxury trade (deep-sea fishing is also a measure of specialization)	Species wealth: presence/absence
	Local/wild			Fish, birds, mammals, antler	Hunting, pests & scavengers	Analysis of oxygen isotopes from teeth may pinpoint locations where animals were raised
	Local/domestic			Cattle, sheep, pig, horse, goat, Poultry, pigeon, rabbit, dog	Backyard farming	
	Remote/domestic			Cattle, sheep	Droving	
2 Husbandry	*Cattle (horse)*	*Sheep (goat)*	*Pig*			*Age/sex structure*
Which animals were reared and what this tells us of agricultural regimes	Neonates			Neonate mortality	Rearing of animals on site representing backyard, urban, or rural farming	Presence/absence neonate bones
			Piglets	Piglets (3–9 months) selected for consumption	Control of/access to cull by consumer, taking of tribute/access to estate production	
		Lambs / Kids		For consumption & skin/hides	By-product of dairying (Legge 1981) & of selection for skin/hide. A high juvenile sheep cull at Danebury may represent the use of skins for tribute or trade (Grant 1984)	Tooth eruption and wear, epiphyseal fusion
	Calves			Under 6 months, mainly male	Veal & hide production (calf-skin). Indicative of tribute, estate production, consumer demand, or dairying (Maltby 1994)	
	12–24 months			Mainly male	By-product of dairying. Fattening before slaughter to enhance yield (McCormick 1983), skins important	As above, also measurement data, anatomical distinction of sex
	18–36 months	18–36 months	12–36 months	Near equal male (or castrate) female sex ratio	Meat production, possibly commercial (Legge 1981); skins & horns also important	As above, also tooth annuli
	4-8 yrs			Mainly castrate & some females	Meat production in extensive system (no shortage of posture) where herd size may define status	Tooth wear & annuli, epiphyseal fusion
		60-72 months		Adults, mainly wethers and ewes	Wool production (Noddle 1980)	As above, also measurement data & anatomical distinction of sex
	6–14 yrs	3–8 yrs	>3 yrs	Mainly females, with some adult males	Dairying & breeding stock (McCormick 1983). Source could be extensive system with many subsistence units, with livestock integrated into crop-production regimes	As above, but epiphyseal data for latest fusing only
	8-20 yrs			Male & female, possibly with some pathologies	Breeding stock & draught animals (eg Dobney et al 1996, 420-1)	As above (but epiphyseal fusion relevant from vertebrae only) – also pathologies
	Birds			Chicken, geese, ducks	Mainly for meat & eggs; species bias may reflect settlement status	Fragment counts & frequency data; sieving
3 Character of livestock at point of slaughter	Proportion of wild to domestic species				Access to game can mark status (eg venison at Barnard Castle & Prudhoe — Jones et al 1986)	Quantification, fragment counts, bone weight, frequency data
Variables in the choice of animals for butchery	Importance of different domestic species as meat staples				Preferences reflect farming strategies (eg more mutton in the diet follows wool production), ethnic identity (Ijzereef 1989) & ritual practice (Leviton 1993)	Non-metrical traits, measurement data, DNA studies
	Diversity of sizes & types (multiple populations) within species (morphological differences in skulls, etc)				A feature of broad supply networks, in which many sources – possibly from different regions (eg hill & lowland sheep) – were exploited	Measurement data
	Changes in size of types available				Medieval Dublin exploited smaller cattle than earlier monasteries in the area (McCormick 1983), perhaps because of increased demand. See Armitage (1982) on differences between town & castle in Tudor London	
	Morphological peculiarities, pathological features				Evidence for use of animals in draught (arable cultivation) & hobbling	Pathologies
	Seasonal exploitation (hunting, fishing, slaughter of domestic stock, etc)				Seasonal fluctuations in supply may be mitigated by processing foodstuffs for preservation	Tooth wear & annuli, epiphyseal fusion (early), measurement data (ie fish size), otolith & scale annuli, seasonal/migratory species

Research topic	Resource	Character	Interpretation, references	Criteria
4 Butchery and post-mortem processing	Consumption of entire carcass	All body parts present	The animals were bred on site or obtained whole. Whole carcasses can witness farming, feasting, and ritual sacrifice	Bone element analysis by count, weight or MAU (fragmentation analysis relevant)
	Primary butchery waste	Over-representation of head & feet	Specialised butchery associated with cattle rearing & processing	Element analysis, butchery & fragmentation
How the butchered animal parts were distributed	Skinning and tanning waste	Over-representation of metapodials & phalanges	Specialised processing of butchery waste, if not specialised stock rearing for hides (leather)	
	Secondary processing: – horners & craft industries	Horn cores, antler, metapodials, etc	Workshop production (industrial or domestic) can witness specialist supply of raw materials or exchange of products	As above, also evidence for use of tools such as drills & lathes in bone working
	– foodstuffs	Long bones smashed for marrow; hanging, curing & processing of meat	Large scale processing of marrowbone may sometimes relate to the use of fats as a preserving medium to facilitate transportation (Maltby 1994). Hook damage to scapulae witnesses beef curing (Dobney et al 1996)	Fragmentation analysis; human post-mortem impacts
	Selection of high or low meat value elements or other specific joints	Bias towards upper or lower limb bones, etc	The differential distribution of resources reflects status & can indicate the operation of 'tribute' & 'market' systems (eg deer hind legs at Barnard Castle: Jones et al 1986), also relates to specific processing practices	Element analysis as above
5 Consumption	Food preparation	Cooking & table waste in primary deposits	Direct evidence for the consumption of animals as food	Contextual & element analysis (incl. pie slice); burning, butchery & fragmentation study
6 Disposal	Activity areas & structured disposal	Differential distribution within & between sites	Spatial patterning of activities described in stages 1–4 above (eg Halstead et al 1978, Wilson 1996)	Fragmentation analysis and preservation
Patterning in the distribution of refuse	Taphonomy	Structured deposition in primary, secondary & tertiary deposits: middens, pits, etc	Disposal mechanisms (night soil, manuring), types of midden (eg town & castle ditches: Rackham 1981); processes of deposition, scavenging, and decay (D Rackham 1996); reworking of deposits & residuality. Social attitudes to rubbish (distinctions between urban & rural environments)	Element and species analysis, fragmentation analysis, analysis of preservation condition

absorption levels) will share a common cause in the local environment.

The description of species abundance normally relies on sieved samples, to counter recovery bias between small and larger vertebrates. However, subdivision of the assemblage into classes (edible mammals, birds, fish, and shellfish), facilitates comparison between sieved and unsieved assemblages, since recovery is less likely to be selective for a particular species within these categories. Simple presence/absence measures can distinguish between assemblages in terms of access to species, although the relationship between sample size and sample richness (the larger the sample the greater the variety) must be taken into account in any comparative analysis. There are many different statistical measures of diversity, but most are inapplicable to archaeological data. Bone samples from different sites are identified to a range of different taxonomic levels, and it can be difficult to establish comparability. Scientific methods for describing diversity cannot easily accommodate such fuzzy data.

Stage 2 Animal husbandry

The specialised exploitation of animals is frequently geared to the supply of towns and other consumer sites. General indicators of urban-type supply are a lack of infant and juvenile skeletal parts, and evidence for systematic butchery. The 'primary' economic use of an animal (eg for draught, dairying, or meat) can often be recognised from the age and sex ratio of the animals slaughtered. This reflects the selective removal of animals from the 'domestic mode' of production and provides sensitive indicators of changes in agricultural regime (Fig 1). It also illustrates the role of small-scale livestock farming in towns (eg O'Connor 1989b; 1991; 1994) and the extent of consumer control (eg the cull structure of pigs at Westminster Abbey in the 11th century suggests controlled supply: Rackham 1994b, 52–3).

An animal's sex can be identified from a limited number of skeletal elements, although good data is rare and this is a difficult area of study. The inferences that can be drawn vary according to species. Overall, age-at-death statistics can be used to reveal subsistence supply, controlled victualling, food rents, or market-dedicated production. Maltby (1994) has shown differences in the urban and rural slaughter profile of Roman cattle, and suggests that towns may have been the most important suppliers for some components, with veal a by-product of local dairying.

Pathologies and trauma can derive from an animal's use in specific activities or rearing conditions. For example, wear patterns on cattle shoulder bones and pelvis may reflect the use of animals in ploughing and milking. Distinctive patterns of dental attrition may indicate penning. Pathologies associated with draught may occur on the feet of cattle and in skull perforations although there are significant problems of diagnosis (Baker and Brothwell 1980; Brothwell et al 1996).

Stage 3 Characteristics of livestock reaching the point of slaughter

In considering the resources a town drew upon for its supply, and the extent to which demand encouraged innovation (as in stock improvement), we can study:

- Comparative proportions of wild/domestic species reaching a settlement (Stage 1);
- The availability of domesticated stocks and importance of meat staples, with implications for specialised husbandry and the importance of urban consumption in dictating rural production (Stage 2);
- The relative homogeneity of livestock populations, distinguishing between settlements drawing on dispersed sources and those reliant on discrete territories with more intensive husbandry practices. At present this can be done with limited success using metrical data and non-metrical skeletal traits (eg O'Connor 1982b; 1989b; Albarella and Davis 1996) but little is published. More detailed study may permit the description of the populations exploited by individual settlements. With the advent of polymerase chain reaction (PCR) in DNA studies it should eventually be possible to draw more precise genetic relationships between samples;
- Comparison of stock sizes at maturity (using metrical data) within and between contemporary sites. Evidence of stock improvement can be seen as a response to demand, and access to different populations can indicate the resource range of an urban centre;
- Bone pathologies indicative of the role of stock in systems of agrarian production, eg for traction and dairy herds (see Stage 2);

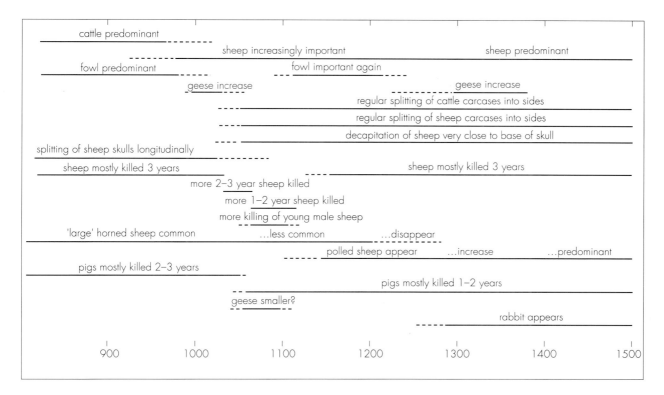

cattle predominant

sheep increasingly important   sheep predominant

fowl predominant   fowl important again

geese increase   geese increase

regular splitting of cattle carcases into sides

regular splitting of sheep carcases into sides

decapitation of sheep very close to base of skull

splitting of sheep skulls longitudinally

sheep mostly killed 3 years   sheep mostly killed 3 years

more 2–3 year sheep killed

more 1–2 year sheep killed

more killing of young male sheep

'large' horned sheep common   ...less common   ...disappear

polled sheep appear   ...increase   ...predominant

pigs mostly killed 2–3 years

pigs mostly killed 1–2 years

geese smaller?

rabbit appears

900   1000   1100   1200   1300   1400   1500

- Indications of the seasonal exploitation of particular species in circumstances where demand is likely to have been constant. Changes in culling patterns may reflect changing demand and the development of husbandry techniques, and might also be evident in the provision of storage for preserved meat products (eg ceramic storage vessels).

Stage 4 Variation in carcass processing after slaughter

Patterns of carcass processing can be diagnostic of urban consumption (O'Connor 1989b). Normally all parts of the animal were available at rural sites, where livestock was killed, butchered, and consumed. The urban butcher is more likely to have supplied a variety of specialist consumers. As a consequence, animal parts were widely distributed. Some elements were discarded (such as the skull), others went to the horner (horn cores), some to the skinner or tanner (phalanges and perhaps metapodials), some were used in bone working (metapodials, ribs, and perhaps radii) and others were distributed in food supply (with high-status consumers taking choice parts). Consequently bone assemblages from different parts of a settlement may contain complementary bone collections (eg Rackham 1987, fig 1). Selective assemblages are readily recognised and may be species or element specific (Holmes 1981;

Fig 1 A Reconstruction of the patterns of urban demand and rural supply derived from the study of variables noted in animal bones from Flaxengate, Lincoln, c 870–1500 (after O'Connor 1982a)

Maltby 1984; O'Connor 1984). It is first necessary to distinguish between patterning because of depletion or addition (O'Connor 1993). Are carcass parts under-represented because they had been removed for use elsewhere, or is the disparity instead a consequence of the importation of the other elements of the animal for specialist consumption? More frequently, however, disposal practices are likely to have resulted in the re-amalgamation of these waste assemblages.

Variability in the skeletal elements present will distinguish between primary processing (splitting/dressing of the carcass; removal of the hides and lower limb elements), secondary processing (separation of specific joints from the carcass; working of bone/antler/horn; breaking of bone components for marrow) and tertiary processing/consumption (meat taken off the bone; disposal of inedible detritus). Where suitable elements are available (see Watson 1972; Rackham 1986a) the following issues can be investigated:

- The relative frequency with which different bones or joints reached a particular site, as indicated by the fragment percentages of the assemblage those bones represent,

- The bias towards the body parts of particular species, implying carcass part selection and specialist processing/consumption (eg Dobney *et al* 1996),
- Indications of butchery techniques related to bulk processing, or the preparation of specific joints of meat and other resources,
- Variations in these characteristics between assemblages, context groups, and sites indicating diversity of specialisation and processing activities within a given settlement.

Stage 5 Food preparation and consumption

Debris associated with meat consumption represents food consumed at a site, as distinct from foods processed at a site but consumed elsewhere. Recognition of cuts of meat diagnostic of consumption 'off the bone', or of bones fragmented as a result of cooking pits and kitchen middens, can be compared with the species pattern represented in 'processing' assemblages. Information from contemporary contexts permits the comparison of what was consumed in the settlement with what arrived 'on the hoof'; discrepancies between these could indicate the processing of certain species for distribution and ultimate consumption elsewhere. This in turn could have significant implications for the usual view of urban food supply being overwhelmingly dominated by a handful of species.

Indications of post-mortem impacts on skeletal elements can identify butchery techniques and methods whereby cuts of meat were cured, stored, and transported (eg perforation of scapulae for hanging shoulder joints). Maltby (1984; 1989) has illustrated differences between rural and urban butchery on Roman sites in Southern England, although this requires a level of data not always collected by other analysts. In his 1989 paper he gives a framework within which such evidence can be recorded, and it may be possible to apply this, at least crudely, to other data. The waste from craft activities, tanning, skins, bone working, and antler working are also of interest, particularly if the waste indicates the use of specialised 'professional' tools.

Stage 6 Discard and disposal

Food preparation and disposal, and subsequent taphonomic processes, are reflected in the way in which bones fragment and decay. Urban butchery practices tend to result in more coarse debris being found in disposal/demolition areas, with smaller pieces associated with domestic activities (Wilson 1994a). Disposal practices could vary considerably through time. For instance rubbish in early Roman towns was often removed for disposal elsewhere, but appears to have been discarded close to its point of use in late antiquity. Differences in disposal practice will affect the quality, integrity, and reliability of the sample recovered. It is first necessary to establish whether or not the bone is in a primary context, such as a rubbish pit associated with the use of a building, or comes from reworked levelling horizons. The reworking of deposits is a particular problem. We need information on the context, spatial variability, condition, and fragmentation of the bone assemblages in order to assess the potential of the material.

3.1.2 Describing assemblages

Animal bone assemblages are not easy to use (Binford and Bertram 1977; Brain 1967; Lyman 1994; Shipman 1981; O'Connor 1996), and several factors introduce bias. These include:

- *Survival bias (taphonomy)*: the problems of differential preservation, reworking, and residuality are especially acute with animal bones due to their variable robustness and the fact that few are diagnostic of date;
- *collection bias:* the value of many assemblages is compromised by the method of collection. Many questions require information on smaller species (birds, fish, and small mammals) whose bones are often missed in excavation (Payne 1972);
- *Description bias:* there are problems with the identification, description, and interpretation of bone (Gilbert and Singer 1982; Meadows 1980; Rackham 1983; Uerpmann 1973).

Different methods can be applied for describing taxa, quantifying species, and bone frequencies (Perkins 1973; Gautier 1984; Watson 1979; Rackham 1986b), interpreting ageing data (Maltby 1982), identifying the sex structure (Wilson *et al* 1982), butchery, and palaeo-pathology. Different characterisations reveal different aspects of the patterns of consumption, but can limit comparability. Species quantification is perhaps the most important in terms of comparing differences between rural

Table 2 Some techniques employed in the description of comparative quantities of animal bones in archaeological assemblages. Other techniques include estimated number of individuals (Krantz 1968; Lie 1980; Fieller & Turner 1982; Wild & Nichol 1983; Ducos 1984; Winder 1993), fragmentation analysis (Watson 1972; 1979; Rackham 1986a; Moreno-Garcia et al 1996); and relative frequency (Perkins 1973)

Method	Criteria and applicability	Sources
Weight	This offers a crude measure of the major components of an assemblage, but distorts the relative importance of some species since there is no direct relationship between bone weight and animal weight/numbers	Kubasiewicz 1956, Uerpmann 1973, Casteel 1978, Grayson 1984, O'Connor 1991
Fragment counts Number of Identified Specimens (NISP)	This is the most widely used measure, but since bone fragmentation varies because of cultural & taphonomic processes it can give distorted results. NISP data is only directly comparable between like contexts	Chaplin 1971, Grayson 1984
Minimum Number of Individuals (MNI)	Estimates the no of individuals present (from diagonostic elements). Can be misleading because of the depletion/enrichment of assemblages in post-slaughter processing	Chaplin 1971, Grayson 1984
Minimal Animall Unit (MAU)	This identifies units of a butchered carcass. The contribution of each species is assessed by the no of MAUs present. Allied to estimates of 'meat value' it indicates the economic contribution made by each species. This facilitates the comparison of urban and rural assemblages, but is laborious	Binford & Bertram 1977
Frequency of occurrence in contexts and bone frequency per context	This measures the likelihood that a deposit will include elements from a species. The rarer the species the larger the assemblage must be to include it, or the more contexts must be sampled to find it. This reduces the impact of exceptional assemblages & reflects the frequency with which a species was present, irrespective of its meat contribution. This may be a better measure for characterising sites than weight, fragments or MNIs. The method is applicable to published data	

'producer', rural 'consumer', and urban 'consumer' sites. Ringrose (1993) has reviewed the range of techniques available for such study and the most relevant are summarised in Table 2. The selection of a quantitative technique should depend on the questions being asked, and more labour-intensive methods require justification in terms of expected information yield. Descriptions of assemblages based on fragment counts (NISP) remain the most generally applicable, although the limitations of this technique can be offset by the use of other methods (eg Minimal Animal Unit in the detailed analysis of assemblages, or frequency of occurrence by context in comparing settlements). For the purposes of comparison different sample levels can be defined, which acknowledge the different levels of description that can be obtained from recorded data. Three levels are proposed.

Level 1

In contrasting the animal bone assemblages from a range of sites, both rural and urban, it is sensible to draw on measures recorded by most analysts, and included in published accounts. Large samples are not always essential, but there is little point in comparing assemblages that can not be dated. The following features can be compared:

- Overall species abundance. Small collections of hand-collected bone can be utilised,
- Relative proportions of cattle, pig, sheep, and horse (on the basis of NISP or MNI, see Table 2). Sample sizes should exceed 500 identified fragments,
- The relative frequency of sheep, wildfowl, freshwater fish, marine fish, etc (on the basis of context/sample frequency not bone frequency),
- Proportion of game animals in the assemblage. Sample sizes in excess of 500 identified fragments are probably needed.

Level 2

Larger samples are usually needed to generate reliable descriptions of age, sex, and stature. Such descriptions generally need raw data rather than the summary information found in published accounts. Information of this nature is usually available in catalogues of recently studied material, but older collections may require restudy. Useful data include:

- Cull profiles of cattle and sheep,
- The proportion of neonate bones or teeth in cattle, sheep, and pig populations (after Grant 1982 or Payne 1973). Large samples (ie over 2000 identified specimens) are more reliable,
- Bone measurements to describe sexual dimor-

phism, stock improvements, introduction and multiple sourcing. Twenty to thirty examples of each measurement used are usually needed, but small assemblages from a range of sites can be amalgamated. Log-ratio methods can be used to increase the utility of small samples, and allow biometrical analysis to be conducted with just a few measurements from each of several different bones of one species (T O'Connor, pers comm). This also allows the detailed unpicking of amalgamated samples to investigate, for example, the presence of different morphotypes.

Level 3

Descriptions of bone fragmentation and butchery permit a higher level of comparative analysis. Assemblages are best described in Minimum Animal Units (MAU). Recording should allow the separation of the proximal and distal ends of the bone by recording the frequency of fragments with epiphyses or diagnostic zones. If these data are to be analysed by a program such as Pie Slice (Moreno-Garcia *et al* 1996) then the diagnostic zones or some other systematic fragment recording system is required. Samples should include contexts with over 50-100 identified fragments. Some reanalysis of published and archive information may be required for fragmentation analysis (eg Dobney and Reilly 1988), and butchery recording (eg Maltby 1989). Ideally, contextual information should

permit the comparison of assemblages from different classes of deposit and allow for intra-site spatial analysis.

The study of animal bone is central to the research proposed in this report. Several issues raised in this section are developed further in the case studies described in chapter 4 (see, in particular, sections 4.2.4, 4.4.4, and 4.6.4, all of which rely on the approaches and methodologies described here).

Future work will benefit from the broader horizons that are being established for osteological studies. The work of Dobney *et al* (1998) on the supply mechanisms in 4th-century Lincoln illustrates the benefits of more integrated approaches. Animal bone studies also benefit from the development of models of spatial and temporal catchment to underpin the site-specific categorisations more usually undertaken (O'Connor 1996). These approaches to the description of animal bone assemblages provide a powerful tool for the description of systems of site, where studies address specific research questions drawing on comparable data from an appropriate range of locales (Crabtree 1996 is a useful illustration of what can be achieved, see p 98). The emphasis placed on the development of models of catchment landscapes and on studies that integrate animal bone data with other classes of information is particularly welcome. It is to these other classes of information that our attention now turns.

3.2 Archaeobotanical assemblages

Plants provided food, fodder, fuel, and building materials, and their exploitation illustrates changing approaches to the organisation of production as well as providing a measure of environmental change. Three principal classes of botanical evidence are the subject of specialist archaeological study:

- *Pollen*. This is the main source of evidence for the study of former vegetation landscapes, and is particularly useful in describing patterns of rural forestation and agricultural clearance. Urban pollen is less useful, except in charting the progress of initial urbanisation, because samples from later contexts usually contain too much residual material and can only offer a very general confirmation of the urban character of the environment.

- *Wood* (including charcoal). Species

identifications and dendrochronology allow the detailed reconstruction of regional woodland management regimes and of patterns of urban supply;

- *Other plant macrofossils* (eg leaves, twigs, and seeds, and their impressions left in materials like pottery and mudbrick). Individual assemblages describe aspects of diet, crop processing, and the local environment. Diatoms (algae) provide a particularly sensitive measure of water quality and character (eg Boyd 1981).

Examples of the contribution that these types of information can make to our study are illustrated in Table 3. This summarises the potential of archaeobotanical evidence in the study of urban supply and its impact on the rural environment, with reference to the factors that affect survival. This table follows the model used in describing animal bone, and is set out according to the successive stages of production, processing, consumption, and disposal of plant resources.

Different factors affect the survival of botanical materials, and it is largely because good assemblages are difficult to obtain that plant remains provide a less useful general measure of the differences between archaeological sites than pottery and animal bone. But where remains are well preserved the information yield is high. Waterlogged contexts are the most valuable, and urban waterfronts have been a rich source of biological material, especially structural timbers and primary waste. The particular circumstances of cesspits favour the survival of seeds that had passed through the gut, and can generate comparable species lists of plants exploited in local diet. Carbonised and otherwise mineralised survivals are another important source of information (especially for burnt cereal crops and fuel residues). Botanical data is best used in conjunction with the study of insect remains and foraminifera. Leguminous crops, for instance, survive infrequently, but their exploitation can sometimes be deduced from the presence of the bean weevil.

Stages in analysis

Stage 1 Supply

Charred residues witness the range of plant species introduced as fuel. From this evidence it may be possible to establish whether a single source dominated supply, or whether diverse stocks were exploited. The materials used can provide information on the management of woodland resources. Differences between the fuels in domestic and industrial contexts may indicate dedicated supply, the specialisation of activities, and their alienation from domestic production. This analysis requires samples from securely identified sources (hearths, ovens, kilns, corn driers etc). The use of agricultural by-products as fuel can provide information about the state of the processing of plant material entering a settlement (see below, Stage 3).

Structural timbers permit the reconstruction of woodland management, such as coppicing and pollarding, and illustrate the range of timber available to the settlement. At a macro level, the pattern of survival of timber suitable for dendrochronological dating (ie with 50+ rings) may offer insights into woodland management and timber availability.

Between c AD 300 and AD 500, for example, the absence of timbers suitable for dating may imply either a shortage of older trees, or a deliberate policy of felling trees at a specific stage in their growth – perhaps 'stands' of trees grown for building purposes (Tyers et al 1994).

Plant macrofossils and pollen assemblages may characterise the urban flora, where soil conditions allow (as in wet or charred/desiccated conditions). There are, however, acute problems in distinguishing pollen 'indigenous' to an urban site from human or wind-borne imports (Greig 1982). Grain crops, such as barley, wheat, oats, and rye, were generally imported to town for consumption. Such crops are not mobile (unlike livestock), so the options for the state of processing when the material is brought to town are greater (cf Moffett 1994). The source of some crops can be identified through the weeds and pests that accompanied them (Kenward and Allison 1994b; Moffett 1994). The introduction of plants and insects can lead them to colonise urban environments, and their presence may, therefore, be indicative of much earlier importation. Because of such colonisation, it is not always possible to establish if weeds reflect the circumstances of crop cultivation and processing, or the subsequent pollution of the crop after its arrival in town (in storage or after discard). In the case of a diachronic study of a particular urban site this distinction may not always be significant; a simple list of the species identified can be linked to likely original habitats, showing that material from these sources was introduced at some point.

But our concern with the changing agrarian regimes that supplied towns is better served if we can isolate the likely sources of the components of a crop assemblage. Taphonomy and post-burial reworking are therefore as relevant to plant assemblages as they are in the study of animal bone. There is some prospect that the combination of pollen, invertebrate (insect), and plant macrofossil data may help isolate the source of the material. Inferences of this nature require well-preserved, substantial, in situ assemblages from primary contexts (eg Kenward and Williams 1979, 69–74).

The range of introduced species found at a settlement can be a measure of urbanisation, since urban-type supply encourages colonisation (Gilbert 1991, 10). This is not a particularly useful archaeological measure because of sample bias (richer samples define sites where soil conditions favour survival rather than anything else), but

Table 3. Environmental data: a table of resources pertinent to this study with a review of their character and potential

Research topic	Resource	Character	Interpretation, references	Criteria
1 Supply *Wood and Timber* How the landscape was managed to supply fuel and timber	Domestic fuel (including shops, etc)	Wood (brush & coppice), smallwood/faggots, charcoal, reused timber, peat, cereal waste, straw, dung, heather, etc — usually obtained from local sources	Low diversity represents managed woodland & organised supply. High diversity reflects multi-sourcing. Evidence describes regional woodland types & clearance, and agrarian regimes (Huntley & Stallibrass 1995)	Samples from primary contexts (hearths, ovens, kilns, flue/stoke holes, corn driers & pits), for study of species, character (roundwood, timber, twigs, etc) & coppicing (annual rings, growth rate, coppice heels, wood diameter)
	Industrial fuel	Coal and charcoal (season of felling & use, evidence for drying prior to charcoal production) — sometimes imported from remote sources against specific industrial uses	eg Woolaston Roman iron-smelting site (Figueiral pers comm.)	Source of coal (microscopic study); presence of clinker, hammerscale, or slag; wood species id; character of charcoal (stem diameter, ring counts, growth rate)
	Structural timber	Oak, beech, elm, alder, pine; imported timber (eg Baltic oak & pine) — from diverse sources and potentially reused	Tree ring sequence matches indicate if multiple or single source (Tyers et al 1994)	Species identifications; dimensions; dendrochronology; evidence for coppicing & management (annual rings, growth rate, coppice heels, stem diameter), same tree-to-source timber
	Wattle, hurdles, posts	Wide utilisation of immature timber/underwood (consistency of size & age) from local & regional sources (NB also the use of grass etc as temper in daub & mudbrick)	Woodland, coppice with standards, oak, hazel, alder & other species	
Foodstuffs Changing crop regimes and their relationship to urban settlement	Cereals	Glume wheats: spelt and emmer Free threshing cereals: breadwheat, rivet wheat, barley, rye Hulled grain: barley, oats Seasonal sowings: autumn wheat & rye, spring barley & oats	Regional/climate variation; introduction of new crops; use of traditional varieties. Diversity can reflect specialised consumption (eg brewing, baking, pottage, fodder)	Sampled context description essential, cereal & weed species identifications; species abundance & frequency
	Weeds (associated with crops)	Weed ecology reflects soils under cultivation (eg *Scandix pectenveneris, Silene noctiflora* - chalky soils; *Anthemis cotula* –heavy soils; *Capsella bursapastoris, Sherardia arvensis* – light soils) & season of sowing (eg *Allium aparine* – autumn sown; *Fallopia convolvulus* – spring sown)		Species identifications; proportions of species in *Secalietea* & *Chenopodietea* communities in samples
	Beans & peas	Seeds (generally carbonised)	Greig 1988, M K Jones 1981	
	Vegetables	Normally only identifiable from waterlogged deposits	Van der Veen 1992, Campbell 1994	Species identification, abundance & frequency
	Fruit	Fruit stones (eg from cess pits, sometimes mineralised), exotics include grape, date, olive & fig; domestic & wild species include elder, crowberry, hawthorn, etc	Often major crops (Kenward & Hall 1995), but poor survival. Variety in domestic species suggests orchards & market gardening; wild species variety reflects seasonal gathering.	Waterlogged, mineralised, or carbonised survivals important for all categories
	Nuts	Mainly hazelnut & walnut		
Landscape The impact of cultivation on the landscape. The physical evidence for changing strategies in response to urban demands	Changing land use: loss of woodland & pasture to arable, or woodland to pasture	Pollen evidence for change; rural plant macrofossil evidence for cultivation of new soils, access to timber, change in cereal proportions & introduction of new varieties; gross changes in cereal grain density at rural sites		Pollen spectra within chronological framework; plant macrofossil identifications; wood identifications; density/litre cereal evidence
	Drainage to 'reclaim' land for cultivation & pasture	Landscape studies linked with environmental data. Sedimentation, mollusc, diatom, *foraminifera*, etc show changing water regimes, salination & pollution.	Polders, fens, river floodplains, warping, etc (eg Hall & Coles 1994)	
	Expansion of arable onto marginal land	Landscape study with plant macrofossil analysis, pollen analysis		
	Evidence for surplus production	Landscape change, structural features (eg corn driers, barns, farm buildings, storage pits, etc).		

Research topic	Resource	Character	Interpretation, references	Criteria
2 Processing	*Primary processing – producer/consumer Sites*			*Cereal grain/chaff/weed seed ratios; straw; weed seed type and size*
Crops and their waste products - the organisation of production and urban supply	Threshing	1 free grain, fine chaff, some broken straw, rachises & weed heads and seeds 2 bulk of straw, most rachises and coarse weeds	Product for winnowing Straw for thatching & flooring. Waste for fuel, fodder & temper	Little opportunity for carbonisation May be carbonised on discard
	Winnowing	1 grain, heavy straw nodes, some rachises, most weed seeds 2 light chaff, straw fragments, awns, lightest weed heads & seeds	Product for sieving Waste for fuel, fodder or temper	Little opportunity for carbonisation May be carbonised when discarded
	Coarse & medium sieving	1 clean grain, weed seeds of same size & some rachis fragments 2 straw nodes, tail grain, weed heads, small weed seeds & some rachis segments and awns	Product for storage, etc Waste for discard	May be carbonised during drying May be carbonised when discarded
	Corn drying	Grain dried to avoid spoiling and germination	Corn driers indicate bulk processing Jones 1981; Van der Veen 1992	
	Secondary processing – consumer sites			
	Fine sieving & hand sorting	1 prime grain & weed seeds same size as grain	Product for parching, milling, boiling, consumption, etc	Accidentally carbonised fine sieve product during parching before milling.
		2 small seeds, tail grain, some glume bases & seeds same size as grain	Discard into fire?	Discarded fine sieve by-product
	Brewing	Malted grain, particularly barley and oats		Many germinating grain
	Bread making	Not clearly identifiable	Normally fragmented cereal testa, 'bran', in waterlogged material (eg Dickson 1987; Kenward & Hall 1995)	
	Animal fodder	Material brought in to feed stabled animals	eg Kenward & Hall 1995	See by-products above, also possible products for some species such as oats
	Commodity production			
	Flax, hemp, dyes, fibres, medicines, ritual, oils	Normally from waterlogged contexts. Possible medicinal plants; evidence for textile dyeing, wool cleaning, fulling & teasing	eg Kenward & Hall 1995; Campbell 1994 for flax & possible retting	Species & fibre identifications
3 Consumption	Food species	Plant macrofossils, pollen from human/animal faeces, cess-pits & manure deposits	Diet - eg Warnock & Reinhard 1992	Coprolites, cess deposits, stable manure/ordure, animal sheds & pens
4 Disposal	Seeds	Urban seed flora, background; sources of seed bank in archaeological deposits (reeds/rushes, hay, straw, heather, peat)	Management of waste products, pollution, social attitudes to dirt, urban complexity (Kenward & Allison 1994a; 1994b; Kenward & Hall 1995)	Information required on sample context & strategy. Waterlogging generally necessary. Species identifications, abundance & frequency; diversity indices; ecological analyses
How waste products describe the urban environment	Hygiene & living conditions	Parasite presence & density (human or animal), beetle & insect fauna, particularly evidence for fleas, ticks, lice, etc & household/domestic pests; species associated with urban fauna		
	Water supply & conditions	Possible changes in range of freshwater fish due to changes in river quality (pollution); incidence of parasites, cess material and eutrophic/stagnant conditions in drains, conduits, etc		Fish species id; parasite density; diatom flora, aquatic invertebrate assemblages, industrial
	Structural timbers reused	Oak, beech, elm, alder, pine, imported timber	Changing supply mechanisms	waste products, metal salts, heavy minerals, etc

where like circumstances prevail it may be possible to use ecological complexity (described initially as species lists) to complement architectural measures of urbanisation.

Characterisation of patterns of rural production through pollen data requires samples from a broad range of rural contexts. Sedimentary taphonomy, and the biases produced by highly localised concentrations of particular species (such as the disproportionate representation of pollen from trees fringing lacustrine environments, which frequently provide the most productive 'pollen traps', in otherwise 'open' landscapes), must be characterised and taken account of. Developing such an approach to study a particular urban hinterland will require extensive and targeted retrieval of pollen samples from a wide range of environments.

Stage 2 Processing

The state in which foodstuffs are brought into a settlement, and the range of processing methods evidenced as residues, provides a sensitive indicator of the functions of that settlement in relation to its agrarian hinterland, and the organisation of production within that hinterland. Well-preserved plant macrofossils can indicate the stage of processing of grain crops (ie cut, winnowed, partially or fully cleaned) with the presence/absence of chaff indicating the state of cleaning, and the nature of chaff components providing information about harvesting methods. Moffett's (1994) study of cereal waste used as fuel in 10th-century Stafford illustrates the potential of such material. Conclusions could be drawn about the likely origin of the grain crop, the harvesting methods employed, and aspects of the wider organisation of cereal crop production. Well-preserved assemblages are essential for the extraction of detailed information of this kind.

Stage 3 Consumption

Plant-based foodstuffs characteristically leave less evidence for their consumption, as distinct from production and processing, than do animal resources. The purpose of importation of plant material – as food resource, animal feed, building/furnishing material (eg thatch) – may vary, but implications for the exploitation of hinterlands exist in each case. The question 'what is the by-product of what?' requires careful consideration in the interpretation of archaeobotanical data. Human and animal cess deposits from pits, middens, or structures can provide information on the consumption of various grain types – subject to the recovery of pollen or plant macrofossils from such deposits (eg Warnock and Reinhard 1992).

Stage 4 Disposal

Again, evidence for this is less easily accessible than is the case with animal bones. Contrasts may be drawn between carefully 'targeted' disposal within pits and specified midden areas, and less structured discard. Variations in this have ramifications for the urban domestic environment, and important considerations such as the quality of available water supply. Discard practice may be illuminated by the study of other material classes, such as animal bone, but it should be noted that the inoffensive nature of the processing by-products of plant-based foodstuffs compared to animal carcasses may result in a wholly different pattern. In any case it is likely that the very preservation of usable data of this type will derive from structured deposition, in pits or in association with features such as hearths and ovens.

This raises an important issue in considering the potential of archaeobotanical study to investigate urban supply. Variations in cereal crops present on urban sites have been described from very low densities (eg from deposits with c 10–12 grains per 10 litres of soil: Green 1982). It is debatable whether these are significant, or the equivalent of the 'background noise', as defined by O'Connor (1989a) in bone assemblages. This begs the question of whether, for example, the apparent shift in emphasis between oats, barley and wheat in Winchester identified by Green (1982), represents anything more than variation within expected limits of probability.

This in turn raises the issue of the nature of the background noise: what does it comprise, and could it represent overall patterns of crop (and animal) consumption within a settlement? Attempts to reconstruct typical urban environments, and to regard deposits associated with specific activities as distorting the picture, encourages the systematic retrieval of low-quality, randomised data. This approach should not take precedence over the study of high-quality samples. Some of the best results obtained have come from the detailed study of large and well-preserved assemblages from tightly dated contexts. Good assemblages are to be prized.

3.3 Ceramics

Pottery is an invaluable aid to research because of its durability, widespread use, and typological variability. It can be used to establish relative and absolute chronologies, and describe patterns of distribution and exchange. The measurement of the relative proportions of different classes of pottery, and the comparison of such differences between assemblages, provides the basis on which the 'reach' of a particular settlement can be assessed. Changing patterns of relationship between a settlement, its immediate hinterland, and more distant sites can thereby be explored.

3.3.1 Pottery production, use, and discard

Aspects of pottery production, use, and discard that illustrate relationships between settlements and their hinterlands are summarised in Table 4. This sets out a series of key stages:

Stage 1 Sources of ceramics

Quantified distribution maps are used to illustrate the relative importance of supply from recognisable sources (eg Going 1987). These maps usually exclude a substantial residue of undiagnostic coarse and greywares, which, whilst assumed to be local, cannot be accurately provenanced. This is true of all periods under study here. Discriminating between these types is essential to the study of local supply networks (an issue we return to in more detail below). Petrological (Vince 1989) and clay-mineral characterisation techniques (Arnold *et al* 1991) can help isolate specific fabric types.

Stage 2 Methods and context of production

Ceramics were usually but one component of wider agrarian production. The potter's access to resources can be indicated by the quality of the clay, the temper that was used, the production technique (handmade or wheel thrown), the firing temperature, and the surface treatment (decoration). This has implications for resource management in the agrarian regime serviced by the potter (cf Costin 1991). Centralisation of production, involving the 'integration' of agrarian producers into a system of production across a wider region (cf Slofstra 1983), can witness substantial changes in the organisation of rural production. The other implications and consequences of such centralisation are:

- The intensification of ceramic use,
- A greater investment at production sites,
- A possibly decrease in the total expenditure on production across a locality or a region,
- Consistent, local access to raw materials at specific locations,
- Increasing specialisation of labour.

The process of centralisation usually involves the development of more complex processes of manufacture (eg clay preparation, wheel throwing, kiln firing), and a greater consistency of form and fabric, recognisable over wider areas of distribution.

Stage 3 Distribution mechanisms

Research has focused on the refinement of typologies and chronologies, and the interpretation of ceramics distributions frequently employs unquantified data and assumptions regarding the dynamics of production and exchange.

Distributions of particular types have frequently been equated with the extent of discrete social groups or 'cultures'. Altered patterns of distribution are often attributed to migrations, or the diffusion of cultural traits *via* acculturation. This paradigm still informs the classification and interpretation of ceramics in Roman, Anglo-Saxon, and Anglo-Scandinavian contexts. The application of culture-historical precepts has been superseded by a realisation of the potential of ceramics distributions to define economic networks. The variety of the overlapping pottery distributions in Roman Britain testify to complex structures articulating production and exchange, and these are generally held to include a demand-led free market influenced by transport costs, if distorted by state interference designed to provide for its own institutions. Similar *a priori* assumptions have informed approaches to later periods. Distinctive Middle Saxon pottery associated with *emporia* – whether imported from continental Europe or of insular manufacture – is seen as an indicator of trade; initially controlled by the royal authority (7th/8th centuries), but subsequently the product of market economies integrated at regional level (9th/10th centuries). Medieval sources indicate complex hierarchies of market towns, and the inter-

Table 4 Processes of ceramic production, distribution, use and discard relevant to the study of urban/rural interrelationships

Research topic	Resource	Character	Interpretation, references	Criteria
1 Source & class of ceramics	Vessel fabric	General fabric character; nature of temper; clay mineral identification. Surface treatments & decoration (see below)	Location of find spot relative to source (mapping of kiln sites)	Visual & petrological characterisations (Orton et al 1993; Peacock 1969); compositional analysis
2 Methods & context of production	Vessel fabric	Clay types (primary, secondary). Temper medium (coarse, fine) in original clay matrix or subsequently added	Distinctions between hand-made vessels fired at low temperatures (c. 500 C – 800 C), wheelthrown vessels fired at higher temperatures (c. 800 C+) with improved kiln technology. Production methods related to wider aspects of agrarian production & access to resources (labour, fuel, raw materials), resulting from changing social relations	Macro/microscopic visual characterisation / identification/ classification
	Vessel form	Regularity/irregularity of form within & between vessels		Visual comparison, measurement
	Surface detail	Marks of coil/slab manufacture, wheelthrowing, mould-forming; composites (eg handmade body, wheelthrown rim & finishing). Treatment of surface (burnishing, impressed/incised/applied decoration, slips, glazes, etc)		Macro-/microscopic examination
	Firing temperature	Hardness of ceramic		Experimental results; Mohs scale; microscopic examination (Orton & Tyers 1992)
3 Distribution patterns & mechanisms	Vessel fabric	Spatial patterning of ware types of known source(s)	Distribution from specific production sites. Distinctions between patterns resulting from kinship obligations/reciprocity; tribute; estate production; state imposed taxation & consumption; market exchange, etc	Presence on different site types (eg Fulford 1975; Young 1977; Lyne & Jefferies 1979)
				Site-catchment analysis of individual sites (eg Going 1987)
				Distributions of specific ware types (eg Loughlin 1977)
				Statistical analysis/interpretation of quantified distributions (eg Hodder 1979; Allen & Fulford 1996)
4 Use of vessels ('in situ', ie after original dispersal from production site)	Vessel form	Use of particular vessels for specific functions	Processing, storage, transport & consumption of agricultural products	Classification on basis of ethnographic analogy (incl. documentary records eg Moorhouse 1978), experimental research & analyses of contexts
	Vessel fabric	Suitability of fabric for specific purpose(s). Post-manufacture impacts (eg scorching, wear patterns)	Probable intended use of vessel, including 'non-functional' roles in respect of status & prestige	Macro-/microscopic examination (eg Holly 1983)
	Vessel contents	Identification of vessel contents to infer function	Traces of actual use made of vessel	Organic residues (lipids, DNA, etc) (Heron & Pollard 1987)
5 Secondary use ('non-portable')	Vessels	Utilised in 'non-recoverable' contexts; eg : drains, cisterns, pipes : ritual/votive/burial	Re-cycling – local provision of facilities. Vessels as indicators of status/ prestige, reinforcing social structure, incorporation into belief system	Examination/interpretation of context of vessels
	Sherds	Used as building/foundation material	Recycling	
6 Circumstances of discard / deposition	Microdistributions of ceramics & contextual associations	Vessels 'in situ' with reference to final use ('primary discard'). Vessels collected & discarded close to immediate context of final use ('secondary discard #1'). Vessels collected & discarded at distance from immediate context of final use ('secondary discard #2')	Contemporary treatment of ceramic debris, rubbish disposal practices; status of assemblage; contemporaneity of constituent components. functional associations; distribution of assemblage; suitability for research into specific questions regarding whole assemblage	Interpretation of context (Millett 1979), identification of taphonomic processes affecting assemblage & deposit (Evans & Millett 1992), soil micromorphology (MacPhail 1994), assemblage characteristics (Millett & Graham 1986)
7 Post-depositional taphonomy	Chronological homogeneity of assemblage characteristics of parent context(s)		Closeness of vessels/sherds & assemblages to original context of use & discard; suitability for research into specific questions regarding assemblage as a whole	As above, and see also Carver 1985

Table 5 Some techniques employed in the description (quantification) of pottery assemblages (see Orton *et al* 1993)

Method	Criteria and applicability
Weight	This compares quantities of like fabrics between assemblages (eg proportions of BB1 to samian). Weight comparisons can be misleading because of the varying density of different wares (eg amphorae can so dominate weight measurements that the comparative importance of finewares can not be established). If there are significant quantities of a fabric type in one assemblage but not in another, this will also skew calculations. A 'density index' can facilitate comparison by weight within assemblages, and vessel numbers can sometimes be estimated when the 'standard weight' of a complete pot in any given fabric is known. Alternatively an index of the volume represented by pottery types can be estimated (eg from total surface area). Such measures include all sherds within an assemblage, which is not the case with other methods designed to avoid the biases found in weight and sherd count
Sherd count	Sherd count can be contrasted with weight. The probability of recovery of different fabrics varies according to degree of fragmentation (highly breakable wares will be over-represented where completeness is low but under-represented where completeness is high). There is a tendency for a greater proportion of robust vessels to be recovered, compared to fragile ones, because larger fragments are more easily seen (recovery rates are also affected by fabric colour). This introduces other biases to the comparative description of assemblages: • within assemblages according to robustness/fragility of fabrics • between assemblages according to depositional characteristics of assemblage • within and between assemblage according to deliberate selection for breakage/preservation
Estimated Vessels Represented (evrep)	This measure varies according to decisions as to whether or not sherds belong to the same vessel. It is difficult to assess variability in attribution between assemblages recorded by different workers, especially where records from a number of discrete contexts are amalgamated to create a single statistic. Identifying conjoining sherds from the same vessel is time consuming. The statistics derived are also affected by the degree of fragmentation and 'lumpy' distributions
Estimated Vessel Equivalent (eve)	A cumulative total of the percentage of vessels represented in an assemblage can be assessed, usually from the evidence of rim sherds (and sometimes bases) as a fraction of a whole. This comparative measure is unbiased by differences in fabric weight and vessel fragmentation. The measure makes more efficient use of the available data than estimated vessels represented and offers greater reliability in statistical analysis, allowing also the calculation of standard deviations to determine whether differences between proportions within an assemblage are significant. The results can be converted via 'pseudo-count transformations' into 'pottery information equivalents' ('pies')

pretation of ceramic assemblages is more than ever interpreted in terms of the economic 'pull' of such settlements.

This summary of the pervasiveness of the free-market model of production and exchange is necessary because of the effect it has had on ceramic studies, and on the interpretation of patterns of pottery supply to urban settlements. It has had a determining influence not just on the interpretation of distributions, but in deciding which pottery types are studied, and how certain types are classified and dated. If ceramic assemblages are to be utilised effectively in understanding relationships between the urban and rural spheres, such enveloping assumptions seem inappropriate.

Recent overviews of Roman (Fulford and Huddleston 1991) and medieval (Mellor 1994) pottery studies emphasise the need for research to be pursued in the light of a range of models for social dynamics and settlement interaction, and in concert with research on related issues pursued through other artefact categories. Some of the models which ceramic data may be used to investigate have already been described (see chapter 2 of this study), but some general points can usefully be rehearsed.

Ceramic assemblages within urban systems offer varying degrees of contrast. These involve changes in the characteristics of vessels and assemblages; a greater range of types and functions, and a greater range of processes involved in the production of these types. Sharper contrasts are evident in patterns of dispersal from production sites, with increased dispersal from some, and continued dispersal at the same level – or cessation of production altogether – from others. Concentrations of consumption/discard of 'specialised' assemblages are characteristic of 'urban' and other consumer sites.

Techniques for identifying sources and distribution patterns of ceramics include:

- Fabrics from known kiln sites (the recognition of similarities in fabric/form, supported by petrological analysis to distinguish between similar fabrics from disparate sources),
- Sourcing according to the clay matrix/inclusions (where compositional and petrological analysis may identify a production source from a clay 'fingerprint' which can be related to specific clay outcrops or establish – via macro-examination/thin-sectioning – the presence of geological inclusions specific to a production area),
- 'Grouping'/differentiation of ceramics of unknown provenance with those from known kiln sites ('workshop sourcing'),
- 'Grouping' of ceramics of unknown provenance.

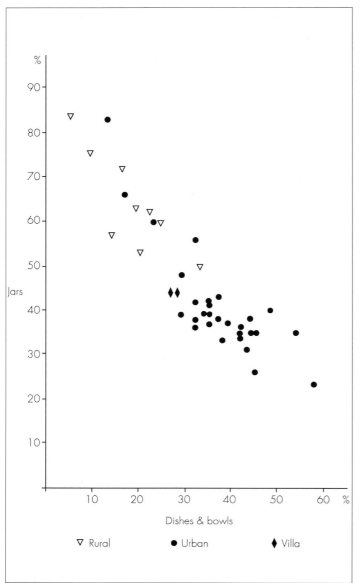

Fig 2 Pottery assemblages on rural sites of the Roman period are usually dominated by storage vessels such as jars. The presence of a higher proportion of dishes and bowls (tablewares) marks out the higher status and more urban sites. Here these characteristics of ceramic assemblages are compared from a series of excavations in south-western Britain (after Evans 2001)

Stage 4 Use of vessels

As well as being an integral part of agricultural production, ceramics – especially coarse wares and jars – were used in the storage and transportation of agrarian produce. Although certain vessels – notably Roman amphorae – have been well studied from this perspective, many studies view pots as commodities in themselves. The study of vessel function needs to be integrated with the evidence for food resources provided by archaeobotanical and archaeozoological assemblages. Quantification by

vessel form and (inferred) function as well as fabric should be undertaken, and programmes of residue analysis integrated into such research. Such studies offer the prospect of a more refined and contextualised understanding of ceramic distributions than has previously been possible.

Such issues can be addressed via study of form and function, drawing on:

- Indices of diversity of shape, utility, and inferred function,
- Evidence of contents and indicators of processes to which the vessels were subjected (ie the study of residues and wear patterns),
- Contextual evidence built from macro/micro, inter/intra site distributions,
- Associations with other finds, especially archaeozoological and archaeobotanical data.

Such contextualised studies can then be integrated into the procedures for establishing the location and diversity of ceramic sources (as above).

Stage 5 Secondary use

The study of the reuse of pottery – whether as intact vessels in functional contexts or broken up as building material in foundations – is unlikely to add significantly to the analyses proposed above.

Stages 6 and 7 Circumstances of discard/deposition and post-depositional taphonomy

Ceramic assemblages are subject to many of the post-depositional disturbances that affect animal bone assemblages. Requirements of chronological homogeneity and representativeness of sample mean that the taphonomic characteristics of relevant deposits need to be characterised.

3.3.2 Describing assemblages

Pursuing these aims requires the quantification of ceramic assemblages, for which a range of methods is available (cf Pollard 1990). Quantification can be carried out:

- by *fabric* – to establish the relative importance of different production sites in the supply of ceramics,
- by *form* – to establish the relative importance of different vessel types and the functional bias of assemblages.

The principal methods of quantification are summarised in Table 5. Detailed comparative study would benefit from the consistent application of the more ambitious measure (EVEs), where resources permit and assemblages are suitably complex. This is a proper goal for future programmes of post-excavation study (below p 129). On the other hand surveys of information that has already been recovered need not be deterred by the fact that disparate measures of quantities were employed. The study of Black-burnished pottery (BB1) distribution patterns by Allen and Fulford (1996) shows what can be achieved from existing data and provides a methodology for further study. In particular the contour mapping of distributions is a valuable tool, and can be developed to map contrasting patterns of product penetration in regional landscapes. The observation that less intensive approaches to quantification can be equally effective seems a reassuring one, although it is not entirely clear how this conclusion was reached.

The most important point to make here is that the subject of our study must be the entire assemblage, rather than its component parts. Evans's recent work (2001) on Roman pottery in northern Britain illustrates the exciting potential of the comparative study of assemblages, quantified by form, from different settlement landscapes. Clear differences can be established between the types of pottery discarded on different classes of site. The material culture illustrates a range of cultural and economic choices; particularly those involved in display at the dining table. Differing regional identities and urban and rural lifestyles can be identified from this evidence (Fig 2).

3.4 Coin

Coinage is clearly an important source of information for this study. Coin was usually issued and controlled by states or ruling elites, and employed to extract surplus through taxation or tribute. Once in circulation it could serve as both a material representation of wealth and a means of mediating exchange. Monetisation thus facilitated the movement of wealth, and served to improve the efficiency and scope of exchange.

The specific rationale for coin production in different periods remains a subject of debate. Was it a device to procure tribute or revenue in a portable and disposable form, or intended to facilitate trade, expand production, and generate (taxable) wealth (eg Hendy 1988)? Was it introduced as a response to increasing production aimed at obtaining commercial profit, or as an aspect of the reorganisation of production and surplus expropriation by a ruling class? What proportion of the population used money, to what extent, and how? The arguments underlying these debates, concerning the relationship between production, exchange, and consumption, and the roles of social relations, state mechanisms, and markets in structuring these, are central to the understanding of town/hinterland relationships.

Numismatic studies have generally been concerned with chronology, issue sequences, coin metrology, and mint output and organisation. Such studies thus describe the fiscal/financial policies of the issuing authorities, inferring episodes of economic expansion, recession, and inflation, often with scant reference to the social context within which these monetary systems operated. Empirical studies of coinage from different historical periods have developed in different directions. Medieval coinages have been intensively studied, classified, and catalogued, and issues such as mint output, sequence, and location researched in detail. The spatial distributions of some specific types have been mapped and discussed with reference to variation between regions and site types (Metcalf 1974; Hinton 1986), and attempts have been made to characterise coin circulation in this period (Metcalf 1988; Blackburn 1993). In contrast, studies of Romano-British coinage have embraced numerically based methodologies, allowing objective comparison of patterns of coin deposition between assemblages, and the application of statistical techniques to group them according to degrees of similarity. This approach has identified intriguing contrasts in the coin-loss profiles of different site types and regions in Roman Britain. Post-Roman coins may not have been lost in sufficient quantities to make similar analyses possible. Nevertheless, some preliminary investigation along these lines might highlight national or regional patterning in coin issue and supply, and would discourage the naive interpretation of coin loss as a direct measure of economic activity (cf Leahy, forthcoming).

In both Roman and medieval studies, attempts to demonstrate relationships between coin use, production, exchange, and settlement type are in their infancy. Ryan, in his survey of late Roman coins in Britain (1988, 6–23), notes how little attention has been paid to the comparative study of provincial coin pools, evidence which could be used to understand both the manner and degree to which settlements were integrated into a monetised economy, and the nature of that economic system. Studies of Roman coinage have begun to recognise the value of contextual associations (cf Reece 1993), and of studying assemblages from stratified archaeological sequences (eg Guest 1998). Although in their infancy, such studies offer the prospect of associating episodes of coin discard with evidence for contemporary activities, and as such an opportunity to investigate the context of final use.

Two specific characteristics of coin assemblages offer potential for the study of relationships between urban and rural spheres, namely:

- Changes in the pattern of coin deposition on individual sites, and comparisons between the coin profiles of groups of sites (comparing changes in site use represented by coin loss, and linking coin patterning to other classes of data);
- The identification of coins produced at a specific mint and the distribution of such products across the landscape (reflecting limits of circulation from specific mints).

Stages in analysis

Stages 1–4 Production, distribution, and circulation

Tables 6 and 7 present a model for the manufacture, distribution, circulation, and deposition of coinage. Stages 1, 2, and 3 include the processes usually addressed in numismatic studies: the metrology of particular types, and their chronology, based on the identity of the issuing authority. On the basis of such studies typological distributions may be mapped. Studies relevant to Stage 4 attempt a detailed understanding of the methods and circumstances of production, and offer the possibility of refining understanding of coin distribution and circulation by identifying distinctions such as mint, workshop, moneyer, and batch. Of particular relevance to this study is the production of 'copy' issues, especially in the 3rd and 4th centuries AD, indicating devolved control of monetary production and

possibly highly localised and sensitive indicators of patterns of exchange (see below p 82). All of these aspects of study relate to production, and are concerned with the creation of typologies that allow the identification of patterning in coin supply at various scales.

Stage 5 Distribution and circulation

The identification of areas of coin circulation may define a political or economic territory. The late pre-Roman Iron Age and early medieval issues of southern England are well suited to such studies. Middle Saxon coins – *sceattas* and *stycas* – bear distinctive designs and have distinct distributions beyond the limits of which coinage is frequently absent. Later Saxon coins in southern England bear mint marks denoting their place of origin, and distinctive characteristics of coin design can also be used to identify the mint at which the coin was struck.

By contrast, the overwhelming bulk of official Roman coinage in Britain was imported, and in most cases the same coin types were probably issued from any number of distribution points. There will therefore be no distinctive attributes on these coins to distinguish their points of origin in insular circulation. Such coins appear to have no utility in attempts to isolate regional patterns of circulation.

Both of these observations are, however, subject to qualification. Firstly, Anglo-Saxon coins are rare as site finds. The repeated recoining of the 10th century reduced the amount of coin entering the archaeological record; although thousands of 10th-century products of southern English mints are known, the overwhelming majority derive from hoards – in which contexts they are of little use in determining patterns of circulation.

Secondly, although official coinage in Roman Britain was imported, a considerable quantity of coinage in use consisted of copies, especially after AD 260. The mint locations of these counterfeits are unknown, but most must have been produced in Britain. The diversity of product inherent in decentralised, intermittent, unofficial copying offers the possibility of distinguishing between the output of particular workshops. It may be possible to establish and discriminate between groups on the basis of coin design (identifying recognisable production 'hands' rather than die-links), metal composition, and manufacturing technique. A combined study of these attributes may allow the identification of production centres and circulation patterns (below p 88).

Table 6 Processes of coin production and distribution (see Table 7 for later stages)

Research topic	Resource	Character	Interpretation, references	Criteria
1 Relative/ intrinsic value of coin	Precious/base metal content & weight of coin	Precious metal	Value independent of specific context of exchange, defined & sustained by issuing authority	Metrological analysis; weight of coin (Reece 1987a; Dolley 1976)
		Base metal	Coinage suitable for use in lower value transactions	
		Alloy	Function of area over which issuing authority needed to maintain monetised economy & available resources of precious metals? Issuing authority may fix relationship between intrinsic & face/exchange value	Measurement of debasement/improvement of coinage (changing ratio of precious/base metals)
2 Source of metal	Metallurgical/chemical characteristics of coin	Metal refined from ore	Results can identify common/disparate sources & 'circulation zones', especially when assessed alongside other coin attributes (eg Ponting & Zeepvat 1994)	Metallic composition of coins can provide recognisable 'fingerprints', allowing grouping of coins by their constituent materials. Recycling of coinage & of other artefacts in mint output complicates the picture
		Metal recycled from artefacts		
		Metal recycled from coinage		
3 Identity of issuing authority/chronology of coin	Design of coin	Selection of motif - obverse (issuing authority)	Linkage to specified issuing authority & absolute chronology	Numismatic classification (eg Ryan 1988)
		Selection of motif – reverse	Scale of coin output in specific period	Ditto; die linkages
		Symbol/design chosen with intent	Context of coin issue	Numismatic classification
			Regional distributions of specific types	Point/quantified distribution maps
4 Methods & scale of manufacture & distribution of coinage	Manufacturing process	Mould cast from molten metal	Related to scale of production.	Quantification of distribution/scale of production
		Produce obverse/reverse dies	Scale of production calculable from use life of dies & number of combinations of obverse/reverse designs	Die-linkage analysis employing estimated use life of dies (Reece 1987a; Dolley 1976)
		Manufacture/strike pellets		
		Manufacture/strike blanks		
		Strikeover existing coin	Possibly localised/unofficial reuse of coin	Identification of 'overstrikes'
	Division of production	By mint (located by mark)	Extent of distribution from mint, index of localised/regional circulation from specified centre	Identification of distribution of mint-mark (Metcalf 1980; Blackburn & Lyon 1986)
		By workshop (identified by mark)	Identification of 'batches' delivered to specific regions in context of centralised coin production	Identification of distribution of characteristic motifs (Kenyon 1993; Pirie 1987)
		By moneyer (identified by mark)	Circulation of products of particular moneyer	Identification of moneyers marks/engraver's style & their distributions (Brickstock 1987; Metcalf 1980)
			Estimates of volume of production (no of different moneyers responsible for some coin type)	
		By 'batch' identified by distinctive motif/ combination of motif	Delivery of coinage with specific motifs to specific regions	Distribution of coins bearing selected motifs

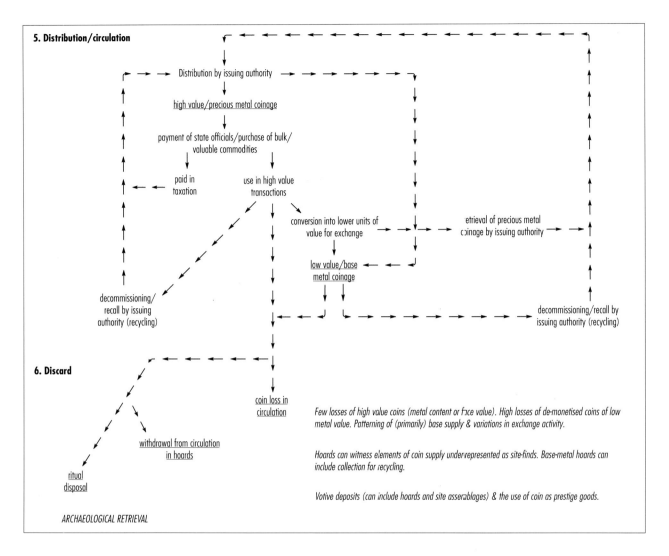

5. Distribution/circulation

Distribution by issuing authority

high value/precious metal coinage

payment of state officials/purchase of bulk/ valuable commodities

paid in taxation

use in high value transactions

conversion into lower units of value for exchange

etrieval of precious metal coinage by issuing authority

low value/base metal coinage

decommissioning/ recall by issuing authority (recycling)

decommissioning/recall by issuing authority (recycling)

6. Discard

coin loss in circulation

Few losses of high value coins (metal content or face value). High losses of de-monetised coins of low metal value. Patterning of (primarily) base supply & variations in exchange activity.

withdrawal from circulation in hoards

Hoards can witness elements of coin supply under-represented as site-finds. Base-metal hoards can include collection for recycling.

ritual disposal

Votive deposits (can include hoards and site assemblages) & the use of coin as prestige goods.

ARCHAEOLOGICAL RETRIEVAL

Table 7 Coin distribution, use, and discard (the stages and processes underlined are those that are archaeologically visible).

It has been stated that one aspect of official imported coinage may be susceptible to the identification of particular spheres of circulation; this concerns the use of specific motifs on the reverse of coins. If issues with specific designs were selected for distribution from particular centres – as occurred in a wider imperial context – it may be possible to detect concentrations of such motifs in regions of Britain, and this attribute could thus be considered alongside those proposed for the indigenous copies.

The contrasting roles of settlements may be investigated through changing patterns of regional coin loss, and the recognition of the degree to which sites conform to the regional pattern. The groundwork for such studies has been established by Richard Reece, who has described a national mean of site finds in Roman Britain by coin period (he

defines 21), representing the gross pattern of coin supply to the province (1988; 1993; 1995). The graphs produced depend on the ratios of various coin types within an assemblage (Fig 3). This takes account of the significance of *new* types as a proportion of coinage already in circulation, rather than simply presenting a static picture of the assemblage as a whole. Such comparative studies involve:

- Creating a 'mean profile' of comparative numbers of coin present, as a proportion of the total assemblage, expressed as coins/per thousand, representing a general pattern of supply,
- The comparison of individual assemblages with the mean to identify deviation,
- Establishing significant variation from the mean to indicate differences in the extent of coin use and therefore to illustrate changing patterns of supply and function.

In these studies Reece has identified significant vari-

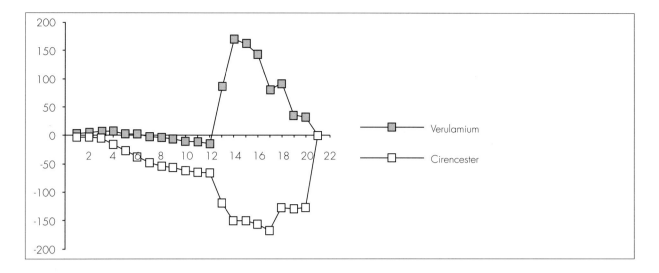

Fig 3 Cumulative frequency diagram of coins from Romano-British excavations (after Reece 1995). The horizontal scale is divided into 22 periods of uneven duration but numismatic integrity (eg Period 4 includes Flavian issues of AD 69–96). The vertical scale shows the deviation of the assemblages from a national mean describing, cumulatively, the percentage of coins belonging to each of the periods. The beginning and end points therefore represent 0% and 100% respectively (see p86 for further description). The illustration shows that *Verulamium* significantly exceeds the mean coin loss for the period after AD 260, but that the opposite is the case at Cirencester

ations from the national mean, as well as several apparently inexplicable similarities between sites remote geographically and of widely differing character. The most striking of his regional variations concerns differences in the pattern of coin deposition between towns in western and eastern Britain in the 4th century. Although coin profiles indicate that there are complexities and variations within individual sites, differences in the aggregate pattern between towns suggests differences in their role in respect of monetised exchange. Further investigation of this phenomenon might serve to clarify differences in urban/rural relationships in this period relating to the role of coinage in mobilising surplus and mediating exchange, with all the implications for wider social organisation which that has.

Stage 6 Deposition and discard

It is usually assumed that coin recovery reflects coin loss and, by extension, reflects the incidence of coin-based transactions. Several studies of patterns of exchange and spheres of economic influence depend on the validity of this premise. It is far from certain, however, that site finds are straightforwardly related to coin use, whatever social constraints or asymmetry of exchange (as in the case of tribute or taxation) may have obtained. Coin finds can usefully be divided into three classes, each subject to its own rules of interpretation:

Site finds

Coins that are lost or discarded are likely to be of low intrinsic value. Such finds may represent the disposal of issues which were not legal tender

(because demonetised or outside their area of currency), illustrate the use of coinage in exchange, derive from ritual discard, or belong to dispersed hoards. Site finds can be associated with specific contexts at a variety of levels of definition: by site type (town, 'small town', villa, temple, monastery, emporia, farm, etc); by structure (forum, barracks, market place, town house, barn, church, etc); or by context (well, butchery or consumer assemblage, pit, floor, manufacturing waste, etc). Distribution within settlements of these types can be mapped. Spatial distributions of distinguishable types (on grounds of date, motif, mint location, die links) may indicate specific, regional episodes of supply and patterns of circulation.

Surface finds

These can be incorporated along with site finds into distribution studies, and it may be possible to integrate distributions with contextual data obtained from remote sensing – geophysics, aerial photography. Retrieval bias can have a huge effect if coin lists obtained without metal detectors are compared with lists from contexts which have been screened in this way.

Hoards

Hoards represent coinage withdrawn from circulation and provide better indication of actual pattern of supply than site finds, albeit biased towards coins of persisting value (ie weight, fineness). A comparison of profiles of coins within hoards can identify regional influxes of coin in specific periods – before mixing through circulation (cf Reece 1987). Coin hoards can be treated as single artefacts, and are portable. Coins derived from hoards may, therefore, not only have no relationship to coins in use, but may equally bear no relationship to the coin pool available for regional use.

Conclusions

The circumstances in which coinage was used are uncertain, and finds do not simply represent fallout from monetary transactions. Recent studies have argued for more contextually specific interpretations, emphasising the importance of social structures, and of belief systems at odds with any supposed economic rationality. Nevertheless, in certain periods the volume of low-denomination coinage, and efforts made to maintain supply, indicate a significant role in mediating exchange, however constrained by custom.

Peaks of site coin loss, even where at odds with nationally or regionally defined background patterns, need not necessarily indicate a peak in economic activity, although this is one possible explanation. Coin loss is, however, unambiguously indicative of the *supply* of specific coin types to a site, by whatever means. Thus, whilst their interpretation in terms of chronology and economic activity is ambiguous, the identification of spatial patterning of supply *does* illustrate links between groups of sites. Where related to known centres of coin production and/or distribution, such networks can serve to define catchments, territories, or other spatial units (continuous or fragmented) which may justify the term hinterland.

3.5 Human bone (and burial archaeology)

Townspeople lived and died differently from their rural counterparts, and such differences can be described from the archaeological study of cemetery populations. This is not, however, an easy source of information to use. Archaeological assemblages are not the same as death assemblages, and these in turn differ from the living community from which they derived (Mays 1998, fig 2.1). As Waldron (1994, 22) has observed, cemeteries present a social or cultural and not a biological sample. Death, burial ritual, decay, and disturbance transform populations. The process of archaeological discovery, sampling and recovery further reduces this selective sample. Such problems are compounded by the fact that published accounts of cemeteries involve a high level of interpretative synthesis, which makes comparative analysis difficult if not impossible, although Conheeney (2000) has described some of the ways in which reporter bias can be mitigated in the comparative study of skeletal assemblages.

Notwithstanding these problems, human remains offer important insight into the character of both urban and rural communities. Table 8 sets out ways in which this information can contribute to our research. The emphasis here is on the study of human remains and the broader subject of burial archaeology is treated more briefly. The importance of social ritual is, however, critical. Not only does such social practice introduce bias to the sample but it also offers a supplementary source of information against which the osteological data can be compared.

Stages in analysis

Stage 1 Sources of human populations

Towns have generally relied on immigration in order to establish and sustain population levels. Social interaction within heterogeneous communities can contribute to the emergence of new cultural models and economic systems, and the character and dynamic of immigration requires study. Several research questions advanced in chapter 2.5 are directly concerned with the way in which urban communities were formed and contributed to innovation and change (eg Q5, Q23, Q28, and Q33).

The pace of scientific advance in biomolecular archaeology offers much promise. The presence of uncontaminated mitochondrial DNA in archaeological samples and the use of polymerase chain reaction (PCR) techniques to amplify trace amounts

Table 8 Human bone: some research themes relevant to this study

Research topic	Character	Interpretation, references	Criteria
1 Sources and homo geneity of cemetery populations	Genetically influenced variability within & between populations	Kinship groups, racial differences and regional diversity evident in genetic characteristics (eg Oota et al 1995)	Legibility of uncontaminated DNA. Genetically determined metrical variation (Warwick 1968, 152). Scoring of genetic traits (eg metopism, missing third molar, etc) & plotting of anomaly clusters (Berry & Berry 1967; Finnegan 1978). Bio-molecular study (eg Human Leukocyte Antigen)
	Environmental variability	Absorption of isotopes characterises individuals raised in specific environments	Isotopes in dental enamel & bone (Hillson 1996; Mays 2000b)
	Differences between male & female populations. Imbalances in adult sex-ratios	Marked sexual dimorphism may indicate a heterogeneous population, with differential male/female immigration (Molleson 1993, 214). Female-led migration supported medieval towns (Goldberg 1992). Preponderance of male slaves marked Roman households (Harris 1999, 69). Sex-imbalances in military and ecclesiastical communities	Pelvic & skull dimorphism, measurements of femur, humerus, atlas, scapula, clavicle & sacrum (Ferembach et al 1980; Brothwell 1981, 59–63, Bass 1987; Mays & Cox 2000)
	Cultural affiliations of immigrant/native communities	Use of burial in formation & declaration of identity. Evident in grave goods & furniture (esp. dress), burial rite (cremation, inhumation, orientation, etc), commemoration (grave-plates, tombstones, etc.). Burial clusters may represent familial, social, class or ethnic associations	Artefact typologies, stratigraphic & structural data, related to descriptions of skeletal remains & spatial data by inter-relational databases & GIS
2 Lifestyle variations within and between populations repre sented in cemeteries	Demography & mortality	Comparative analysis is difficult because of problems in ageing adult skeletons (Molleson & Cox 1993, Cox & Mays 2000) & establishing sample contemporaneity (eg Barber & Bowsher 2000, 9–11), but see Brothwell (1994) & Grauer (1991) on medieval cemeteries around York. Infant mortality rates offer more reliable comparisons between health status of different populations, although differences in burial practice can present a particularly biased sample (eg McKinley 2000, 266)	Adults aged from teeth (Brothwell 1981, 53; Whittaker 2000); cranial suture fusion (Meindl & Lovejoy 1985); & pubic symphysal ageing (Brooks & Suchey 1990; Suchey et al 1988; McKern & Stewart 1957). Immature skeletons from dental development (Schour & Massler 1941), length of diaphys (Sundick 1978; Ubelaker 1989, 70–1) & epiphyseal fusion (Salter 1984; Bass 1987)
	Stature	Height as a proxy for general health (Molleson 1993; Brothwell 1994)	Metrical data (Trotter & Gleser 1952; 1958)
	Diet	Dietary reconstruction from trace element identification. Lead in bones an indicator of polluted diet/environment (eg Molleson & Cox 1993, 37, but note also the problems of source & diagenesis: Waldron 1994, xi)	Chemical analysis, stable isotope analysis, trace element analysis (Mays 2000b)
	Hygiene	Periodontal disease, caries & abscesses reflect oral hygiene. Parasite infestation & tuberculosis reflect overcrowding & poor hygiene	Skeletal & dental pathology; radiography (to spot lesions, Harris lines, and tooth abscesses) (Roberts & Manchester 1995; Hillson 1996)
	Health/diet related stress & injury (genetic predisposition also relevant)	Tooth wear & malocclusion mark dietary consistency (Hillson 1996, Molleson 1993 on Roman Poundbury). Illness & malnutrition stresses are shown in dental enamel hypoplasias (Dobney & Goodman 1991), prevalence of caries (Molleson 1993), rickets (Molleson 1988), scurvy, Harris's lines & *Cribra orbitalia* (Stuart-Macadam 1991). *Cribra orbitalia* in post-medieval London may reflect environmental deterioration (Molleson & Cox 1993, 44)	The relationship between stressful episodes & formation of defects is indirect. Variables in the causes of stress mean that reliable comparisons cannot be made between populations (Hillson 1996)\n\nStudies of parturition have been hindered by poor field practice, but future study may benefit from improvements in sampling technique (Cox 2000)
	Activity related stress & injury	Repeated activities can cause trauma at muscle insertion points (Stirland 1991), osteoarthritis (Molleson 1993), 'occupational' fractures & pathologies such as Schmorl's nodes (Ortner & Putschar 1981, 357) & squatting facets (Brothwell 1981). Activities can be suggested (eg horse-riding: Farwell & Molleson 1993, 200)	
3 Burial practice	Belief systems	Ideology in selection/preparation of dead for burial (infanticide, excarnation, pyre ritual), grave structure & furniture (suppression of spirits, equipment for afterlife), & burial ritual (processions, wakes, libations, etc)	Burial type, funerary structures, animal bone & ceramic assemblages, evidence of food preparation & offerings (need for systematic flotation of cremation burials & cremation related contexts)
	Social differentiation	Status & wealth represented in burial goods & monuments. Spatial patterning by rank possible (Toynbee 1971)	
4 Post-burial	Commemoration & re-use	Symbolic & ritual uses of burial sites	
	Decay & disturbance	Taphonomic processes (Mays 1998, 17–22)	
	Excavation	Recovery bias (eg Blackfriars, Ipswich: Mays 1991)	

of fragmented DNA, permit the investigation of the genetic composition of cemetery populations. Improved descriptions of population heterogeneity and homogeneity will contribute enormously to understanding of the ways in which towns were formed. It must, however, be noted that genetic variation is not necessarily the same as race or ethnic variation, since group identity is socially constructed (Mirza and Dungworth 1995; Jones 1997). The analysis of oxygen isotope ratios in bone and teeth can also tell us where some individuals had been raised, allowing us to compare place of origin with genetic markers (Mays 2000b). These are expensive and experimental techniques and, at least in the immediate future, are more likely to be used to describe individuals than populations. Metrical skeletal variation, which has been comparatively neglected in British archaeology, can be deployed more cost effectively to describe the characteristics of cemetery populations (Mays 1998, 100–1; 2000a). As Mays (1997) has noted, comparatively little work on population history has been carried out. Much current publication output is concerned with individual case studies and cemeteries: and a more population-based approach is needed. The importance of gender differences in patterns of urban immigration merit particular attention in such study (see Table 8).

Stage 2 Lifestyle variation within and between populations

Palaeo-demographic studies remain problematic (papers addressing current problems and opportunities are found in Cox and Mays 2000). Attempts to estimate age-at-death based on macroscopic techniques are not always reliable (Molleson and Cox 1993, 167–79), and the significance of results obtained from comparative surveys of population morbidity can be questioned. Broad-band descriptions of age are less misleading and facilitate comparison between populations recorded by different specialists (Conheeney 2000, 278). Age estimates for infants are also more reliable. The study of patterns of infant mortality has important research potential. Unfortunately children are often underrepresented in cemeteries and those available to archaeological study represent a partial sample (Conheeney 2000, 278–9; Molleson and Cox 1993, 206–14).

Notwithstanding these problems, Brothwell (1994) and Grauer (1991) have compared survey data from cemeteries in and around medieval York with a view to identifying differences between rural and urban populations. Brothwell notes that contrasting morbidity may reflect differences in growth and nutrition, changing mating patterns in urban groups, differentials affecting migration into towns, stress, effects of work on growth of physique, environmental constraints on growth (including working conditions, pollution and parasite loads), and socio-genetic factors. These issues are all susceptible to study. For instance the rural sample showed greater limb use and stress; a preponderance of *cribra orbitalia* at Wharram Percy might suggest that this small village group was less healthy; villagers at Clopton had lower standards of dental health; religious isolates were generally 'better off'; and so on. These observations suggest directions in which research can be taken, even if the results must be used with caution.

Lewis and Roberts (1997) have explored stress indicators in biological anthropology in an attempt to move away from the description of individual diseases to a more general analysis of malnutrition and infection in past populations. New methodological approaches are emerging. Markers of occupational stress (MOS) include musculoskeletal stress markers (MSM) and robusticity markers (RM). Whilst we can not attribute specific incidences of bone or dental tissue change to a single episode, overall patterns of stress can be described. A significant obstacle to comparative analysis is the absence of agreed standards for making accurate identifications: some basic assumptions may need reassessment, and consistency in use of terminology is required (Kennedy 1998).

Stages 3–4 Burial and post-burial

Burial practice can witness the development of visible social differentiation, and mark increasing social complexity. The evidence illustrates processes that contributed to the development of settlement hierarchies. The search for social ranking within cemeteries, and evidence for the use of the dead in marking status and identity, has generated a considerable literature (see Bassett 1992). Until recently such studies made comparatively little use of skeletal evidence, concentrating instead on grave goods and burial practice. Future research is likely to benefit from the more integrated approach to the evidence that has been adopted in reports now reaching publication (eg Barber and Bowsher 2000).

In this survey we are particularly interested in the location of power in the landscape and in the use of wealth to represent power. The choice of how and where high-status individuals were buried can be revealing (as illustrated by the inferences drawn from the presence of high-status burials in 7th-century Ipswich and London, above p 25). Funeral ritual and the foci provided by graveyards and tombs can also influence expressions of urban identity, settlement pattern, and urban morphology. The dead make an important contribution to urban ideologies and civic ritual, and these complex social themes can not be treated adequately in a summary such as this.

The nature of human burial is such that issues of reworking and residuality are less problematic than is the case, for instance, in the study of animal bone. The processes of selectivity, whereby some burials are preserved intact and others are not, need to be assessed, however, if we are to make meaningful generalisations about populations.

Issues relevant to the description of cemetery populations

The above summary gives some indication of the potential of population studies based on human skeletal material recovered in archaeological excavations. The range of variables that can affect individual assemblages complicates comparative study. For instance populations that live longer have different health status. As a consequence we can not compare like with like, and we need to develop descriptive methodologies that take account of different population structures. Waldron (1994, 90), believes that the prospects of being able to carry out meaningful comparative work on published material are slim. He suggests that comparison might be made possible by computing risk or odds ratios of each age stratum, which can be summed to give a common odds ratio.

Comparison is further limited by the problem of providing reliable chronologies. Many cemeteries lack adequate internal stratigraphy. The irregular presence of datable artefacts, even in cemeteries where grave goods were used, can result in very broad dating (eg Barber and Bowsher 2000, 9–11). Since most identifiable pathologies were acquired at some unknown date before death we are left with little chance of developing a narrative description of comparative changes in diet and health status, except in very general terms. We also need to take account of the fact that place of burial is not necessarily the same as the place of death (eg Molleson and Cox 1993, 206). Some broader patterns of deterioration and improvement may usefully emerge, but these are only likely to provide significant new insight for periods and regions where other, historical, sources are unavailable.

From this summary we identify three areas for future research that deserve emphasis. The first of these is the study of migration in the support of urban populations, as an influence on urban diversity and in defining relationships between town and country. Such study stands to benefit from recent methodological advances, and the greater willingness to confront issues of race, ethnicity, and identity that has come to characterise theoretical writing over the past decade. The second theme is that of the changing nature of settlement environments, as revealed in the pathologies of human populations (drawing on the evidence for diet, pollution, occupational injury, general morbidity, etc). Finally the importance of burial in the definition of status and power remains a critical theme: the study of which can describe the changing relationship between powerful people and places of power.

3.6 Other categories of finds

Before concluding this survey of the ways in which archaeological finds can contribute to the study of the relationship between town and country, several other classes of material deserve attention.

'Small finds'

This catch-all archaeological classification includes a wide range of household items, articles of dress and other artefacts made from a variety of materials (metal, glass, bone, stone, ceramic, etc). Many of these objects – such as jewellery, dress fittings, weapons, horse fittings, and metal tableware – were intended to describe status and identity. Others although essentially practical – like tools, loomweights, spindlewhorls, and whetstones – also witness the distribution of occupations and resources. Johnson (1996) correlates the range of new artefacts evident in the early post-medieval period with fundamental changes in the way people saw themselves (although see also MacFarlane 1978). Swift's (2000) survey of late-antique dress accessories in Rome's north-west provinces provides an impressive illustration of how finds can be used to reveal changing approaches to group affiliation (involving the interplay of status, culture, gender, and ethnicity). Similarly the work of Allason-Jones on the small finds assemblages from turrets along Hadrian's wall (2001) has shown how quantitative work can be used to characterise sites, reveal networks of association, and challenge preconceived ideas about settlement character.

Portable artefacts of base, precious, and alloyed metals occur in a wide range of forms. These can be classified according to their metallurgical composition and the manufacturing technique employed in their fabrication, as well as on stylistic and functional grounds. These different classifications make it possible to map distributions and explore ways in which such products reached consumers. The evidence of industrial residues can also identify production sites.

Metal objects are durable and easy to recycle, and are less likely to enter rubbish assemblages than most other artefacts. Their value was not a constant and their discard depends on the ease of securing replacements, recycling value, and fashion redundancy. Other factors include the role of such objects in ritual deposition (including their use as grave goods, in metalwork hoards and as votive deposits at springs and wells), and their association with production and recycling sites. Because of such factors it is not possible to rely on comparative ratios in describing the circulation of such items, except where there are grounds for assuming a common level of redundancy.

Small finds are relatively easy to identify and quantify, and can be used to map functional and social zoning, both within households (as Hingley 1989, 43–4, but see Smith 1997, 37, for a critique of this study), or across entire settlements (Margeson 1993). The huge number of small finds (>6500) from excavations in Winchester has allowed a detailed study of spatial patterning by material type and small find use (Biddle 1990). This established a strong correlation between some classes of artefact and the status of the urban sites (eg weapons were associated with the castle, tacks were unusually abundant at the minster and bishop's palace, etc). This approach can be extended to exploit the evidence already available in published finds catalogues in order to describe broader landscapes.

Building materials

Ceramic building material (brick and tile) and building stone can be used to similar research ends as pottery (see chapter 3.3), but are usually a less subtle source of evidence because of the comparative lack of typological variety. These were bulky commodities. Their production and distribution required a considerable investment. The identification of sources of production and quarrying, and patterns of distribution illustrate complex urban supply networks. The involvement of civic and other authorities in some aspects of supply, and the occasional use of stamps to mark kiln products, adds important detail. Certain classes of material (flue tile, marble, glazed floor tiles, painted wall plaster, etc) provide simple measures of the specialisation, status, and sophistication of the settlements where they were used.

The widespread reuse of building materials at certain periods (notably in the 3rd–5th centuries, 9th–10th centuries, and from the 13th century onwards), illustrates a different form of supply, as redundant buildings were recycled. Patterns of reuse, and the transportation of materials from 'urban quarries' for use in the construction of new settlements in the environs offers an opportunity to record relationships between town and countryside in periods of urban regeneration or the reorientation of settlement systems.

Glass

Glass is difficult to use. Gross differences in the character and sources of glass at different periods can sometimes be established from compositional analysis, but the widespread recycling of glass makes this a complex issue. Many production centres relied almost exclusively on reused cullet and therefore do not present a clear signature. The active collection of glass for reuse as cullet can be reflected in the archaeological record by average fragment size. Processes of recovery were often more exhaustive where local glassworks provided a ready market for the material, and differences between urban and rural approaches have been noted (Price and Cottam 1998, 7). In any case glass has nothing like the utility of pottery in the study of patterns of supply and marketing, since there were fewer sources of production and the archaeological assemblages from which such patterns can be reconstructed are smaller.

The study of glass does, however, add important detail to research into industrial organisation and the social location of industry (urban, rural, monastic, etc). Glass products were frequently important status markers and glassworks are comparatively archaeologically visible. These can mark high-status sites. There are, also, important links between the different forms of tableware (ceramic, glass, metal), and these need to be described in order to provide a context for the interpretation of the pottery.

Landscape features

Our main concern here has been to focus attention on the value of material culture in describing approaches that have guided the relationship between town and country. We have concentrated on the loose finds that can be recovered in excavation because these lend themselves readily to comparative study. Buildings and landscapes can also be used in such study, although the complexity of these archaeological artefacts makes it difficult to reduce the evidence to convenient typological classifications. The control of land sustains power, and relict landscapes and settlement morphologies witness the production and mobilisation of surplus. Sources of evidence include: aerial photography, landscape survey, surface artefact distributions, geophysical prospection, phosphate and other soil chemistry analyses, and building survey.

Gross changes in landscape organisation, evident in various periods in various parts of the country as a result of aerial and landscape survey, are obviously of prime significance. However, detailed understanding of more subtle changes and developments is essential in monitoring shifts in the pattern and emphasis of rural production in specific regions.

This can be achieved through fieldwalking, geophysics, phosphate and related analyses, and excavation. Two issues are crucial:

- The chronology of landscape development, particularly with regard to field systems and their dating. The basis on which field systems are dated should be subject to rigorous appraisal, particularly with regard to the context of materials found in boundary ditches. Issues of residuality are crucial here;
- Research designs for landscape studies should combine different types of data. Where appropriate information is available, fieldwalking, geophysical, and geochemical analyses should be conducted within a framework which takes account of visible evidence of landscape organisation (eg aerial visibility of field systems). Recording should be carried out at a level of detail that allows the accurate integration of the results of different techniques. The enhanced recognition of relict ancient landscapes offered by developed remote-sensing techniques, such as aerial multi-spectral scanning, offer the best starting point for attempts to integrate and target ground-based survey.

Building archaeology draws on both artefactual and structural evidence in the classification of building types and traditions, and the social analysis of domestic space. Some of the problems of using such evidence, in particular those of establishing consistent approaches to site description and dating, have been described in our review of rural settlement in Roman Britain (p 22). Where the evidence survives, house design reflects regional differences in social and family structure (see p 115), and witnesses processes of cultural adaptation (eg Perring 2002).

3.7 Integrated approaches to finds assemblages

Each class of material described in this chapter has generated an extensive specialist literature. Most specialists are keenly aware of the need to integrate results from separate fields of research to better describe assemblages, but this proper ambition can be difficult to achieve because of the fragmented nature of archaeological research. The importance of the study of the relationships between different material classes has already been stressed at several points, but three themes merit elaboration: how archaeological samples are formed and how these relate back to original populations; how variables

within these populations may have interacted; how archaeological descriptions of such variables might be achieved.

The nature of archaeological assemblages

The classes of information summarised here offer very different clues to our reading of the past, because of the diverse paths taken from life assemblages to death assemblages. Different types of material enter the ground for different reasons, and once buried are subject to different processes of decay and recovery. Archaeological evidence offers an incomplete and potentially misleading sample of original populations, although the reconstruction of the processes that have created our samples are highly informative. For instance, in our discussion of animal bone we noted the problems of depletion and enrichment of assemblages that occur because of the supply of select parts of an animal carcass to specialist consumers (p 39). In describing the potential of seeds and insects we touched on the issue of colonisation, which makes it difficult to distinguish between imported elements of an assemblage (a crop accompanied by weeds and pests), and those that occurred locally because of previous episodes of importation (p 43). Artefact assemblages are instead the product of the decisions taken about value and redundancy, which influenced patterns of breakage, recycling, loss, and burial.

Most finds occur in rubbish assemblages. The processes of how and why things become rubbish are central to the study of consumer behaviour and the display of status (Hodder 1989; Tilley 1990). Rubbish is subject to extensive reworking, both on its way to the midden and once in the ground. This is a particular problem in built-up areas, where the export of rubbish results in dispersal and recycling (hence the scarcity of late-medieval rubbish deposits described above p 30). The presence of a high proportion of residual finds is a characteristic of many urban deposits, and a feature of ploughsoil archaeology. The interpretation of reworked assemblages is always a difficult matter, and this is particularly the case where finds can not be independently dated on typological grounds (as is the case for most botanical and faunal material). The study of residuality is an important area for research. Two classes of residual finds are often defined: items that remained in circulation beyond their normal period of currency ('heirlooms'), and finds that had been redeposited ('rubbish survivals'). It is not usually possible to distinguish between these, although it would be instructive to study 'heirloom' survivals in accidental loss assemblages such as fire horizons. The issue of how rubbish is curated, reused, and disposed is, however, enormously complex.

Most of the work undertaken has concentrated on the evidence of individual artefact classes, especially pottery. Dated pottery types can be traced through stratigraphic sequences to establish base measures of residuality: sherd size and abrasion can be measured to describe reworking; and cross-joining used to trace the dispersal of individual vessels

(Millett *et al* nd; Evans and Millett 1992; Orton and Orton 1975). But studies which have drawn on more than one source of evidence show that different types of find behave differently. The Romsey Rubbish Project combined environmental and artefactual evidence to describe site formation processes (Green and Lockyear 1994). This study included descriptions of sherd abrasion and size to assess residuality. Residuality indices, based on the evidence of fragmentation and abrasion of pottery and bone, were also developed to assist in the study of finds from excavations in Lincoln (Dobney *et al* 1996). The evidence of the two classes of material does not coincide, such that unabraded pottery can be accompanied by abraded bone and vice versa. This suggests that different types of rubbish were differently curated, and archaeological deposits were composed of material drawn from different sources.

Descriptions of assemblages in terms of primary, secondary, and tertiary deposition (Schiffer 1976; La Motta and Schiffer 1999), provide a starting point for further study, but do not touch on the range of ways in which assemblages were formed. For instance, broken pottery can be collected for secondary use as a building material, and the nature of this assemblage may change through a series of stages as it is collected, stored, sorted, and used. It is therefore necessary to identify the value transforms that might have been involved in the discovery of new uses for old rubbish. There are important distinctions to be made between curated rubbish which may still be seen to hold residual value, and the uncurated finds that can then be reworked as the unconscious consequence of post-burial processes. Some aspects of these processes of change are impossible to reconstruct, but the relationship between stratigraphic context and the character of finds assemblages demands closer attention and would benefit from the application of a wider range of analytical techniques. For instance soil micromorphology has under-exploited potential in the study of the mechanics of stratification processes (eg Boivin and French 1999).

In its review of the subject, the Council for British Archaeology gave strongest emphasis to the need for integrated studies of the relationship between find and context (Millett *et al* nd). It also suggested that we need to understand variations in ratios between different classes of artefact. Cool (Cool *et al* 1995) has experimented with methodologies based on correspondance analysis in order to describe and compare assemblages made up of a range of types of archaeological finds from discrete urban contexts in York. Comparison would be made easier if some base line descriptive measure could be established, against which all other evidence of presence or absence could be compared. One underused approach is to measure soil volume during the process of excavation, and to use this as a base for establishing comparative quantification (Evans and Millett 1992). The objective is to describe variations in the supply of different materials through time, although this can only be properly achieved where we are able to compare the supply of items that share a similar degree of redundancy and robusticity. This is an issue we return to in our concluding discussion (p 128).

Food webs

Although the relationship between archaeological assemblages and original populations is indirect, it remains the case that our interpretative models need to work back from the evidence in order to describe variation in production and supply. This means that we have to attempt descriptions of the original populations.

The whole topic of urban food supply is implicitly a study of food webs, and hence of energy flows and stores via crops, livestock, people, and detritivores. Different environments, different agricultural regimes, and different patterns of consumption support different food webs. These can be modelled and compared to patterns identified in archaeological assemblages. An example of how this might be done is provided by Bond and O'Connor (1999, 420), who describe the development of urban habitats in medieval York (see also O'Connor 2000). The evidence of refuse disposal is taken as a starting point, and it is shown how this source of food supported a population of vertebrate and invertebrate scavengers (Fig 4). These populations sustained predators, whilst the enhanced nitrogen and phosphorus content of the soil affected plant colonisation. Several variables can be introduced to the model, and the relationship between these can be expressed numerically. Detailed ecological modelling of this type, built from reasonable assumptions about habitat and population behaviour, can be tested against the archaeological evidence.

This is also a field of study where recent advances in archaeological science permit more ambitious modelling of change than has previously

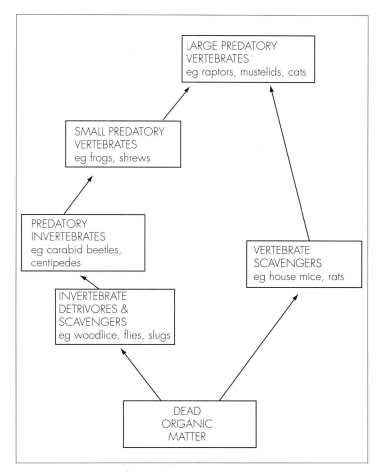

Fig 4 A simplified diagram of a food web that might be supported by urban organic refuse (after O'Connor 2000)

been possible. Molecular, chemical, and radiometric analysis can all contribute to studies of the place of humans in past food webs. For instance human teeth, bones, and faeces, and food vessels provide information on diet by chemical and isotopic means (see Table 8). As Martin Jones has observed (1992), bioarchaeological data can identify ecological stress within past human food webs, the consequences of which can be seen in soils, nutritional stresses in plant communities, herbivores, in human remains, and in fish assemblages from polluted rivers. Another direction is the focus on the physiological response of plants and animals during their lives to human actions (eg skeletal responses of domestic animals and human populations, harvest time, and fruit stone morphology).

Interpretative models of past food webs and habitats involve a considerable degree of conjecture, but changes in one parameter ought to be reflected by changes in another and this provides a valuable test of the inferences drawn.

Comparing different classes of archaeological find

Many important conclusions can be drawn without the need for detailed statistical analysis. It is often sufficient for synthetic accounts of specialist reports to be aware that the different materials may have come from a common source and been produced within the same system of agrarian production (eg Evans 1995). Pottery distributions can be compared with sources of building stone, or storage vessels can be studied in the context of bone assemblages indicative of the processing of meat products for transportation within such vessels. Ceramic forms and manufacturing techniques also provide clues to the agrarian context of their original production, and, where the source area is known, can provide a starting point from which to examine local food production. The study of some aspects of specialist production necessarily draws on information from a range of sources. A demand for cheese, for instance, might leave evidence in the form of mortaria, colanders, and cheese presses; briquetage; and distinctive herd profiles.

Quantitative descriptive techniques make it possible to compare assemblages at an intra- and inter-site level (Tomber 1988). Many characteristics can be described as comparative ratios. These include the types of material present (eg weight ratio of iron to bronze), artefacts of similar functions in different materials (eg ratio of glass vessels to comparable pottery ones), functional characteristics (eg ratio of tableware to kitchenware), and sources of supply (eg products of kiln x to kiln y). Such attributes highlight aspects of the manufacture, distribution, and use of the commodities involved and characterise sources of supply.

The use of multivariate statistical methods permits a more ambitious range of comparative study, and can highlight unexpected congruencies and dissimilarities. Published research has concentrated on spatial and functional variations within established material classes (eg Redman 1979). Correspondence analysis permits comparisons in the composition of assemblages in two criteria (Baxter 1994). Although applicable to counts of whole objects, it has also been successfully applied to broken objects, such as pottery (the 'Pie slice', Orton and Tyers 1992), animal bone (Moreno-Garcia *et al* 1996; Orton 1996), and glass (Cool 1994). Once quantified, there is flexibility in the level of detail at which comparisons are made, and results can be displayed as a graph, making interpretation easier. The flexibility with which data can be manipulated within Geographic Information Systems has made it considerably easier to experiment with different ways of structuring and presenting comparative data.

We have already referred to Biddle's (1990) work on small finds from medieval Winchester. The statistical basis for this description of social and functional differences within the town relied on the use of contingency tables. A detailed study of stratified assemblages has also been carried out on the late-Iron Age and Roman-period farmstead at Maxey, Cambridgeshire (Pryor *et al* 1985). Here, patterns of disposal of a wide range of artefacts were identified, and changing practices through time explored. Both studies used artefacts that could be easily classified and quantified, in environments where similar patterns of redundancy could be assumed.

There is a risk that ill-defined ambition to 'compare interesting finds' will result in expensive data collection without clear benefits. The nature of archaeological assemblages places severe limits on what can be achieved. Kenward, in discussing the applicability of multivariate analysis to insect assemblages (1978, 41), has observed that many correlates might be largely worthless because of the extreme heterogeneity of the assemblages. The different circumstances of discard and post-depositional decay justify the current practice of dividing site finds according to material class, but we have already described how the study of both deposit formation processes and food webs depends on approaches that cut across the traditional divisions of archaeological material. Further research is needed to assess the extent to which different classes of artefacts can be compared successfully.

3.8 Summary

The archaeological finds reviewed in this chapter describe a landscape of consumption. They witness the creation and disposal of wealth, and the organisation of production and supply. We have already touched on many reasons why this evidence can be difficult to use, but it is the material from which models of the relationship between town and country can be developed and tested.

In order to focus attention on how archaeological finds might contribute to the research described in chapter 2 we have given emphasis to three aspects of the evidence. We have reviewed models that can be developed on the basis of 'lifecycles' of use and exploitation of the resources, we have described critical archaeological properties of different classes of materials, and we have surveyed ways in which the different strands of evidence can be brought together.

Different stages in the use of the resources are illustrated here in a series of tables. These show how archaeological evidence witnesses different farming strategies and systems of exchange. The specialist demands of stratified and urban societies introduced bias into resource use, and the explanation of such bias forms the basis for much of the research described. In reviewing this research we have also offered a critique of explanatory models that exaggerate the importance of market forces in articulating the relationship between town and country, and between producers and consumers. Alternative models may better account for the archaeological evidence.

Different classes of material became rubbish, or were buried, for different reasons – and once buried were subject to different processes of decay. These processes are still only partially understood, and this limits the use we can make of the evidence. Pottery is easily broken and difficult to recycle, but robust. It is therefore one of the most informative components of archaeological assemblages. The utility of pottery in establishing patterns of supply is well established. Here we have stressed the value of extending such studies to locally produced coarsewares, since these have received less attention than finewares but were more closely integrated with local patterns of production and exchange.

Animal bone is perhaps even more useful. Analysis permits the description of the range of species present, the age and sex of the animals slaughtered, and the dispersal of animal bones in butchery and subsequent processing. In order to facilitate the study of systems of sites, some common approaches to the use of this data are recommended (see also p 128). Essentially there are crude approaches that permit the superficial comparison of extensive set-

tlement landscapes, and more intensive studies that permit the detailed study of contrasts within and between assemblages. Archaeobotanical remains (pollen, wood, and plant macrofossils) contribute to many of the same research themes, but variable survival justifies a more selective approach to the use of this evidence. Research is best served by the detailed study of unusually well preserved samples. Complex processes of selectivity also influence patterns of human burial. Dead populations are, in any case, far removed from living ones. Improvements in scientific technique promise important results in the study of patterns of migration, as well as in the study of contrasting environmental conditions.

Metal and glass objects are easily recycled and only enter the archaeological record in exceptional circumstances. Much can, however, be deduced from the supply of coin. Statistically based approaches to the study of Roman coinage, such as the development of coin-loss profiles to characterise different types of sites and regions, have illustrated important contrasts between town and country. Such techniques could also be applied to the study of later periods of coinage, although in most cases the sample base is too small.

The interpretation of this information will benefit from a broader understanding of the way in which assemblages were formed, and how the different components identified relate to each other. Urban assemblages offer excellent data for such study. Several detailed surveys, notably those undertaken in Lincoln and York, are exceptionally important to the research considered here. But much material has not yet been reviewed for its contribution to the study of town/country interaction. This is particularly the case with the finds from lower status rural sites. We need more works of synthesis that compare different classes of site and place data within the context of broader agricultural and urban regimes. In some areas of study an improved sample is first required, elsewhere the sample is adequate but its description less so. In the following chapter we explore these issues in more detail, and test the nature of the available data by developing research proposals for particular archaeological landscapes.

CHAPTER FOUR

Research frameworks

4.1 Introduction

In this chapter we propose a series of case studies. In the face of a wealth of information, of which so many questions can be asked, it is not easy to single out specific projects for particular attention. Numerous programmes of research can be justified. There is a need, however, to draw together some of these threads of argument if specific and viable research strategies can be built from the generalised observations that have been advanced in the preceding chapters.

Following a broadly historical narrative, we start with a study of the late Iron Age and Roman settlement hierarchies of Essex (4.2) and conclude with a base line review of the environmental impact of Roman and medieval London (4.6). Each study explores a specific settlement landscape and offers a framework from which programmes of study can be launched. In each study we include a review of the available data and of the current state of research, before concluding with detailed proposals.

Processes of change

Major changes in past settlement patterns have always excited archaeological attention. The contrasts that can be established at points of change – at critical spatial, temporal, or cultural boundaries – invite explanation. Difference illuminates. Changing approaches to the way in which surplus production supported power systems is a central theme throughout this survey. Towns are a product of the preferences of the powerful and are supported by an uneven distribution of wealth. The functions of

towns were neither constant nor inevitable: social order and hierarchy can survive without towns, just as individual towns can fail in urban societies. In both the late pre-Roman Iron Age and in the early medieval period it is possible to suggest that a critical feature of change was the substitution of kin-based systems, supported by domestic modes of production, with more hierarchical arrangements. In these more complex societies, surplus was extracted through tribute or taxation (see p 13). Such change involved the nucleation of power and established the social platform from which urban choices could be made. Many questions attach to this process. Our primary concerns are with the location of power and its visibility in the landscape, the structure and nature of economic activities attached to towns, the supply mechanisms developed to sustain towns, and the impact that these had on the broader environment (see chapter 2.5: Q4–11).

Our interest in these changes can not concentrate exclusively on urban systems, since many of the relationships being studied could develop without the need for towns. The place of the town can only be established by looking at the range of options that were available, and by comparing the dynamics of the different systems. We have good archaeological evidence for two distinct periods when choices were being made between different types of settlement systems, and from which urban foundations emerged. The changes in settlement dynamics that accompanied the development of *oppida* and their replacement by the first Roman towns in the first century AD are well documented in the archaeological literature but still poorly understood (Q12–16). Complex settlement hierarchies were also a product of the Saxon period, and the processes which resulted in the development of middle Saxon *emporia c* AD 650–850 are the subject of continuing debate (Q20–3). These periods of change are therefore the focus of two of our case studies (4.2 and 4.4 below).

Describing hierarchies of settlement

We introduced this report with a complaint about the site-specific nature of many archaeological studies (p 4). Despite the range of information available, comparatively little research has been conducted into the nature of the relationships between Romano-British settlements. Several different economic forces relevant to the period have been theorised, but archaeological evidence is rarely used to provide anything other than an anecdotal test of these ideas. Many of the published surveys describe marketing strategies. The alternative mechanisms whereby surplus could be distributed, and the ambivalent place held in such systems by towns, are subjects that await study. Such study needs to pay particular attention to the role played in marketing by estate production and by 'small towns' (Q14–19).

Study of such issues in the Saxon period is complicated by our limited understanding of the settlement hierarchy within which the *emporia* were located. It is only by knowing how *emporia* differed from other sites that their role can be described. The issue of how to describe and characterise differences between sites on the basis of their artefactual assemblages requires study (Q20–3).

Here we have attempted to explore ways of describing settlement hierarchies within the context of our studies of processes of change (4.2 and 4.4 below). Although it is implicit in all of the studies discussed here, it is perhaps necessary to stress that the next stage of work, once individual landscapes and hierarchies can be described, is to progress towards descriptions of networks of such sites. There is a risk that some of the case studies reviewed might reinforce a misleading impression of economic territoriality.

Regional identities

Much of the research described in this report is essentially aimed at the understanding of comparatively discrete systems, but, since the diversity of settlement pattern is a vital element of the English landscape, research must also address issues of regional identity and contrast. The ways in which distinctive regional identities emerged has a direct bearing on the attitudes taken to the expression and structure of power.

Amongst several intriguing aspects of the archaeology of late-Roman Britain two appear to be particularly ripe for study. The first of these is the nature of regional contrast. Notwithstanding the assumed homogenising effects of over three centuries of rule from Rome, different regions in Britain developed discrete identities. If anything these divergences were even more evident in the 4th century than they had been in the first (see Woolf 1998, 203, for a similar pattern in Roman Gaul). This greater differentiation was apparently a product of participation in the complex systems of cultural argument that characterised the later Roman empire. The second curious feature is the degree to which the later Romano-British economy had become monetised. A flood of small coin offers an invaluable tool for research, in which it seems likely that local and regional systems of supply and use can be described from the distribution of particular issues (see 4.3 below).

The study of the emergence of regional and national identities in medieval Britain has been given emphasis by English Heritage (1991; see also Thomas 1983, 21), but is an area where archaeology has been slow to deploy results in the service of synthetic study (Q31–6). Fortunately this is an area where historical geography has already developed a range of models and approaches. Our suggestion here is to use archaeology to improve our description and understanding of these models (see 4.5 below).

Other themes

Several other issues deserve brief emphasis in future study. Towns have widely been seen as places of innovation, where new social and economic relationships could be formed, and from which change was transmitted to the countryside (see Collis *et al* nd). In some respects such innovation is an aspect of the processes of change we have already described and an instrumental feature in the development of regional identity. The study of urban fashion deserves emphasis, however, because of its ability to illuminate changing ideological strategies that are not always evident in economic practice.

The study of the ecological impact of urban development requires further base line research. Historically towns have been remarkably successful in supporting large urban populations. In order to do so they have had to adopt a variety of strategies to survive and to mitigate their environmental impact. Archaeological data has an important contribution to make to the study of the ways in which ecological impacts associated with the creation and support of towns have been accommodated (Q10–11, see 4.6).

We have also described several problems in the use of archaeological assemblages (above p 62). We do not yet know enough about the ways in which archaeological assemblages were formed and transformed. Without more information on the subject it is difficult to draw reliable inferences about the nature of living populations from the incomplete evidence of dead ones. Different patterns of consumption, redundancy, discard, reworking, and residuality all require attention. In particular we need to better understand the relationship between find and context.

The archaeological database

As we have already explained (above p 6), the research undertaken in order to write this report involved a detailed review of work that had been undertaken in England. We wished to know where excavations and surveys had taken place, and to establish how the available data might contribute to future study. A list of towns was established from published reviews: in particular those of Wacher (1995), Burnham and Wacher (1990), Biddle (1976), Reynolds (1977), Beresford (1967; 1981), Beresford and Finberg (1973), and Heighway (1972). Others are listed in the extensive town surveys being undertaken by English Heritage and in Sites and Monuments Records (SMRs). A database of archaeological sources (archives, excavation reports, pottery reports, etc) was compiled for these sites and for the territories around them.

On the basis of this rapid survey, England's richer archaeological landscapes were provisionally identified. The availability of recent fieldwork data does not, of course, define landscapes where analytical research should be undertaken. Some periods and regions present sparse archaeological data, and research themes specific to these will necessarily be studied on the basis of more limited data. The recent survey of the territorial hinterland of Wroxeter has

tackled such problems in detail (see above p 20). For most studies, however, the availability of data is a prerequisite for closer research. A distinction can be drawn between regions where analysis is feasible on the basis of available data and others where further sampling may be needed.

Most excavation has taken place in lowland Britain, following the pattern of both past settlement and modern redevelopment, and this area presents the richest source of information. There is therefore a bias in the available data towards landscapes in the south-east of the country. The five counties of East Anglia are particularly well placed for advancing several of the research themes discussed here. This is not just because of the range of data available, and the settlement history of the region, but also because of the existence of a structured research framework tested by a series of review conferences (Buckley 1997). The development of similar frameworks for other parts of the country, combined with the introduction of robust and agreed regional artefact typologies, will broaden the base within which constructive work on the themes discussed here can be advanced.

Summary

At the outset we described this survey as a study of models (systems and ideas), variables (classes of evidence) and samples (sites and landscapes). The case studies presented below are therefore structured to explore the potential of a range of different sources of information (animal bone, pottery, coin, ecofacts, small finds, historical data, buildings archaeology) from particular archaeological landscape in order to test particular interpretative models. These are necessarily individual studies. Coherence is provided by our abiding concern with power, hierarchy, exploitation, and consumption.

The proposals concentrate attention on periods of change when urban strategies were more actively promoted and when modes of production and exploitation changed most radically (the late-Iron Age and early-Roman period; the 7th–9th centuries; and in the later medieval spread of urbanism). Each proposal is made specific to key landscapes and outlines some of the ways in which research could be advanced.

An exploration of contrasting social and economic strategies adopted in response to late-Iron Age and early-Roman urbanisation in the Colchester area (4.2) is followed by a study of the ways in which increasing coin use in late Roman Britain affected the relationship between town and country (4.3). The early-medieval settlement hierarchy is the subject of a further study, and explores the role of *emporia* (*wics*), using both *Hamwic* and Ipswich as examples (4.4). The contrast between nucleated and dispersed areas of settlement in the medieval period, and the ways in which this might relate to domestic arrangements and urban change are considered in the context of both Warwickshire and Norfolk (in 4.5). The final case study (4.6) considers the environmental and ecological impact of London in the context of studies of urban sustainability.

Several important research topics are not explored in these case studies. Most significantly we have not proposed a research framework for the study of the economic and social character of the late Saxon *burh* (Q24–9). Nor have we come up with a suggested approach to the study of the place of the town in later medieval development cycles, specialisation and innovation (Q34–6). These are but the most glaring of omissions on a list that could easily be extended. Our neglect of certain themes and regions is not intended to imply that these missing areas of research are somehow less important.

4.2 Iron Age to Roman

Frances Condron with Dominic Perring

4.2.1 Background

The study of Britain's urban beginnings has usually concentrated on unravelling the political choices that preceded and attended Roman conquest and rule. As we have seen in chapter 2 archaeological research has been particularly interested in the processes by which power came to be located in urban central places and which resulted in the creation of Romano-British culture. The big questions have been concerned with the contributions made to urban outcomes by military commanders and local elites. The narrative of imperial expansion and the evidence of the selective introduction of Romanised patterns of consumption within the province have made it possible to describe settlement and culture in terms of a stark polarity between 'Roman' and 'native'. More recent scholarship has sensibly moved beyond this rather restrictive model and describes a plurality of economic and social relationships within the Roman world.

After the Roman conquest, Britain accommodated a variety of systems of social allegiance that were underwritten by different mechanisms for manipulating surplus. In some areas kin groups owning land in common may have persisted in self-sufficient, 'subsistence' farming, little touched by a Romanised urban society. Elsewhere landowners may have operated slave-run estates, drawn on rents from tenants, or used tied and wage labour directly to produce agricultural surplus. Throughout the province the army, subsidised by taxation and commanding a massive supply of labour, was

directly involved in production and exchange, as well as being a principal consumer. Extensive imperial estates and public lands must have further complicated the relationship between the forces of production and consumption. At the gates of the Roman camps, and in some towns, merchants and traders could earn profit through state commissions or in the market place. In this environment commercial forces may occasionally have escaped social control. This is perhaps even more likely to have occurred in the extra-mural and roadside settlements, although even here it seems likely that most economic relations remained socially embedded. In most contexts, surplus was probably extracted by tax rent, but the ways in which it was directed into the support of power could differ considerably.

Goods would have navigated networks of patronage and dependency built around interests of tribe, country, class, office, gender, and faith. It is important to stress that abstract economic considerations are rarely paramount. There is, therefore, a potentially confusing range of alternative influences operating within any given settlement hierarchy.

In this chapter we review some of the ways in which it might be possible to describe the changes in settlement dynamics that accompanied the development of Iron Age *oppida* and their replacement by a Roman-inspired settlement hierarchy. For reasons explained in more detail below we believe that such study is best conducted in a region encompassing most of modern Essex, which area roughly coincides with the assumed territory of the pre-Roman tribe of the Trinovantes. The research objectives are based on those set out in chapter 2, and are most particularly concerned with the impact of town-based systems on structures of late Iron Age and Romano-British economic power. In general terms this involves a study of how power was expressed in the landscape and how the settlement pattern represented changing relationships (see 2.5: Q4–7).

Five models of exchange can be described and tested in this study area:

- Rural exchange networks, bypassing central places,
- Town-based markets,
- Domainal supply systems based on villa and urban estates,
- Military/state provisioning,
- Long-distance exchange.

The study of these contrasting economic pathways and networks involves first determining the extent to which it is possible to identify and differentiate between them. This is not a straightforward matter and the archaeological evidence may not be conclusive. Studies of the changing patterns of building material supply to Roman sites along the south-east coast have shown, however, that changes in the nature of the command economy (as influenced by institutions such as the *classis Britannica*) can be described from archaeological finds (Allen and Fulford 1999). Other exchange systems are implicit in the descriptions obtained of local material culture from both urban and rural sites within the region. This evidence tempts our further attention.

The aim is to understand the context in which specialist exchange, such as long-distance supply, town provisioning, and specialist craft production, operated. There are two ways in which we can investigate these different economic relationships:

- Through measurements of the degree of economic integration between rural areas and consumer sites (although establishing dating frameworks will be difficult on low-status sites). This requires a review of the full range of sites within the settlement hierarchy, and a measure of the variation in adoption of practices and products representative of the different approaches to settlement organisation and exchange;
- Through patterns of consumption in towns and forts.

Comparisons can be made in the composition of assemblages from a wide range of settlements, and in the spatial distribution of diagnostic artefacts both within and between them. Settlements can be defined primarily by the type of rubbish they generate, rather than by morphological typology (as suggested in Burnham *et al* 2001). Such an approach recognises the great variation in settlements traditionally classified as belonging to the same type, and therefore offers a more sophisticated description of past settlement patterns. The following questions can be asked of this material:

- How comparable are the artefactual signatures of *oppida*, early towns, military sites, and low-status rural sites? To what extent were the legal distinctions apparently drawn between the different classes of urban foundation reflected in the way in which culture was framed and economies supported?
- How did access to resources and the evidence of specialist consumption differ through the settlement hierarchy? The adoption of certain aspects of Roman culture, as evidenced by both imported goods and local patterns of social display, did not occur at the same pace on all sites. A detailed regional survey of the progress of cultural change would clarify the social and economic forces involved.

As has been made clear in chapter 3, animal bone and pottery are particularly useful to the study of these themes. Study can focus on identifying local and regional herding strategies and the impact of Roman urbanisation on supply and consumption. Study of the animal bone should be conducted with the following questions in mind:

- How were *oppida* qualitatively different to contemporary sites in dietary habits and their consumption of surplus? How was such consumption supported and what impact might it have had on rural production?
- How important was local supply (in particular of cattle) to the provisioning of conquest-period military sites? What different supply mechanisms can be identified and what does this tell us about the relationship between new power structures and established mechanisms of rural production?
- To what extent can faunal assemblages be used to identify 'Romanised' and 'native' animal husbandry practices and diet? Can diverse urban/rural identities be measured through diet, and how did conquest and the foundation of towns change such identities?

- Did urban populations have access to more exotic foods? How far down the settlement hierarchy can exotic consumption be traced, for instance do villas have more exotic assemblages than other rural settlements (King 1991)?
- Did the founding of towns result in a change in agricultural practices in their environs? To what extent are changes also seen around small towns, many of which show their greatest development in the early 2nd century?
- Is there any evidence for a late Roman 'ruralisation' of urban faunal assemblages, as is assumed in some models for the period (although see Dobney et al 1998)? How do major and small towns compare?

Maltby (1994) has undertaken work of similar scope in the Hampshire basin, where he has compared differences in the relative abundance, mortality patterns, morphology, and butchery of domestic mammals in assemblages from urban, suburban, and rural sites centred on Dorchester and Winchester.

Research would also involve a detailed investigation of access to imported, regionally and locally produced ceramics. Important information on exchange networks at a variety of levels can be gleaned from ceramic assemblages (see Millett 1990, 166–73).

- Long-distance marketing and exchange can be explored through samian distribution, to test Going's (1992) model of fluctuations in its supply to Britain,
- Variation in access to the major Romano-British wares needs to be explored both through time and between sites (based on Pomel 1984),
- Local exchange networks are poorly understood, and the sources and distributions of local products need to be established.

Building material can also be exploited in studies of the Roman settlement hierarchy. Comparison of major civic, imperial/military, and private buildings shows differences in the range of building materials being used. This is most evident in variability in the use of imported building stone (eg Allen and Fulford 1999), and in the use of tile and brick, but may also have had an influence on access to more local supplies of building material.

- Can different systems of building material supply be located within the different models of exchange (military/imperial supply, market supply, estate provisioning, etc)? If so how can

sites be characterised within such systems, and what types of interaction can be deduced?
- What relationship can be established between architectural complexity and finds assemblages? How different are settlement hierarchies described on the basis of architectural style from those defined by patterns of consumption and discard?

Here we have concentrated on the ways in which archaeological finds can shed light on the economic basis of power, but the study of the material culture must also take account of the ways in which it can be used to describe patterns of identity and affiliation. Jones (1994; 1997) has shown how assumptions about the bounded nature of ethnicity have constrained previous studies of this relationship between culture and identity. She stresses the need to examine social and cultural processes that transcended the conquest, and uses the archaeological evidence of Essex and Hertfordshire to illustrate some of the problems that must be addressed. There are significant areas of common interest between the research platform she describes and our own.

In order to explore the use of Roman-style material culture in the negotiation of ethnicity it is necessary to adopt a contextual approach. Social and cultural groups can not be used as the primary unit of analysis. Variation can instead be studied through a series of 'locales': rural settlements, nucleated settlements, forts, extra-mural settlements, etc. A contextual study of stylistic variation in pottery, buildings, and dress fittings can describe approaches to cultural affiliation, although our ability to compare fashion statements is compromised by the fact that most dating frameworks depend on the evidence of typological variation (Jones 1997, 129–32; and see Willis 1994).

4.2.2 Sample areas and databases

South-east England offers the best opportunities to explore transformations in power structures attendant on the Roman conquest, in part because of the greater archaeological visibility of the pre-Roman elite in this region but also because of the intensity of fieldwork that has taken place here. This potential is recognised in local research frameworks (Bryant 1997, 28). Indeed it has been argued that Hertfordshire is one of the best areas in which to study the late Iron Age in Europe (Hertfordshire County Council 1997, 9). Models developed in this

Fig 5 The distribution of settlements known as *oppida* in late pre-Roman Iron Age Britain (after Millett 1990)

Table 9 Archaeological data available for the study of late Iron Age and Roman sites in Essex: the principal urban sites

Site	Pottery reports	Animal bone reports	Building material	References
Colchester Gosbecks	Hawkes & Hull 1947: discussion of forms & fabrics from large assemblages	Dunnett 1971 very brief review	Archive held at Colchester museum	
Sheepen	Dunnett 1971 brief discussion of fabrics and forms, and samian stamps	Niblett 1985 full details of contexts, quantified by fragment count, MNI. Detailed discussion included		
	Niblett 1985 full details of contexts, quantified by sherd number. Amphorae also by minimum no. of vessels. Histograms of relative frequency according to four main periods			
	Hawkes & Crummy 1995 details of dykes (few finds)			
Stanway	Crummy 1995 on assemblages from burials			
Colchester *Colonia*	Symonds & Wade 1999 detailed synthesis of Roman pottery. Site reports also discuss pottery, but do not list contexts in which the groups were found. Crummy 1992 for the fortress	Luff 1993 detailed synthesis of animal bones. Published accounts do not list contexts/features in which bones were found. Brasier 1986 animal bones were not analysed. High quality of information, but problems of residuality	Benfield & Garrod 1992 good assemblage of building material, not yet analysed. Shimmin & Carter 1996 range of building material, needs analysis	Brasier 1986; Crummy N 1987; Crummy 1981 & 1984; Crummy *et al* 1993; Dunnett 1971; Hawkes & Hull 1947; Shimmin 1994
Chelmsford	Very large assemblages. Going 1987: detailed discussion of some mansio groups, but EVES presented in summary form only. Samian incompletely published	Drury 1988 & Luff 1982 publication of groups from *mansio*. Well fill published in detail (MNI; age; sex; size; butchery. Also plant & shellfish remains)	Drury 1988 discusses mansio, but material was not quantified	Drury 1972; Martin & Wallace unpub
	Wickenden 1992 detailed discussion of two temple groups (fully quantified by EVE and weight) but no totals for the whole site	Wallis 1988 discussion of horse burial	Wickenden 1992 descriptive discussion	
	Further work is planned for 2002–03	Wickenden 1992 publishes temple groups (2,537 id frags); quantified as MNI; age; meat weight; sex; cattle skeletal elements; sheep slaughter patterns		

region, where pre-Roman social hierarchies were perhaps most developed, will not necessarily apply elsewhere. They do, however, offer a starting point for comparative research.

This review takes the period immediately prior to the Roman conquest as its starting point, and places emphasis on the social and economic processes associated with the establishment and use of *oppida*. The study of this process must necessarily look to those parts of the country where it took place and this places limitations on our choice of study area. Millet (1990, 24), has listed the main *oppida* and related sites presently known in England (Fig 5). The presence of an elite residential enclosure marks out places which may have combined symbolic functions with administrative ones, and which might justify the description of 'tribal town' (Millett 1990, 26–8). Only three places: Colchester, St Albans (*Verulamium*), and Silchester present these characteristics.

The Roman presence in Britain has generated a much more substantial body of data than that available for the study of the pre-Roman Iron Age. More than 30 Romano-British towns have been investigated over the last 50 years. These include the five main 'chartered' towns of the province, most *civitas* capitals, and a number of small towns. The

Romano-British countryside has also been intensively studied, most usually in the context of site-specific investigations although several regional landscape surveys have also been undertaken. Hertfordshire and Essex have both witnessed busy programmes of excavation. More high-status sites of the late-Iron Age and early-Roman period (including 40 Roman villas) have been studied in Hertfordshire than in any equivalent area in England. It has consequently been argued that 'in terms of known sites, the *Verulamium* area offers the best opportunity for discussing the nature of Romano-British settlement' (Hunn 1995). Unfortunately the artefactual and ecofactual evidence available from *Verulamium* requires reassessment. A review of the dating of the coarse pottery has been identified as a research objective in a consultation paper (Niblett 1994), and further work is needed on the pottery typologies for the entire region.

In contrast it has been claimed that 'the current approach to Roman pottery in Essex offers the greatest opportunity within Britain for achieving major advances in the understanding of urban and rural marketing' (Fulford and Huddleston 1991). Excavations have been carried out on a wide range of relevant sites in Essex (Tables 9–12 and Fig 6). It is this combination of extensive excavation

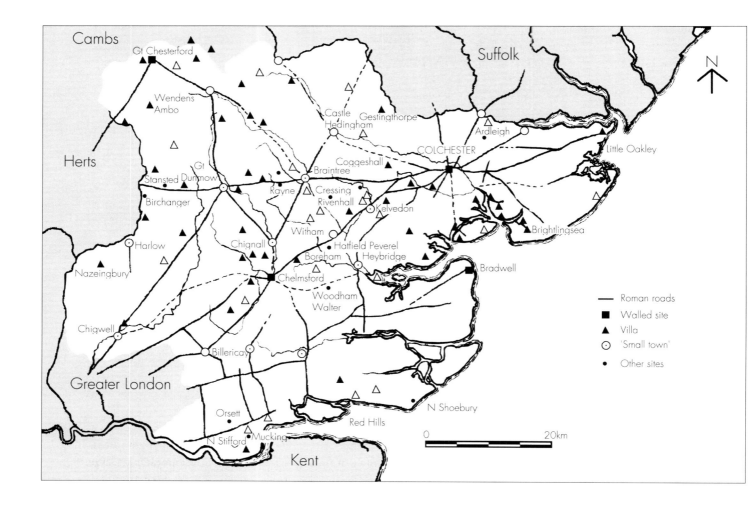

Fig 6 Essex: Roman sites with good finds assemblages (after Barford, 2002)

supported by a sophisticated understanding of pottery typologies that makes this a particularly promising area for synthetic study. The establishment at Colchester of a legionary fortress and colony also allows us to explore the changes that their introduction involved. The study of the earliest phase of Roman occupation is given further value by deposits associated with the Boudiccan destruction of Colchester, which provide independently dated assemblages including crops, pottery, and bone. Contemporary fire horizons in *Verulamium* and London provide valuable comparative data.

The research framework offered here is therefore most closely concerned with the potential of Essex and southern Suffolk, but aspects of this work could usefully be extended to include adjacent areas. There are important issues that can not be explored in the proposed study area. In the first place any regional based survey will fail to properly address the divergent experiences of different regions and communities. There is therefore also scope for adding a comparative dimension to this

study, contrasting the network of relationships established around Colchester with those attendant on other urban foundations within the province. In particular issues of military/civilian interaction, can only be studied effectively in regions with a longer military presence, such as the territories of the *Corieltauvi* (Leicester and Lincoln) or *Brigantia* (Aldborough). The paucity of easily datable finds on many rural sites in the north means that somewhat different approaches will be needed to those described here. But in any case no single model can be made to apply uniformly.

The study of changing patterns of rural settlement and urban demands in late antiquity might be better addressed in the west of Britain. The apparent prosperity of the Chilterns, with its flourishing villa economy can be contrasted with settlement in the upper Thames valley, where work on gravel extraction sites has generated a good sample of Romano-British farmsteads and some excellent archaeobotanic data (Lambrick 1992). For present purposes, however, it is more useful to concentrate our attention on the particulars of a single proposal. To this end we dedicate the remaining part of this section to a study of the archaeology of late-Iron Age and Roman Essex and its surrounds.

4.2.3 Review of previous work

Pre-Conquest settlement

The economy of Iron Age Britain was almost entirely rural, and the 1st-century landscape of Essex was characterised by a pattern of dispersed farmsteads engaged in mixed farming, in which cattle and sheep figured importantly (Kemble 2001, 78–9). A complex settlement hierarchy had, however, developed in the course of the 1st century AD with Colchester (*Camulodunum*) at its apex. Several parts of this *oppida* have been investigated. Numerous dykes were cut from the late 1st century BC, and were still being modified after the Roman conquest (Hawkes and Crummy 1995). The industrial area at Sheepen, investigated in the 1930s and 1970, appears to have been occupied from *c* AD 5 to its destruction in the Boudiccan revolt (Hawkes and Hull 1947; Niblett 1985). A temple and theatre complex has been studied at Gosbecks. At Lexden an impressive tumulus opened up in the late 19th century contained a rich cremation burial dated to around 10 BC (Foster 1986). Other high-status burials have been found within the region, including the discovery at Stanway of a series of enclosures surrounding rich cremation burials. Provisional dating suggests that this cemetery remained in use to around AD 60 (R Havis, pers comm). Excavation of these and other pre-conquest and conquest-period cemeteries shows that imported goods were incorporated into local burial rituals (eg Drury 1978a; Wickenden 1988). In the 1st century AD such imports were generally more common in cemeteries than on occupation sites. The distribution of wealthy burials and religious complexes across the presumed tribal territory suggests a tribal structure made up of separate lineages or septs (Millett 1990). Although *Camulodunum* may have served as a multi-focal centre for a wide region, its importance in articulating exchange needs to be evaluated against these alternative centres. These include the ritual complexes at Harlow,

Chelmsford, and Stansted, and the more complex settlements such as Heybridge and Hacheston (see Table 10).

Pre-Roman occupation has also been studied at a series of other sites in the region. Archaeological assemblages suitable for the study proposed here have been recovered from excavations at Billericay, Birchanger, Bishop's Stortford, Ivy Chimneys, Witham (settlement and religious complex), Kelvedon, Little Waltham, Mucking, Nazeingbury, Orsett and Rivenhall. There is also evidence for salt production from the late 1st century BC into the 2nd century AD from the Red Hills of south-east of Essex (Fawn *et al* 1990; Sealey 1995).

Most of these late-Iron Age sites continued in occupation after the conquest. The study of change across the period of conquest is complicated by the problems of dating settlements that were not strongly or obviously integrated into exchange networks. In the absence of diagnostic imports, archaeological dating structures are generally reliant on the evidence of local ceramic traditions and building styles. Continuity of later Iron Age pottery traditions into the 1st century AD is, however, attested to the north and west of the study area, particularly in the tribal territory of the *Iceni*. Even though wheel-thrown Gallo-Belgic type wares were adopted in Essex and Hertfordshire from the 1st century BC, handmade traditions also continued in use here (Bryant 1997). This chronology makes it difficult to distinguish between pre and post-Conquest assemblages. Similarly the typical late-Iron Age timber-built roundhouse set in a rectilinear ditched enclosure continued as a settlement form to at least the 2nd century AD (Drury 1978b).

Early post-Conquest sites

The only early military sites to have been studied in detail in the region are those in and around Colchester. The legionary fortress here became the focus of the subsequent *colonia*, and barrack blocks were used to accommodate the early civilian population (Crummy 1997). Early post-conquest occupation layers can be separated from later ones by burnt layers representing the Boudiccan sack of the city. The possible military supply base at Fingringhoe was quarried away in the early 20th century, although finds were recovered unsystematically and the assemblage contains important early-conquest material (Willis 1990). Aerial photography has also

Table 10 Archaeological data available for the study of late Iron Age and Roman sites in Essex: lesser nucleated sites

Site	Pottery reports	Animal bone reports	Building material	References
Heybridge, Maldon	Post-excavation work nearing conclusion. Good potential for LPRIA and early Roman, including large amphora (Dressel 1) assemblage	Post-excavation in progress	Ongoing research. Includes temple complex, timber domestic structures	Wickenden 1986; Martin & Wallace unpub; Atkinson & Preston 1998
Great Chesterford	Draper 1988: much residual material Miller 1989 samian only Crossan et al 1990: general discussion Brooks & Wallis 1991 summary discussion Miller 1996: 2 unquantified groups only Further work programmed for 2002-3	Draper summarises 3rd-4th century groups. Partial recovery of bone Miller discusses bone briefly 69 bone fragments found. Brooks & Wallace animal bones not quantified	Miller 1996 brief discussion of (unquantified) building material	Collins 1996; Essex County Council 1996; Martin & Wallace unpub Archives at Saffron Walden & Cambridge museums.
Braintree	Bedwin 1985 (Mount House) discusses fabrics and forms (1,100 sherds), not quantified. Milton 1986 summarises unstratified collection Havis 1993: 2 sites (inc. Sandpit Rd. with 3,996 sherds) quantified by EVE or sherd number & weight Other sites await analysis	Drury 1976 offers basic analysis Bedwin 1985 lists seven fragments. Milton 1986 lists 108 identified fragments (unstratified) Havis 1993 quantifies two bone-rich features (2,215 identified frags) by MNI; age; meat weight; sex; cattle skeletal elements; sheep slaughter patterns Not all bone was kept.	Drury 1976 summary of tile Havis 1993 includes discussion of building material (not quantified)	Martin & Wallace unpub
Kelvedon	Clarke 1988a brief discussion of late 1st century assemblage Rodwell 1988 discussion of samian & brief unquantified review of other wares Assemblages in need of re-analysis	Rodwell 1988 discussion of 747 identified fragments, quantified as MNI		Eddy 1982; Eddy 1995; Ellis 1981; Martin & Wallace unpub
Great Dunmow	Small assemblages. Wickenden 1988 discusses three groups in detail, fully quantified (cemetery, shrine, large pit). Most pot residual	Wickenden 1988 general discussion of bone only	Wickenden 1988 discussion of shrine	
Billericay	Rudling 1990: part of 1987 excavation assemblage. Further analysis needed	Rudling 1990: small assemblage. More may be available from other excavations. Needs analysis	Rudling 1990 covers part of assemblage. Analysis needed	Kemble 2001, 115; Martin & Wallace unpub
Ivy Chimneys, Witham	Thorough description and quantification of 1.5 tonnes of pottery, with EVEs			Turner 1999
Chigwell, Little London	Excavations by the West Essex Archaeological Group (Clarke et al 1998)			Martin & Wallace unpub
Harlow	France & Gobel 1985 discuss mostly unstratified material. Martins refers to good 2nd century groups			Millar 1974
Stansted	Excavations by Frameworks Archaeology			

revealed two forts at Great Chesterford, and another two at Coddenham in Suffolk, but these sites have not been investigated or dated (for other possible early sites of Roman forts see Kemble 2001, 87–9). V-shaped ditches found in excavations at Chelmsford might also be from a military base (Eddy 1995).

As we have already seen several lesser urban sites and villages had their origins in the pre-conquest period. These include Billericay, Chelmsford, Heybridge, and Kelvedon. Cult centres have also been found at Harlow and Ivy Chimneys (near Witham). The finds recovered from the settlements at Chelmsford and Heybridge are particularly useful, since these sites have seen extensive programmes of excavation which additionally permit the intra-site analysis of patterns of consumption. Other nucleated sites that appear to have had slightly later origins, with little or no evidence for pre-conquest occupation, include Coggeshall, Great Chesterford and Great Dunmow. Important landscape surveys have also been undertaken in the Blackwater Estuary and a major programme of work is in progress at Stansted.

Villas and the countryside

Few villas have been identified within the study

area, although this may be a problem with recognition because of the local emphasis on timber and earth-walled construction. The greatest concentration of known villa sites is in the Colne valley, although others are known to both east and west of Colchester. It seems likely that most of these villas would have been in the economic and social orbit of Colchester. Few of the known sites have been subjected to detailed archaeological excavation. Material is, however, available from the Boreham 'principia', Gestingthorpe, Ipswich Castle Hill, Chignall, Nazeingbury, and Rivenhall. The results of the excavations of these last three sites have been published, although the finds merit further attention. Evidence for rural settlement has also been found at several other sites, such as Castle Hedingham and Rayne, where it is not entirely clear if these had been part of villa estates. The sample is a poor one and not entirely representative (Going 1997) but is probably adequate for the purposes of comparative analysis. Some further excavation of representative sites might be justified if the opportunity arose, particularly in the Colne valley.

The southern part of Essex, and in particular the Thames estuary, was characterised by a very different form of landscape (see Rodwell 1978, although some of the conclusions drawn about the planned nature of the field systems here have yet to be substantiated). Here there were fewer elite properties but more evidence of industrial production. One possibility is that this area was imperially owned and administered by the London-based procurator (Perring 1991, 48). Pottery kilns have been found at Mucking, Billericay, Grays, and Orsett Cock, whilst there is good evidence for salt production and cattle droving. Pottery production in this area was perhaps associated with the preservation and transportation of agricultural surplus. It would be instructive to compare the range of products and their distribution with the output of the early kilns at Colchester.

Later sites

Late military sites include the forts at Bradwell (Othona), Walton Castle, and Farnham. The extent to which these places were integrated into local economies and social hierarchies needs to be explored. This is a complex theme that should be addressed within the context of the broader pattern of commerce along the North Sea littoral. A survey of building stone used in coastal sites in the later

2nd and 3rd centuries illustrates some long-distance supply patterns that may have been the product of the command economy developed to support the classis Britannica (Allen and Fulford 1999). Comparable supply systems appear also to have influenced distributions of Black-burnished pottery (BB2) likely to have been produced in the Thames estuary from c AD 100. In the later period, however, most building material seems to have been obtained from local sources, perhaps reflecting administrative changes. The modelling of the impact of the command economy on the region will need to take such changing circumstances into account.

Third century changes in the urban role of Colchester (see p 22) are possibly evidenced by farming within the town (Faulkner 1994) and by a reduction in the significance of pottery production (Going 1997). Comparisons between the later assemblages of Colchester and small towns in the civitas are needed to measure any changes in Colchester's economic primacy within the regional settlement hierarchy. An important question to address is whether 'small towns' emerge as significant market centres in the later Roman period.

Methodological approaches

The quality of the sample from this area has been enhanced by the development of a regional pottery type series (see p 74), by the number of sieved animal bone assemblages that have been obtained, and by the general accessibility of the archive.

Broad exchange zones in the study area have been identified through patterns of distributions that have been recorded in late-Iron Age pottery, in particular using 'Gallo-Belgic' types, to explore variation in access to imported wares. Sites in east Essex and Hertfordshire generally contain lower proportions of this wheel-thrown pottery, compared with the rest of Essex and southern Suffolk (Martin 1988). However, adoption of Gallo-Belgic type wares is not even across all sites, as shown by the presence of local, handmade and imported wares at Wendens Ambo (Hodder 1982). This highlights the importance of improving our understanding of local and regional exchange networks. Access to imported vessels should therefore be compared with locally produced diagnostic sherds, in particular Black-burnished (BB2) ware.

Several different supply systems can by hypothesised from the archaeological and topographical evidence. A landowning elite based at Colchester

Table 11 Archaeological data available for the study of late Iron Age and Roman sites in Essex: higher status rural sites (principally villas)

Site	Pottery reports	Animal bone reports	Building material	References
Chignall	Wallace and Turner Walker 1998. Good assemblage, especially of later Roman material (although much influenced by taphonomy). Only late material published in detail, but not quantified by EVEs	Luff 1998: 6102 bone fragments in a good state of preservation, published in full	Brief consideration of Roman building material in Clarke 1998	Other specialist reports found in Clarke 1998
Boreham (Great Holts Farm)	Lavender 1993: unquantified lists of wares found. Further work is in progress	396 fragments identified to species only. Albarella 1997: describes two 3rd-4th century groups in full	Report on two buildings in Lavender 1995	Murphy 1997
Gestingthorpe	Draper 1985 covers samian in detail; other forms by fabric and form. Not quantified. Mostly surface collections	Draper 1985 covers worked bone only. No excavated groups	Draper 1985 discusses tiles only (unquantified)	
Nazeingbury	Huggins 1978 discussion of range of wares, unquantified	Huggins 1978 bones quantified as MNI	Huggins 1978 brief discussion only, unquantified	
Rivenhall	Rodwell & Rodwell 1985; 1993: one group fully quantified only (including EVEs). Much residual pot	Rodwell & Rodwell 1985; 1993: small assemblage	Rodwell & Rodwell 1985; 1993: unquantified discussion of range of materials present	
Coggeshall	Clarke 1988b discusses some groups, quantified by weight only. Isserlin 1995 divided by phase, quantified by weight only	Clarke 1988b uses 600 identified fragments, identified to species only	Clarke 1988b: summary of tile. Isserlin 1995 on 878 tile fragments, sorted by form and sherd number. Not all tile was kept	
Brightlingsea, Noah's Ark	Martin 1996 describes large 2nd century group			
Little Oakley	Barford 2002 discusses stratified assemblages. Not quantified	Some bone quantified as MNI		
Wickford (Beauchamps farm)	Excavations by Rodwell – unpublished.			Kemble 2001, 161

would have controlled much of the surplus wealth produced from this region, but as we have already noted this model may not apply in parts of the Thames estuary where the Roman fleet may have dominated supply (Allen and Fulford 1999).

The presence of oyster shells on inland sites might illustrate the operation of complex supply networks. The remains of the epifauna that lived on the shells can sometimes point to the oyster beds that were being exploited, whilst changes in shell size can reflect on the organisation and impact of the farming of such beds (Winder 1992).

Ceramics have limited potential to identify local exchange networks, as it is not possible to pinpoint the production sites of locally produced wares using fabric analysis. Although within Essex there is a well-developed methodology for using building remains, it may be difficult to make comparisons with other areas as different standards are being used.

4.2.4 Research proposals and conclusions

Further study can make use of reports and archives listed in Tables 9–12. These archives should be assessed for their potential to contribute to research themes described here and to establish if there is any unnecessary duplication in terms of the type and class of site/assemblage. Lacunae in the databases can be defined on the basis of this assessment, and recommendations established for future sampling.

Faunal remains

Work can be taken forward on the basis of Luff's (1993) survey of the main domesticates in Roman and medieval Essex. Faunal assemblages will need to be identified by species, and quantified as MNI, with further consideration of age at death, sex, pathology, and butchery marks (see p 41). This will entail further examination of those assemblages with greatest potential. Study should include:

Table 12 Archaeological data available for the study of late Iron Age and Roman sites in Essex: lower status rural sites

Site	Pottery reports	Animal bone reports	Building material	References
Orsett	Carter 1998 full quantification, including EVEs, of pottery from kilns. Full description of decorated samian			
Birchanger	Medlycott 1994: basic quantification of 1,546 sherds	637 frags identified to species only	N/A	
Hatfield Peverel, Witham	Ecclestone & Havis 1996 brief discussion of fabric and form only. Some unusual aspects to assemblage (lack of storage vessels)	Ecclestone & Havis 1996: 286 identified fragments (range of species) only		
Rayne	Smoothy 1989 discussion of quantified pot (EVEs, weight, sherd number). Samian treated differently	Smoothy 1989 discussion of 1,871 identified fragments, quantified by number, weight, MNI, meat weight. Discussion of ages at death	Groarke in Smoothy 1989 (quantified by weight, decoration).	
Castle Hedingham	Lavender 1996 general discussion, not quantified (1,192 sherds)	Lavender 1996: 57 fragments only found	Lavender 1996 brief discussion. More details available in archive (SH92, Braintree museum)	
Grays	Kilns producing pottery dated AD 150–250, unpublished			Kemble 2001, 134
Mucking				Birss 1982; Jones 1973; Jones & Rodwell 1973
'Red Hills' - various sites				Fawn et al 1990; Rodwell 1966; Sealey 1995
Tilbury, Gun Hill				Drury & Rodwell 1973
Wendens Ambo	Hodder 1982 discusses formation processes			
Ardleigh	Brown 1999 pottery kilns and early groups. Not quantified			
Woodham Walter	Late Iron Age and 2nd century groups. Not quantified			Priddy & Buckley, 1987
North Stifford	Early assemblages. Not quantified by EVES	Summary report only		Wilkinson 1998
North Shoebury	Report on 2,300 sherds, mainly 2nd century. Not fully quantified			Wymer & Brown 1995

- A comparison of theoretical models for changing practices in animal husbandry (eg King 1989; Grant 1989). Which settlements reveal changes in faunal assemblages in the 1st century AD? How soon after conquest did these changes take effect?
- The construction of a range of cull profiles for the main domestic species, to investigate variations in practices of animal exploitation (for meat, hides, wool, and dairy products, eg Grant 1984).
- The preparation of a model of assemblage profiles to reflect different stages in the processing and discard of animal remains (above p 35), which can be compared with observed assemblages. Collation of rural settlement assemblages may be necessary for some comparisons, though differences in the disposal of animal bones on urban and rural sites are expected (Wilson 1994b).
- The identification of key variables indicative of high status in the LPRIA and early-Roman periods within the study area: these to include relative measurements of dependency on sheep/pig/cattle in charting the degree of integration of different patterns of consumption (as set out by King 1991) and of fowl and pig bones in order to identify and characterise backyard penning.
- Comparative evidence for the consumption of wild animals and fish (within the context of the evidence for the main domesticates), to assess the extent to which cultural identity, status, or wealth may have shaped faunal assemblages. Evidence for hunting and of dietary taboos should be assessed.

- Explorations of the extent of residuality in faunal remains, by assessment of variation in bone fragmentation, wear, and colour from single contexts (K Dobney, pers comm). Work should concentrate on individual contexts with 50 bone fragments or more, and act as an essential control for the results of other faunal analyses. Work in this area is still experimental.
- Studies of the distribution of oyster shells through the study area. Is there a set of sites that does not have access to this widely available food?

This study will focus on the primary occupation layers wherever possible, in order to reduce the problems of residuality and reworking. Attention will also focus on assemblages from sieved deposits, although this is not crucial for all aspects of the comparative analysis.

Ceramics

Work should build on Going's (1987) study of 1st-century ceramic supply to Chelmsford, and on Pomel's (1984) study of later Roman pottery. The study should use assemblages quantified following the guidelines of Young (1980), involving measurement by sherd number, weight, and EVE by fabric and form. Sample size is also an issue. Willis (1996) follows Evans' (1985) minimum requirements of well-dated groups (not whole site assemblages) consisting of at least 50 sherds, 1.0 RE (rim equivalent), and 0.75kg in weight or more. Some smaller collections could be collated for inclusion in analysis (Orton *et al* 1993, 175). Results should be displayed as distribution maps, weighted where relevant. It is difficult to integrate samian into these analyses because of different recording practices, and the recommendations of Willis (1997) should be adopted. This will require some re-quantification of published groups.

Some additional post-excavation analysis may be recommended for critical assemblages where data is not already available (following Fulford and Huddleston 1991). The identification of these assemblages is an important aspect of this project, particularly for rural sites. Ongoing work on material from the recent Elms Farm, Heybridge, excavations will add to this picture. Work is required to redress the past neglect of so-called Romanised locally produced pottery in excavation reports for

the sites in Essex and Hertfordshire (Jones 1997, 36–8).

Imported assemblages

Assemblages should be compared to define variations through time and between types of site. At Colchester and Chelmsford some aspects of intra-site variation can also be included in the analysis (eg intra-mural and extra-mural). A system of ceramic phasing should be proposed to facilitate comparison, and this should distinguish between pre-conquest, conquest, Neronian, Flavian, Hadrianic/Antonine, and later assemblages. Evidence for variation needs to be measured across the entire settlement landscape and charted through time (eg is Lyons ware restricted to military sites in the study area?). Characteristics to be recorded should include:

- Presence of imported ceramics by class (eg *terra nigra*, *terra rubra*, *terra sigillata*, Dressel 1 and 2–4 amphorae, etc) and form (eg samian Drag 29, 15/17, etc). The database should allow for the separation of wares by possible function and cultural association. For instance it has been suggested that oil *amphorae* are more common on military sites and wine *amphorae* on civilian sites (Willis 1996),
- Plain and decorated forms used in the study area, as a means of refining local settlement chronologies (Willis 1997, 7),
- Attitudes towards non-local objects and foodstuffs. First-century AD cemeteries are a particularly rich source of information within the study area,
- Ratio of decorated/plain terra sigillata. For instance were decorated pieces more valued than plain, or were decorated bowls more valued because of their form? (Willis 1997, 26–32, 36),
- Comparison of assemblage composition with regard to imported wares and glass. Variation may distinguish sites that were incorporated into glass 'recycling' networks (presumably those with markets) from those that were not.

It may also be possible to explore differential access to particular forms of terra sigillata. At a basic level differences between decorated and plain forms may be discernible for the 1st century AD. Some forms were more common than others, the Drag 31 bowl for example. Changing ratios in locally manufactured drinking vessels may instead define higher status sites, where imported forms were not preferred (see Evans 1993). Thus the ratio of jars (typical LPRIA form) to cups and flagons is another useful measure. Differences in contemporary assemblages from ritual, funerary, and occupation sites will also repay attention.

For later periods, site-specific variation in access to products of the Oxfordshire, Nene Valley, and Colchester (BB2) kilns can be explored within the context of the regional patterning described by Pomel (1984). Important locally produced wares include Hadham ware. Further work is needed to distinguish between local products, which are an essential source of information in a study of settlement interaction. Possible techniques include neutron activation, and detailed microscope fabric analysis. A feasibility study as to the appropriate physical analysis should be undertaken.

Regional distribution and exchange

The following areas of study also merit inclusion within this programme of proposed research:

- A general review of the assemblage composition at Colchester with other major towns in the region, specifically London and *Verulamium*. Closely dated contexts ought to be identified, and the importance of Colchester as a regional market evaluated;
- Comparison of assemblage composition with regard to the major regional wares (percentage ratio of Oxfordshire, Verulamium, Colchester, and BB2). This will have two strands. Firstly it will involve drawing comparisons between urban settlements, particularly small towns, to identify any variation in the significance of these sites as markets. Secondly it will entail drawing contrasts between individual urban sites and rural settlements, in order to examine the strength and pervasiveness of any markets;
- Comparison of the ratio of specific wares across the study area to describe variations in their availability and use.

The study of these characteristics will be used to describe a hierarchy of consumption and discard, which can be compared with classifications based on the evidence of settlement scale and architectural complexity. From such an analysis it should be possible to describe the significance of urban markets

within the regional economy. This sort of analysis is most easily taken forward with diagnostic finds, such as imported and regional pottery (eg Oxfordshire colour coats), and distinctive products from town-based kilns at sites within the region (most notably the products of the potteries at Colchester). The extent to which access to urban mediated production and supply was restricted, or conversely the extent to which towns were excluded from exchange systems, can be revealed through distorted distribution patterns. Some weight will also have to be given in such studies to the role of communication routes in facilitating supply.

Our ability to describe patterns of local exchange would be considerably improved if we could trace the distributions of other locally produced wares, such as the products of the kilns in the Thames estuary. Unfortunately the exploitation of glacial outcrops for clay supply in Essex makes it difficult to isolate fabric types that clearly distinguish between these local products.

Building material

Although timber and clay were the most important resources exploited in the construction of the houses and settlements within the study area, research is better served by modelling the changing patterns of use of more robust materials. Research should, however, commence with a review of the range of materials employed (including timber and mud-brick) and its impact on the archaeological visibility of settlement remains. This would build from the survey by Williams (1971) and allow the construction of models reflecting different modes of production and supply of building material (estate/ domainal, imperial supply, and reuse), including the analysis by Allen and Fulford for the later period (1999). Further research can build from this to incorporate inland sites, extend the temporal range, and look more closely at contrasting patterns in the use of locally available materials. In any modelling, separate approaches will have to be adopted for the consideration of timber, locally quarried materials, imported stonework, and brick. Much new work has appeared since Rodwell's (1982) assessment of tile production and exchange in the study area. The models provided by McWhirr for production and exchange of brick and tile in the Roman period (Darvill and McWhirr 1984) also need to be tested against more recent work.

In addition to modelling patterns of supply, research can also explore the following:

- Comparison of assemblage composition for a range of different types of buildings and sites, as a possible means of distinguishing between civic, imperial, and private building projects,
- Comparative descriptions of patterns of recycling building material,
- Development of a suitable recording strategy for tile and brick based on a fabric and form series (a fabric series is being developed by Hilary Major). Quantification should permit comparisons with other categories of find.

Attention should be limited to assemblages where recovery strategies were documented, and assessment can be made as to how representative the sample is. Such a study would draw attention to the under-utilised potential of bulk finds in archaeological research, and develop recommendations for the recovery and analysis of building material.

Comparative analysis

It is anticipated that the supply networks for ceramics, animal bone, and building materials operated differently both between and within settlements. Comparative analysis of these different systems provides an opportunity to improve our understanding of the complexity of economic exchange in Roman Britain, and should be structured to encourage cooperation amongst specialists in regional and national syntheses.

Integrated studies drawing on the evidence of both pottery and animal bone can be structured to describe dairy production (distinctive herd profiles, colander/cheese presses, and salt/briquetage); meat or fish preservation (inland finds of briquetage, distinctive fish or animal skeletal parts); and drinking customs (glass and ceramic flagons, bottles and cup/beakers, amphorae). Descriptions of settlements deriving from such comparative analyses can be used to redefine the settlement hierarchy in terms of access to and consumption of local, regional, and imported produce, and to reconstruct the transition from LPRIA to Roman Britain in terms of shifting control over people and land. Areas for investigation are:

- Comparison of assemblage composition both within and between sites,
- Development of methodology for comparing different categories of finds as a means of constructing new syntheses of the material remains (see above p 64),
- Identification of diverse artefact categories involved in a particular production process or activity (such as dairying, meat/fish preservation, drinking).

For the third element, research will borrow from ethnographic studies of food preparation and combine these with ancient documentary sources as a means of building models for comparison with the material remains. This has particular potential in the study of assemblages from *Camulodunum* (Sheepen) and Colchester, where spatial analysis can also be undertaken for a wide range of objects. The burnt layer representing the Boudiccan sack of the city enables early post-conquest contexts to be identified securely.

4.3 Coin and late Romano-British exchange

Mark Whyman

4.3.1 Background

This chapter reviews the potential of late Romano-British coinage for the study of market-based exchange, regional economic differences, and the role of towns in mediating such exchange. Five contrasting regions have been identified within which significant differences in the character of the regional economy can be proposed: these are Gloucestershire and the lower Avon; Essex; East Anglia; East Yorkshire; and a 'northern frontier zone' south of Hadrian's Wall.

The review presented in chapter 2 describes how late Roman towns were qualitatively different from those of the 2nd century (p 22). Transformations in the organisation of production and exchange are evident in both town and country, and developments in the late-Roman countryside have been interpreted as illustrating the growth of rural market-based exchange (Millett 1990). One of the strands of evidence drawn upon in these arguments is the increase in the volume of coinage in use after *c* AD 260.

Archaeological evidence allows a detailed study

Fig 7 Map showing regions of coin analysis as referred to in the text

of patterns of coin loss. For no other period do we have such a fine tool for the study of the way in which a pre-modern monetary economy functioned, and this is an area with enormous potential for the advance of archaeological technique. Relationships between the imperial state, its agents, and the Romano-British population can be described through the study of coinage. The research questions that can be addressed from this evidence have already been described (chapter 2.5, Q8–9 and Q17–19).

The character of the archaeology of late-Roman Britain is by no means uniform. Variations in artefact style, settlement form, landscape organisation, and decorative art serve to differentiate regions. Although these require further definition and study, it is apparent that the 4th century must be understood in these regional terms, and with greater resolution than straightforward notions of 'east/west' and 'lowland/highland' divisions. Furthermore, whilst elements of these differences may have roots in earlier and pre-Roman institutions and stylistic repertoires, they should not simply be seen as statements of traditional identities. Many of these differences represent transformations in relations of production and exchange, and consequent patterns of consumption, and evidence the degree and direction of such changes. In order to understand urban hinterlands in late Roman Britain we need to study a range of contrasting regions.

The proposed research involves the creation of regional coin-loss profiles to compare the integration of sites and site types into monetised exchange systems, and variations in this over time. Distribution patterns of specific coin types, both official and counterfeit, can be used to find patterns of coin circulation around different centres. Contrasts in the patterning of coinage from the major copying episodes may be sensitive indicators of change in the later 3rd and 4th centuries.

The existence of these patterns lends support to the argument that a system of markets and monetised exchange contributed to the transformation of the late Roman countryside, albeit that the reasons this system arose are open to debate. The investigation of patterns of monetary supply to late Roman sites allows us to address the role of specific towns as central places by:

- Defining their economic hinterlands in terms of coin circulation,
- Understanding the degree to which different

rural sites and site types were integrated into those hinterlands,
- Recognising changes in these patterns between the mid 3rd and late 4th/early 5th centuries.

The central role of coinage in mediating exchange, and variations in its issuing, mean that the results of this research will have major implications for the relationship between the imperial state, its regional and local agents, and the wider Romano-British population.

4.3.2 Sample areas and databases

Five regions have been selected for study because of their contrasting regional developments in the later 3rd and 4th centuries (Fig 7). These are defined topographically. Here we have avoided definitions based on assumptions about the extent of ancient territories, or on anachronistic county boundaries. This is not to assume that such topographically defined areas approximate late Roman political or administrative realities (although they might). Nor is it to adopt a rigid geographical determinism. It can nevertheless be maintained that many basic aspects of production, exchange, and consumption will have been specific to defined regions. Following Todd's discussion of villa estates the study seeks to understand how holdings were managed and exchange within them articulated 'though the vital tenurial links between estates and their dependent properties will remain elusive' (Todd 1989, 14).

It is recognised that different patterns may emerge within the regions, just as patterns across them are unlikely to be limited by their boundaries. Further study can work outwards from these core areas to identify the limits of any recognisable patterning, and it might eventually be appropriate to extend the results to establish a province-wide survey.

Gloucestershire, Avon and the lower Severn

The region encompasses the lower Severn basin, bounded to the west by the Black Mountains and the River Usk, south by the Mendips and the edge of the Marlborough and Lambourn Downs, and east by the River Cherwell. To the north a line connecting Banbury, Stratford-upon-Avon, Alcester, Worcester, and extending westwards to Hereford establishes a notional boundary.

The region includes the *colonia* at Gloucester

(*Colonia Glevensis*) and the *civitas* capital at Cirencester (*Corinium*). Both have seen extensive excavation of Roman deposits. The heartlands of the region are a byword for late Roman affluence and a flourishing agricultural landscape, characterised by the number of wealthy villas that have been investigated here (eg Barnsley Park, Chedworth, Littlecote, and Woodchester in Gloucestershire, North Leigh in Oxfordshire, and Gatcombe in Somerset). The region figures heavily in the studies of late Roman coinage (eg Brickstock 1987, 66, fig 5; Ryan 1988, 61, fig 4.1), although only the southern fringe of the region is included in Davies' (1988) study of barbarous radiates.

Essex

The region is defined by the coastline to the east and the Thames estuary to the south. To the west it is limited by the Rivers Lea and Cam, and north by the Stour. Roman Essex has been intensively studied, with major campaigns of excavation of the *colonia* at Colchester (*Camulodunum*) and the 'small town' of Chelmsford (*Caesaromagus*). In addition the county has seen substantial excavations in lower order settlements (Table 12), and extensive field survey has mapped large areas of the rural landscape.

There has been surprisingly little dedicated study of Roman coinage from Essex. The publication of coins from Colchester (Reece and Crummy 1987) represents a landmark in the presentation of coins from an extensively excavated Roman town, and the region figures prominently in Kenyon's study of Claudian bronze copies (Kenyon 1993). For later coinage, however, little synthesis appears to have been undertaken. Davies included a few sites in his thesis on barbarous radiates, appended to his main area of study as an afterthought (1988). Sites in the county are all but absent from the surveys of Ryan (1988) and Brickstock (1987). However, recent work on the coin assemblage from Elm's Farm, Heybridge, by Peter Guest (pers comm) has included coverage of the majority of Essex sites, providing comprehensive and up-to-date data.

East Anglia: Suffolk and Norfolk

The region is defined by the coast to east and north, the Rivers Great Ouse and Cam to the west, and the Stour to the south. The only major Roman town in this region is Caistor-St-Edmund (or 'Caistor-by-

Norwich'), *Venta Icenorum*. Archaeological attention has concentrated on coastal sites, such as the forts at Burgh Castle, Caistor-by-Yarmouth, and Brancaster, and their associated settlements. Most significant for this project, however, is the volume of survey on Roman rural settlement landscapes, combined with a huge quantity of coins recorded as a result of liaison between archaeologists and metal detector users. In the late-Roman period, East Anglia is noted for an apparent lack of villas, in spite of obvious evidence of intense agricultural production, including the draining of significant areas of fenland in the east of the region. The presence of numerous late Roman gold and silver hoards (eg Johns and Bland 1994) suggests the presence of a wealthy elite.

Only a handful of sites from East Anglia are included in the surveys of Ryan (1988) and Brickstock (1987), and the region is beyond the limits of Davies' 1988 study. The one published regional study, covering the entire Roman period, collates and analyses (using loss profiles) coins from sites within the probable tribal limits of the *Iceni*, roughly equivalent to the modern county of Norfolk (Davies and Gregory 1991). A point of particular interest in the context of this study is the slight indication of an earlier end date to coin lists in the northern two-thirds of the county than in the southern third. This is a pattern that should be tested by comparison with data from Suffolk and Essex.

York and eastern Yorkshire

The region is defined by the coastline to the east, the Humber estuary to the south, the River Ouse as far north as York and the Foss northwards from York to the west, and the uplands of the North York Moors/Cleveland Hills to the north.

York itself (*Eburacum*) has seen several major excavations, although it is not well understood in comparison with similarly important towns elsewhere in Britain (eg Gloucester and Colchester). Excavations have taken place at the supposed *civitas* capital at Brough-on-Humber (*Petuaria*) and the 'small town' at Malton (*Derventio*). The contemporary rural landscape is less well studied. This situation is being redressed by research projects at Holme-on-Spalding Moor and Shiptonthorpe, but much data awaits synthesis and analysis. The level of systematic fieldwork contrasts sharply with, for example, Essex and East Anglia. It is clear that the region was heavily involved in supplying the northern frontier from the late 3rd century onwards (Evans 1988). It is likely that this development involved major changes to the level and organisation of rural production in the region, but the data remains inaccessible.

Roman coins from York found before the late 1980s have been studied but not published (R Brickstock, pers comm). Coin lists are available for older sites, and the important sites of Malton and the villa at Beadlam have recently been published, but much of the data from east Yorkshire remains either in manuscript or archive. The importance of the region (and York itself), in administering and supplying the settlement infrastructure north of the rivers Mersey and Humber makes the study of this area an essential complement to that of the frontier zone itself.

Carlisle, Corbridge, and the northern frontier zone

The region is delimited to the north by the line of Hadrian's Wall (see Casey 1984) and west by the Irish Sea, and incorporates the Solway Plain, the Eden and Lune catchments as far south as Kendal, and the territory to the north of the Roman road from Brough-under-Stainmore to Catterick and north of the Cleveland Hills. The North Sea coast defines the eastern limit.

The bulk of archaeological research into Roman settlement in the region has been carried out on military installations and their associated settlements, in particular on Hadrian's Wall. Work beyond these enclaves has been less extensive. Indeed, the very existence of other settlement types displaying 'Romanised' material culture is in some doubt (only two possible 'villas' are known: Scott 1993, 56). Settlements that can be described as towns have been excavated at Carlisle, Catterick, and Corbridge. The military preoccupations of much research have emphasised the earlier histories of many sites, although more recent excavations (eg South Shields, Birdoswald) have produced high-quality evidence for the later period.

Differences in the coin-loss profile characteristic of the northern frontier zone and lowland southern Britain have been noted by Casey (1984), who attributes the weakening of late coin lists there to the effects of the *annona militaris* and consequent taxation in kind rather than coin. There also appear to be differences in coin supply between the eastern and western seaboards. Shotter (1989) has noted the sparseness of coin finds from the western region

around Carlisle, although there is now a substantial assemblage from the town itself. He also suggests a regional or local production centre for 'barbarous radiates' there, based on a concentration of finds from the Blackfriars Street excavation, whilst Brickstock (1987) proposes Piercebridge as a centre for the manufacture of *Fel Temp Reparatio* copies and a complementary local or regional distribution. Of particular interest will be a comparison between coin supply and deposition with that in eastern Yorkshire, an area that clearly had important contacts with this region.

4.3.3 Review of previous work

The starting point for research into regional patterning of 3rd and 4th-century coinage is the 'coin-loss profile', established by Reece (p 54). His division of Roman Britain into four periods – A (to AD 259), B (AD 260–294), C (AD 295–330), and D (AD 330–402) – permits the comparison of sites on the basis of similar ratios of coin loss. Although the time scales and geographical diversity involved inhibit interpretation, Reece (1991) has identified distinctive 'urban' and 'rural' patterns of coin loss, and regional differences. Comparison has also revealed some startling and unexpected concordances between dissimilar site types and remote locations, seemingly inexplicable in terms of current understanding of the character of Romano-British settlement.

Reece's recent work has eschewed clustering techniques, and in order to provide a rapid visual comparison he has returned to coin-profile graphs. Coin loss on each site is represented as a cumulative frequency diagram, after the British mean coin loss has been subtracted from the figure for each coin period. Distinctive profiles can be rapidly identified and displayed on a series of diagrams of sites exhibiting comparable patterns of coin loss. This allows comparison without the imposition of pre-selection criteria, and avoids the reductionist effects of sample size experienced when unsorted data are analysed statistically.

All of Reece's numerical analyses have involved the comparison of specific coin-loss profiles against a mean derived from sites throughout southern Britain. There are indications of distinctive regional characteristics. The most pronounced of these is a contrast between major towns in eastern and western Britain. The former exhibit a high rate of coin loss in the third quarter of the 3rd century compared with that of the middle 4th century, in the west this situation is reversed (1991). Ryan (1988, 92, fig 4.13) has further observed that sites in western central England produce above-average concentrations of coinage minted after AD 388. Reece argues (1987b) that these regional variations need detailed measurement in order to understand variations in coin supply and exchange, both regionally and at specific sites.

The number of coins lost in Britain prior to AD 260 was low when expressed as a percentage of total Roman coin loss, and their early occurrence outside towns and military sites is rare (Reece 1974b; 1987). Reece argues that this coin served the needs of the state, in taxation and payment of soldiers and officials, and was otherwise little used as a medium of exchange. The pattern is transformed from c AD 260, after which low-value bronze and debased 'silver' are found in large quantities on a wider range of sites: approximately 85% of site finds in Roman Britain are attributable to this period (Reece 1974b, 65: fig 1). This seems to imply that monetised transactions were more widespread: more people used coins in the exchange of goods of lower value at more places.

The apparent significance of low-denomination coinage to economic exchange in the later 3rd and 4th centuries is emphasised by recurring episodes of counterfeiting – those of AD 274–286, AD 341–346, and AD 348–364 being particularly significant. These, Reece (1987) has argued, represent the local provision of coin when fresh supplies from the imperial mints did not materialise. Such improvisation would seem to confirm that a regular supply of coin was important, and that it played a significant role in mediating exchange at regional and local levels.

On many multi-period archaeological sites, late-Roman coins occur in far greater quantities than those of any other period (Ryan 1988, 34), including the early-modern period when coinage was in near universal use. This profligacy led Ryan to suggest that much of the late-Roman material had been deliberately abandoned, perhaps as a result of legal or social prohibition, or discarded after having been demonetised, or in a votive context (ibid, 151–2). He further argued that many coins retrieved as 'site finds' were originally deposited in hoards, subsequently dispersed by reworking episodes (ibid, 93).

Studies of Roman coinage have long recognised that hoards and site-find assemblages differ markedly in their contents, in the factors affecting those contents, and consequently in their interpretative potential (cf Reece 1974a; 1974b; 1987; above p oo). Coins retained in hoards are frequently biased towards heavier and/or more valuable coins, in particular issues with a high precious metal content. In the case of site finds, whether casual losses or deliberately discarded, the reverse is true. The two classes of evidence are therefore complementary in establishing the coinage available in any given period. From the mid 4th century, however, hoards of low-value bronze issues occur frequently, their contents largely echoing the issues and types recovered as 'casual losses' (ibid, 69). The presence of coins from disturbed hoards of this nature would introduce an unpredictable level of bias into the recovered assemblage. A single large hoard could significantly distort the apparent pattern of coin loss. If the latter is taken to represent phases of coin use, and sites are compared on this basis – as is implicit in the numerical studies pioneered and developed by Reece – false conclusions are likely to be drawn concerning the significance of coin-loss patterns. Variations in the percentages of different issues present may not be equivalent to variations in the pattern and location of economic exchange.

An alternative interpretation for the volume of base, low-module, late-Roman coinage can be proposed following Boon (1974, 133), who argued that monetary units in this period were created by small bags of coins – folles – rather than individual pieces. Thus the volume of coinage measured by individual finds may exceed the number of transactions represented by a large assemblage. This still does not solve the problem of how the coins came to be 'lost' in such numbers, as a bag of coins is harder to mislay than a single item. Nevertheless, since any group of two or more coins found together is technically considered to be a 'hoard', it raises the possibility that the 'mutually exclusive' division between 3rd and 4th-century bronze hoards and the coins employed in economic transactions is not as clear cut as Ryan implies (1988, 36).

Understanding coin distributions in terms relevant to urban hinterlands presupposes that the coins were used in transactions of some kind. Accepting that the interpretation of coin use and loss is contextually specific, and therefore problematic, there are clear attractions to the study of coin use in late Roman Britain. These include the sheer volume of coin minted and in circulation in this period. The archaeological evidence represents only a small fraction of the number of coins produced. This is testified by the fact that die-linked coins are the exception rather than the rule.

It is implausible that coinage used in these quantities was not used in commodity exchange, even whilst acknowledging Davies' point (1992) that use may have varied between regions. If most low-value coinage was introduced in the course of exchange, then a high rate of presence should indicate a site where such activity was comparatively intense. Variations in this pattern through time, within and between sites, would thus provide evidence for the reorientation of exchange involving coinage, and could be particularly telling in characterising how regional patterns of exchange and the roles of different site types in exchange and articulation of surplus, changed through time.

For the purposes of archaeological study, coin assemblages are most important for what they tell us about supply. This is the phenomenon addressed by quantitative studies, and other observations regarding site chronology and function are subsidiary. Preponderances of different issues at different sites need not mean that exchange varied in accordance with the observed chronological pattern, since differences can reflect continuing circulation of earlier coinage at one location compared to the injection of new coinage into another. Such patterns do, however, provide the means to investigate which sites were receiving specific issues, whether defined in terms of 'coin issue period', 'minimum issue period', obverse/reverse type, or counterfeit variant, in ascending order of detail. Sites can then be compared and grouped according to the presence of these issues, identifying the settlement networks within which they were circulating.

Regional coin-loss profiles

The first stage in the further investigation of regional variation is the creation of mean coin-loss profiles for a series of discrete regions. One study of this type, examining the chronology and distribution of coin loss in Norfolk throughout the Roman period, has already been undertaken (Davies and Gregory 1991).

As the study proposed here is intended to address the period *c* AD 260–402 it will be restricted to Reece's periods X–XXI. The potential to detect regional variations will be enhanced by the refinement of the coin periods employed, breaking them down from 10–23 years to specific issues which can be identified as having been

minted over periods of five years or less (Ryan 1988, 70). 'Minimum issue periods' have been used by Ryan, who identifies significant fluctuations in coin issue and loss within the broader periods usually employed (*ibid* 69). In mapping inter and intra-regional coin-loss variation between sites and types of site, this refinement would appear to be highly desirable. Ryan's study provides a model for future work.

Coin-loss profiles based on minimum issue periods require detailed identifications. This is problematic since not all coins can be identified to their minimum issue period due to illegibility. Furthermore, reporting protocols have frequently involved the attribution of coins to reigns or coin periods (Ryan 1988, 67), so that more detailed characterisation requires reference to an archived catalogue or to the coins themselves.

Patterning of supply/circulation: official issues

Ryan considers that the lack of chronological variation in supply across the country favours Reece's model of a directed state supply of coinage, as opposed to Fulford's suggestion that mints represented in British coinage indicate areas of continental Europe with which Britain's trade was conducted (Ryan 1988, 94). However the coinage was put into circulation, it must have involved the transhipment of substantial quantities from the point of importation to the centres from which it was released. Towns remain the most likely candidates for this for most of the later 3rd and 4th centuries. If any of the structure of the 'batches' in which coins were produced was retained at the point of distribution, the possibility of recognising specific regional patterns of circulation exists. Whilst they may not be recognisable at a level of definition based on coin-issue periods of a few years, there is a further level of detail which may allow detection.

As an appendix to his 1988 study, Ryan listed all of the 'exactly identified' coins covered by his survey, totalling 5994 and forming 27.1% of all 4th-century coins (Ryan, 1988). Of these, over 2000 were types of which more than ten examples were known, representing 142 distinct types defined by combinations of mint and reverse and obverse legends. The number of distinguishable types occurring as site finds in Britain in numbers greater than 10 would seem certain to increase by at least 40%, and possibly more, if coinage minted between AD 259 and AD 310 were to be added to this list (Ryan cites 2905 coins exactly identified from the period pre AD 394, the majority of which probably date from after AD 259). This would provide around 200 distinctive *official* coin types that could be plotted as possible indicators of coin pools defining limits of circulation.

It is well known that specific coin types were differentially distributed between different provinces. The British bias in the distribution of the 'Britannia' reverse legend has long been noted, and Hobley's study (1995) of western imperial bronze coinage in the period AD 81–192 demonstrates patterning in distribution between provinces. Can such patterning also be detected within provinces? Comparatively little 'drift' of bronze coinage occurred between provinces; whether such 'hermetic' coin circulation can also be detected in regions within them through studying the same variable would repay investigation, and might provide a potent means of investigating the reach of late Romano-British urban hinterlands and their regional economies.

Patterning of supply/circulation: counterfeit issues

Counterfeiting reached epidemic proportions in Britain in three particular episodes: between AD 274–286 – barbarous radiates, AD 341–346 – Constantinian copies, and AD 348–364 – *Fel Temp Reparatio* – FTR or Fallen Horseman copies (Reece 1987a, 20–3). It has been argued that these 'unofficial' coins were a substitute for imperial bronze coinage when importation was interrupted (Reece 1987a). The volume of this coinage argues against its interpretation in terms of opportunistic profiteering. Furthermore, a moneyer's hoard associated with the production of 'barbarous radiate' coinage, shows that the metallic content of the 'blanks' on which different denominations of coin were struck was carefully controlled (Ponting 1994). The recovery of large numbers of copies from official (eg military) sites also argues for the recognition and sanction of provincial authorities.

The products of these main copying episodes have each been the subject of major surveys: by Davies (1988), Hammerson (1980), and Brickstock (1987). These have identified regional or local production sites and/or groups defined by dies/style.

Davies' thesis attempted to identify regionally produced issues on the basis of die-linkages and more subjective 'style groups', using a comprehensive photographic record. Although he was successful, the numbers of coins linked in this way

constituted a small fraction of the 16,000 coins examined. He did not find types that were characteristic of specific regions. Davies attributed this fact, at odds with the anticipated result of his survey, to three factors:

- The importation of large quantities of barbarous radiates from northern Gaul, particularly in the earlier phase of their use; die-links and stylistic similarities between British finds and those from northern Gaul appear more frequent and consistent than their equivalents within Britain,
- The widespread circulation of coinage within Britain,
- The existence of a multiplicity of production sites, with coins struck 'in virtually every village and hamlet' and low volumes of production from each die (Davies 1988), resulting in the observed proliferation of different types for which no die-links can be recognised.

It should be noted that the number of die-links both within and between the sites and regions examined by Davies (a study roughly restricted to England south of the Thames) was low. Although he identified seventeen 'style groups', most of which he regarded as having regionally specific characteristics, the numbers identifiable as site finds in each case were usually in single figures. If Davies' assertion of extremely fragmented local production is correct, his argument for extensive circulation of most issues across the province is unnecessary. This conclusion is also suggested by the infrequency of the detectable correspondences between regions. The evidence is more likely to reflect the activities of a multitude of local producers. In this case the coin circulating in any given region would consist of a large number of different types, each unique to a particular locality.

If this is correct it will be difficult to study regional patterning of irregular coinage. The sites at which coin is most likely to have been deposited, such as towns, are likely to have attracted a huge range of local variants, as well as coin from further afield. Nevertheless, unlike the 'wholly mixed' model of widely circulating coinages, this suggestion of 'maximum diversity' does offer the possibility of progress by refining the geographical scale at which similarities are sought.

Hoard evidence suggests some extremely localised production. This is the conclusion drawn by Davies in his study of a hoard from Meare

Heath, Somerset. A large percentage of the low-module minim coinage in this hoard was struck from only a few dies, suggesting 'a tradition of irregular coin production in Avon, Somerset and the South Wales area which continued from the earliest to the latest British radiate copies, with production in many small centres in this region, away from the authority of the large towns in the south-east' (Davies 1986, 117). Similarly a series of groups of die-links recognised within a hoard from Sprotborough, South Yorkshire, indicates that these coins were 'almost certainly of local manufacture' (Mattingly and Dolby 1982). A local production centre for radiate copies has also been suggested in or near Carlisle (Shotter 1990). These examples suggest that the detection of local types as site finds should be possible. The problem is that the sites which produce most coin, and are therefore likely to have the greatest potential for detecting die-links or style groups, are themselves those at which the greatest diversity of coins will have arrived.

Whether later copying episodes follow a similar pattern to that of barbarous radiates is unknown, as no comparable surveys have been carried out. Brickstock (1987, 118) has proposed regional centres for *Fel Temp Reparatio* copies in the Gloucestershire/North Somerset region, the Canterbury/Richborough area, and in County Durham, possibly centred on Piercebridge, but detailed classification and mapping has not been done. Marked contrasts in this respect between different copying episodes reflect differences in the production and use of money between the later 3rd and mid 4th centuries.

4.3.4 Research proposals and conclusions

The chronological and spatial patterning of coin loss offers opportunities to investigate the patterning and structure of urban hinterlands in late Roman Britain. The proposed research programme will involve:

- Comparison of the structure of coin deposition *c* AD 260–402 at a regional level,
- The identification of variations in that structure between sites within regions,
- The isolation of specific issues, whether official or counterfeit, which show clear concentrations in particular regions, and can thus be seen as indicative of monetary circulation around one or more issuing or production centres.

Coin-loss profiles and inter-site comparisons

The intra-regional comparison of towns and other settlements on the basis of coin loss requires that all sites within a given region be measured against regionally derived mean values. This will allow effective comparison between different regions, indicating possible broader-scale differences in the chronology of coin deposition, and thus differences in the mechanisms and patterns of integration of urban and other settlements. This work should be conducted in two stages:

1 The creation of 'regional mean' coin-loss profiles for the period c AD 260–402

These should be presented as cumulative frequency diagrams for the regions, using Reece's coin periods X–XXI; the comparison of individual sites against that mean; and the identification of patterns of variability between sites and site types both within and between regions. Where they exist, published coin lists, either from individual site reports or numismatic overviews (eg Reece 1991) will suffice for the compilation of regional profiles. In the case of unpublished or ongoing sites, the relevant data is easily obtained from archive reports or the researchers working on the material.

2 The creation of similar profiles based on Ryan's 'minimum issue periods'

These will need to be established with consistent criteria for the accuracy of identification required for a coin to be included in the data, and a further search for groups of comparable sites both within and between regions. They will be more difficult to compile, since many reports do not catalogue coins in sufficient detail to allow attribution to the minimum issue period. Ryan's scheme for the 4th century requires extension back to AD 259 to incorporate later 3rd-century coinage. His COIN-DATA database includes pre-AD 294 data that would make this possible (1988, 54). Detailed identifications of coins excluded from Ryan's survey will be required. Although some numismatic reports provide full descriptions with reference to catalogues of official issues (eg Casey 1995), this is not universal. Archive reports will need to be consulted in order to identify specific types. In some instances it may be necessary to return to the coins themselves in order to address particular lacunae.

Patterning of supply/circulation: official issues

These approaches allow the comparison of sites in terms of coin deposition over time. At their most basic level coin-loss profiles present data pertaining to different coin types, with chronological variability being the primary consideration. Ryan's 'minimum issue periods' provide a finer mesh for detecting variations in the spatial distribution of chronologically differentiated issues, and thus identify groups of sites sharing a common coin supply in particular periods.

This approach can be refined by cataloguing exactly identifiable coin types, and plotting their distributions in search of significant regional clustering. As we have seen, Ryan's research indicates that only 27.1% of the total of post-AD 294 coins were exactly identifiable, and this will present difficulties on sites producing low numbers of coins, typically rural settlements, as already low numbers will be grossly diminished. Areas in which liaison between archaeologists and metal-detector users is effective offer especial potential.

The use of such restrictive criteria also introduces particular biases into the profiles, as does – in different ways – the inclusion of coins with less precise identifications (Ryan 1988, 71). It is essential that the grounds on which coins are included or excluded in the creation of minimum issue period profiles are consistent within and between regions.

Investigating the possibility that regional circulation of coinage in the period AD 259–402 can be identified through distributions of specific official coin types therefore requires:

* Establishing exactly identified coin types from the period AD 259–309,
* Plotting the distributions of these types within the regions defined for study, if not also over the whole country.

Patterning of supply/circulation: counterfeit issues

Further potential for examining local and regional monetary circulation, and by extension the inter-relationships between settlements which such circulation reflects, is provided by the issues of counterfeit coinage which proliferated in late 3rd and 4th-century Britain.

If the regional and/or local variants suggested by studies of hoards can also be identified as site finds,

the distributions of these irregular coin types, whose production sites are known or can be reliably inferred, offers one of the most powerful means of describing the extent of late-Roman exchange networks. Previous work has shown that it is difficult to recognise patterns of distribution, but their recognition offers considerable rewards in understanding the organisation and articulation of exchange in late-Roman Britain.

Previous studies of the major episodes of counterfeit coinage in later 3rd and 4th century Britain suggest the existence of a proliferation of local and regional variants. The development of these approaches could lead to highly specific and sensitive indications of the extent of coin circulation within localities, forming interlocking networks within regions. Relevant studies in specific regions should lead to a national scheme of classification (already begun by the work of John Davies), and comprehensive definition of local, regional, and imported types. The initial stages of this would involve:

* The classification of style groups and die-links within known hoards from each of five study regions (detailed below),
* Collation of site finds from within each region, their attribution to the groups previously established, and the mapping of their distributions,
* Inter-regional comparisons to identify the degree of 'linkage' of particular types between regions, and the regional concentrations of those types.

These analyses should be carried out for the three major episodes of counterfeiting noted above.

Davies' photographic archive, created as part of his 1988 thesis, forms the starting point for regional analysis of 'barbarous radiates'. It will be necessary to extend this coverage, since none of the regions proposed here were completely dealt with in his study, and East Anglia, East Yorkshire, and the northern frontier were outside it altogether. This will allow systematic comparison of types within and between regions.

Similar research will be necessary to identify types, die-links, and style groups of Constantinian and *Fel Temp Reparatio* copies. For the latter, Brickstock (1987, 89–90) has suggested regional patterning as already noted. However, since he makes no formal classification of the coinage beyond module and prototype (and only the former is used to any extent in his analysis), a detailed search for requisite patterning in type distributions is not yet possible.

Highly localised groups would correspond with the pattern suggested by barbarous radiate hoards, in which extensive die-links thought to be indicative of very localised production are often encountered. This would require examination of assemblages from within more closely defined areas than has previously been attempted, which is itself dependent on the existence of sufficient sites within such areas.

The recovery of sufficient coinage from comparatively small areas beyond towns is likely to be the exception rather than the rule, and, as already noted, areas in which liaison between archaeologists and metal-detector users is effective offer particular potential. Additionally, in some of the regions not wholly covered by, or absent from, Davies' 1988 survey (eg Gloucestershire, East Anglia, Essex), site density and fieldwork/metal-detecting coverage may reveal highly localised patterns.

A major advantage offered by the apparent regional variation of late-Roman irregular coinage is that, if consistent local and sub-regional styles can be established, individual finds can be incorporated into analysis. Whereas approaches based on numerical comparison require coin finds in considerable numbers from a given 'site' (however defined), in this approach single examples can be incorporated, even where precise provenance is uncertain. This has important implications for the value of surface finds to such a study, of particular relevance in regions where the recording of such finds has increased exponentially over the last twenty years (Dobinson and Denison 1995). The Heritage Lot-

tery Fund scheme for finds reporting provides a mechanism whereby new finds within particular regions can be incorporated into a developing research framework.

As a further stage of research, corroboration of regional groupings could be provided by metallurgical and compositional analysis of regionally defined types. Ponting has demonstrated that the Fenny Stratford counterfeiter's hoard comprises blanks and pellets whose respective metal contents were evidently strictly controlled (Ponting 1994), and irregular coinages in different areas may thus be sensitive to discrimination in this way. This opens up the possibility of 'sourcing' worn and illegible examples.

The proposed study of late-Roman irregular coinage is in effect an old-fashioned exercise in classification. Although there is also scope here for the imaginative application of statistical techniques, including multivariate analysis in exploring relationships between metal, reverse, obverse, date, geographical location, and archaeological context. This study permits the investigation of patterns of supply, distribution, and circulation of this coinage. The recognition of distinct regional or local spheres of exchange around specific centres will depend on the particular character of these in the different copying episodes. However, if they were organised in such a way that consistent regional or localised distributions can be recognised, the extent and detail of the information offered by the various unofficial issues is prodigious, and would amply justify the investment in research and classification.

4.4 *Emporia* and early medieval settlement

Mark Whyman

4.4.1 Background

In chapter 2 we summarised current understanding of the role of English *emporia* in the late 7th–9th centuries, and suggested a series of questions to ask of the archaeological evidence (chapter 2.5, Q20–3). These stress the importance of establishing how *emporia* articulated with other elements of the settlement hierarchy, rather than seeing them as the earliest post-Roman manifestation of a single urban process (Astill 1994; Scull 2001). Three *emporia* are reasonably well documented: *Hamwic* (Morton 1992), Ipswich (Wade 1988), and *Lundenwic* (Rackham 1994b); and a fourth can tentatively be

identified at York (Scull 1997; Kemp 1996). Programmes of study are outlined here for the two most intensively studied emporia and their regions: Hamwic and Ipswich.

It is generally accepted that the 7th and 8th centuries saw an increased range of settlement types, and that there is contemporary evidence for a measure of landscape reorganisation (cf Hamerow 1991). Many sites display similar characteristics to the *emporia* in terms of production and consumption. These include monastic sites as well as others where the applicability of terms such as 'monastery' or 'manor' is debated (eg Flixborough, Brandon). Current research is hampered by inconsistent approaches to the classification of site types. Most observed differences can be attributed to shortcomings in sample size and representativeness. Some sites, however, stand out as being comparatively impoverished. For instance Chalton, Cowdery's Down, Maxey, Yeavering, and possibly Willingham and Yarnton, lack evidence for industrial production and consumption.

A descriptive typology of the classes of settlement, based on explicit analytical criteria, is required. This should define sites by economic process and social function, in which settlement morphology and building type are not the sole determinants. The aim is to understand how sites were integrated into local and regional patterns of production and consumption. This will also provide a basis for comparison between *emporia*, both as settlement sites, and in terms of their relationship with the surrounding regions.

The characterisation of artefactual signatures for sites of the period *c* AD 650–850 is therefore an important subject of study, involving a broader review of the evidence than that available from the environs of *Hamwic* and Ipswich. Comparison between settlements requires that discrepancies in the survival and retrieval of different materials be taken into account for existing data and built into methodologies for future data recovery. Animal bone assemblages provide the best evidence for discriminating between sites which are otherwise similar in terms of evidence for craft production and consumption of manufactured and imported commodities. A principal conclusion, however, is that better samples recovered in more comparable circumstances are required.

Current approaches to the classification of early medieval settlement

The interpretation of individual settlements has tended to employ terms and concepts drawn from a range of 'received classifications', which fall into three groups:

- Terms used in contemporary documentary sources: *villa regia, monasterium, caput,*
- Retrospective application of terms used later in the medieval period: 'palace', 'manor', 'market', and 'village',
- Modern classificatory terms: 'productive site', 'estate centre'.

Current usage of these terms is unsatisfactory. The meaning of contemporary terms is frequently ambiguous, and their usage in 7th and 8th-century documents variable. Importing terms from later, better documented contexts can introduce anachronistic assumptions regarding site function. Finally, the coining of comparatively neutral terms can leave discussion stranded at the level of labelling, without developing descriptions to enhance understanding of middle-Saxon settlement and society.

All current systems of classification suffer from not having been defined in terms of material criteria. This weakness is particularly apparent where the identification of non-documented sites as being 'monastic' or 'secular' is concerned, and the notion of monasteries as a distinctive settlement type in the 7th and 8th centuries may be erroneous (cf Carr *et al* 1988, 377). Supposed indicators of monastic life occur on a range of sites without documented monastic associations. These include evidence for literacy (inscriptions and styli: eg Carr *et al* 1988, 375, fig 4; Loveluck 1997, 4, fig 9), planned structural complexes, the use of stone in building construction, specialist craftworking, and long-distance exchange (Loveluck 1997, 9).

Wormald concluded that Christian belief systems and, by extension, material accoutrements were adopted beyond ecclesiastical circles (Wormald 1978, 68). The practice of setting up 'false monasteries', endowed by royal grant, whose inhabitants '(give) themselves up freely to what Bede calls lust, by which he means living the layman's normal family life' (John 1960, 44) is also relevant. Such considerations must qualify speculation about the ecclesiastical origins for sites where this is based on the evidence of material culture (cf Milne and Richards, 1992, 94). Such an approach can be seen as developing the study of early monasteries along lines similar to those pioneered by Rahtz (1973) and developed by Gilchrist and Morris (1993).

Classifications drawn from later historical periods have been employed, often unconsciously, in much of the research into Anglo-Saxon settlement. This has been particularly evident in landscape studies, where concepts about continuity and village origins have led to uncritical use of terms such as 'manor', 'village', and 'market'. In the case of Flixborough, for example, Loveluck (2001) has challenged the site's interpretation as a monastery, and suggested that it was a manorial centre, citing similarities with Wicken Bonhunt, Goltho, and North Elmham, the 8th-century phases of which

Table 13 Excavated Middle Saxon sites in Norfolk, Suffolk and north Essex

Site Name	Characteristics	References
Brandon, Suffolk	'Productive' or 'monastic' site, major unpubl artefactual/ecofactual assemblages	Carr et al 1988; Carr pers comm Crabtree 1996
Burgh Castle, Norfolk	3rd–4th century 'Saxon shore' fort with 7th–8th century cemetery & occupation	Andrews 1992, 22, fig.8; Johnson 1983
Burrow Hill, Butley, Suffolk	Gravel island site with burials, metalwork & coins of 7th–9th century	Fenwick 1984
Caistor-on-Sea, Norfolk	3rd–4th century walled settlement with burials, ceramics & coins of 7th–9th century	Andrews 1992, 22; Darling et al 1993
Ipswich, Suffolk	Emporia site; 30+ excavations to 1996. Substantial unpubl. artefact/ecofact assemblages	Wade 1988 & Wade pers comm; Suffolk cc 1995/6,14
Middle Harling, Norfolk	Coins, metalwork & Ipswich ware sherds, ambiguous ?assoc. with structures, within extensive Ipswich ware scatter	Rogerson 1995
North Elmham, Norfolk	7th–9th century structures & assoc. middle saxon artefacts, interpreted as 'manorial centre'	Wade-Martins 1980a
Wicken Bonhunt, Essex	7th–9th century structures & assoc. mid-sax. artefacts, incl. major animal bone assemblage, interp. as 'manorial centre'	Wade 1980; Crabtree 1994 and 1996

have been labelled manors. All three have produced morphological evidence consistent with this identification from phases closer in time to the known currency of the 'manor' as a physical and institutional entity (Wade 1980, 102; Beresford 1987; Wade-Martins 1978, 140, fig 122). It remains open to question, however, whether the term, and all that it implies in terms of seigniorial control over land and/or population, is appropriate for the earlier settlements on the same sites.

The third option in categorising middle-Saxon settlement types has been to employ empirically based, ostensibly neutral terminology. The term 'estate centre' has been offered as a descriptive definition which, whilst implying a superior relationship with particular land holdings and/or populations, makes fewer assumptions about the mechanisms whereby power was exercised. Currently, the most widely used term of this type is 'productive site', usually employed with reference to settlements or surface scatters of material disproportionately rich in non-ferrous metal artefacts and coins. The term has come to prominence as a result of site recognition by metal-detector users but has also been applied to excavated settlements (Andrews 1992, 19).

The identification of sites as 'estate centres', whilst avoiding obviously anachronistic assumptions, does give rise to the question of what an estate comprised. The notion of a defined unit of land, familiar from medieval and later

circumstances, may be inappropriate. This is important to the understanding of how *emporia* related to their hinterlands. Scull (2001) has proposed that these sites were provisioned from the estates of 8th-century aristocrats with a controlling interest in them. An understanding of the mechanisms whereby *emporia* were supplied in such circumstances depends on the nature of an 'estate' in this context, and Eric John has argued that 8th-century charters represent 'barefaced ... grants of power ... over men and fields ... without a hint of conveyancing in them' (1960, 30–1). Whilst use of the term 'estate centre' may therefore be permissible, its definition in terms of the role of any given settlement, and its interactions with higher and lower order settlements, requires clearer formulation.

The use of the term 'productive site' has been reviewed by Richards (1999), who argues against the view that it represents a distinct class of site, namely periodic markets and/or meeting places. Richards has demonstrated that many excavated settlements conform to the artefact pattern encountered on 'productive sites', that sites identified using that term are only distinctive in the way that they were identified and sampled, and that to view them as a distinctive class of site is misleading. He proposes that the term be abandoned. Richards' study is of a further significance in that it attempts formal, quantitative analysis of sites on the basis of their artefact assemblages. He anticipates that this may

Table 14 Middle Saxon surface artefact concentrations in Norfolk

Site Name	Characteristics	References
Babingley (Fens)	44 sherds middle saxon pottery in 3 concentrations; 'metal detector finds'; church	Andrews 1992, 16, fig. 5b
Bawsey (Fens)	8ha scatter of metal objects & coins, 34 of 7th–8th century, much of area enclosed by ditch; church	ibid, 20
Caistor-by-Norwich (SE)	30 coins and metalwork from dispersed locations	ibid, 23
Hay Green, Terrington St Clement (Fens)	1.5km long, 7ha spread of Ipswich ware, 1000+ sherds	ibid, 15, fig 3; Rogerson & Silvester 1986; Silvester 1988, 37
Longham (Central)	38 middle saxon sherds; church	Andrews 1992, 16, fig. 5c. Wade-Martins 1980, 33-9
Tilney St Lawrence (Fens)	108 sherds Ipswich ware	Andrews 1992, 15, fig. 4b; Silvester 1988
Walpole St Andrew (Fens)	113 mid-sax sherds incl. 108 Ipswich ware: trial excavation	Andrews 1992, 15, fig. 4c; Silvester 1988
Walpole St Peter (Fens)	124 sherds Ipswich ware, two sceattas	Andrews 1992, 15, fig. 4a; Silvester, 1988
West Walton (Fens)	30 sherds Ipswich ware; church: trial excavation	Andrews 1992, 15, fig. 4d; Silvester 1988
West Walton (Ingleborough) (Fens)	Low oval mound, 40 middle saxon sherds including 28 Ipswich ware	Andrews 1992, 15, fig. 5a
Wormegay (Fens)	Sandy island, 166 sherds Ipswich ware c. 1ha extent; church; smelting slag	Andrews 1992, 20–1, fig. 7; Silvester 1988

Table 15 Middle Saxon surface artefact concentrations in Suffolk (source: J Newman)

Site Name	Extent in hectares	Ipswich ware no sherds	Church	Coins and metalwork
Barham	3	30	yes	c.50 sceattas; 60+ mid 7th-mid/late 8th century metal artefacts
Bromeswell (1)	2+	15		9th century & later coins/artefacts
Bromeswell (2)	1	8		7th century Coptic bucket
Bucklesham	1+	16	yes	
Clopton	2	30	yes	
Coddenham	?	?1		much 7th–8th century coins & metalwork, craft manufacturing
Culpho	1+	5	yes	
Culpho/Grundisburgh	1+	4		
Great Bealings	0.5	5	yes	
Grundisburgh	7–8	12	yes	
Martlesham	2	8		
Pettistree	1	5		
Ramsholt	2	6	yes	2 sceattas & 3 other metal objects
Rendlesham	7–13	20	yes	1 ?imported potsherd
Shottisham	1	5		finds up to late 7th century
Sutton	4	50		2 sceattas; 7 other objects

'eventually help us to reconstruct a settlement hierarchy for Anglo-Saxon England', albeit that the study addresses a limited range of variables and uses excavated samples of settlements which the author acknowledges (J Richards, pers comm) are not necessarily representative of those settlements in toto.

4.4.2 Sample areas and databases

Emporia

Hamwic (Southampton), *Lundenwic* (London/Westminster), and Ipswich are the prime *emporia* sites to have been studied. Of these *Hamwic* appears to be in the better studied region and is the type-site from which studies of this class of settlement have advanced. Archaeological fieldwork in Hampshire has retrieved much evidence for settlement *c* AD 650–850, notably from 40 years of excavation in Southampton, the site of *Hamwic* (Morton 1992), but also from excavations at Portchester (Cunliffe 1976), Winchester (Biddle 1975), Chalton (Addyman and Leigh 1973), and Cowdery's Down (Millett and James 1983). These are supplemented by material from Faccombe Netherton, Little Somborne, King's Somborne, Andover (Old Down Farm), and more recent work such as the Meon Valley Survey and the excavations in Romsey by the Test Valley Archaeological Trust.

On the other hand the morphological development of Ipswich is better understood and the distribution of 'Ipswich-ware' throughout Norfolk and Suffolk (Blinkhorn 1999), provides a powerful tool for comparative analysis of the settlement network. The study of Ipswich and its environs benefits from the existence of a range of excavated sites of the period *c* AD 650–850 (Table 13), in addition to which a series of other sites are known from artefact scatters in Suffolk (Table 14) and Norfolk (Table 15). Furthermore East Anglia has probably the most comprehensive distribution of metalwork surface finds of this period from anywhere in England. *Lundenwic* has been excluded from detailed consideration here since the research agenda for this site will inevitably be influenced by the results from the ongoing post-excavation study of the finds from the Royal Opera House excavations.

Two important earlier sites are now being studied: Flixborough and West Heslerton. These are likely to far exceed in quality the data available from West Stow and Mucking.

Types of middle-Saxon sites

Thirty-two middle-Saxon sites were reviewed in order to establish whether or not archaeological data allows for the identification of different classes of site. Only sites excavated on a significant scale were considered, since the intention was to identify differences between sites based on the activities represented on them (Fig 8). The survey thus makes no attempt to be a comprehensive review of excavated middle-Saxon settlements, and only published sources were consulted (down to 1998). Discrimination on the basis of surface survey data is not at present possible, although the need to remedy this situation is emphasised, and some possible steps towards doing so are presented. The sites considered are:

1 Barking Abbey, Essex (Webster and Backhouse 1991, 88–94): 2 Brandon, Suffolk (Carr *et al* 1988): 3 Chalton, Hants (Addyman and Leigh 1973): 4 Cottam, ER Yorks (Richards 1996): 5 Cowdery's Down, Hants (Millett and James 1983): 6 Flixborough, Lincs (Loveluck 1997; 2001): 7 Goltho, Lincs (Beresford 1987): 8 Hartlepool, Co Durham (Daniels 1988): 9 Ipswich, Suffolk (Wade 1988): 10 Jarrow, Tyne and Wear (Cramp 1969): 11 London (Strand and Westminster) (Rackham 1994b): 12 Maxey, Cambs (Addyman 1964): 13 Middle Harling, Norfolk (Rogerson 1995): 14 Monkwearmouth, Tyne and Wear (Cramp 1969): 15 Mucking, Essex (Hamerow 1993): 16 Northampton, Northants (Williams *et al* 1985): 17 North Elmham, Norfolk (Wade-Martins 1978): 18 Portchester, Hants (Cunliffe 1976); 19 Ramsbury, Wilts (Haslam 1980): 20 Raunds, Northants (Cadman 1983): 21 Riby, Lincs (Steedman 1994): 22 Southampton (*Hamwic*), Hants (Bourdillon 1994; Brisbane 1988; Hinton 1996; Morton 1992; Timby 1988): 23 West Heslerton, N Yorks (Powlesland 1998): 24 West Stow, Suffolk (West 1985): 25 Wharram Percy, N Yorks (Milne and Richards 1992): 26 Whitby, N Yorks (Cramp 1976a; 1976b; Johnson 1993; Rahtz 1976; Wilmott 1996): 27 Wicken Bonhunt, Essex (Wade 1980; Crabtree 1994): 28 Willingham, Cambs (Connor and Robinson 1997): 29 Winchester, Hants (Biddle 1975): 30 Yarnton, Oxon (Hey 1997): 31 Yeavering, Northumberland (Hope-Taylor 1977): 32 York (Fishergate), N Yorks. (Kemp 1996; Mainman 1993; O'Connor 1991; Rogers 1993)

Fig 8 Map showing location of mid Saxon sites

4.4.3 Review of previous work

Ipswich and East Anglia

All of the sites listed in Table 13 have produced substantial ceramic, artefactual, and in some cases archaeozoological and ecofactual assemblages. Only Middle Harling and North Elmham are definitively published, the other references are to interim and summary reports, but archive reports are generally available. The *emporium* at Ipswich has produced good assemblages of ceramics (local and imported), ferrous and non-ferrous metalwork (including coinage), glass, animal bone, and environmental data. Brandon is the only other site with a similar range and quality of data.

East Anglia is unusual in that a chronologically diagnostic ceramic type, Ipswich ware, seemingly produced exclusively within or in the immediate environs of the eponymous town, is found throughout Norfolk and Suffolk (Blinkhorn 1999). A comprehensive survey of this material has recently been completed (Blinkhorn forthcoming). Completion of a corpus of Anglo-Saxon material from Suffolk, undertaken by Stanley West, is imminent, and Helen Geake's national survey of middle-Saxon burial provides an up-to-date corpus of grave goods from the region (Geake 1997). Several other surveys will add relevant data. These include the Fenland Survey (P Murphy, pers comm), the East Anglia Kingdom Survey (A Rogerson, pers comm), and the proposed Lark Valley Survey (initiated by Catherine Hills, A Rogerson, pers comm).

Field survey in south-east Suffolk (Newman 1992), south-east Norfolk (Davison 1988; 1990), the Norfolk Fens (Silvester 1988; 1991), Launditch Hundred (Wade-Martins 1980), and Witton, Norfolk (Lawson 1983), has identified numerous middle-Saxon settlements represented by surface artefact scatters (Tables 7 and 8). Furthermore, cooperation with metal detector users and groups across the region has produced the most comprehensive distribution of metalwork surface finds anywhere in the country. New data, particularly finds of surface metalwork, have proliferated and continue to be recorded in quantity (J Newman, pers comm; H Geake, pers comm). These have revealed the existence of a number of major concentrations referred to as 'productive sites' (Andrews 1992, 19; Newman 1995). Amongst these is the putative *emporium* at Burnham on the north coast of Norfolk, which has produced an extensive scatter of

material, including Ipswich and imported wares, and quantities of 8th-century coinage and metalwork (A Rogerson, pers comm).

The lack of anything more than summary publication of most of the major East Anglian sites has inhibited synthetic and analytical treatments of the major assemblages. The exception to this is Blinkhorn's study of Ipswich ware (1999). The occurrence of this pottery type at every known middle-Saxon settlement site within East Anglia leads the author to suggest the existence of a fully fledged 'market economy' here in the 8th century. Beyond East Anglia, its occurrence on 'high-status' sites is taken as evidence of a role in elite exchange. Whilst the pattern is irrefutable, its interpretation could usefully be considered against the other possible models of the dynamics of middle-Saxon society, and in the context of information from other classes of material.

The study of the imported pottery found in the region is less advanced. Imported ceramics have historically been central to studies of the role of *emporia* as ports-of-trade and centres for the distribution of high-status goods (Hodges 1981). Although Ipswich has been the subject of detailed study the results have not been published (Coutts 1991). Furthermore, a range of fabric types which may be of continental origin, or may have been manufactured within the region in imitation of such imports, cannot at present be attributed to a particular source, and may not have been routinely recognised in fieldwork (K Wade, pers comm).

Other interpretative overviews of excavated assemblages include the work of Crabtree (1994), who compares animal bones of domestic species from West Stow and Wicken Bonhunt. This concludes that the preponderance of pigs at the latter site, and the character of the kill pattern, suggest that Wicken Bonhunt received food renders (livestock as tribute, tax, or rent), in contrast with the lack of evidence for anything other than domestic production at West Stow. Murphy (1994) has used archaeobotanical data to suggest localised changes in patterns of cultivation and landscape organisation between the 4th and 9th centuries, but is constrained from drawing wider ranging conclusions by sample limitations. Assessment and analysis of material from Ipswich and Brandon does, however, indicate a quality and range of data to interpret on a firmer basis.

Field survey in East Anglia has primarily been concerned with demonstrating the existence and distribution of settlements, treating them, ultimately, as candidates for excavation, rather than to compare 'sites'. The results have, however, revealed a pattern of apparent nucleation of rural settlement in the period *c* AD 650–850 (Wade 1983; Newman 1992, 34). Interpretation of this pattern has usually been in terms of population or environmental pressures on resources (*cf* Wade 1983). Notwithstanding the possibility that some 'early-Saxon' pottery scatters may in fact be contemporary with middle-Saxon settlements, the pattern is a real one. Its interpretation, however, needs to be considered in the light of other models proposed for the period (p 24) and in conjunction with information provided by other classes of data. A similar pattern has been identified in the Lincolnshire Fenland by Hayes (1988), who proposed the development of field survey for analytical rather than purely distributional ends (1991). These recommendations have not, however, been applied to middle-Saxon data.

Newman (1998) has synthesised data from the Ipswich area, with particular reference to regional distributions of Ipswich ware and *sceatta* coinage. He illustrates clear patterning in the concentration of both distributions within East Anglia, although Ipswich ware is found beyond East Anglia, whereas 'indigenous' East Anglian *sceattas* are not, possibly implying a 'two-tier' exchange system. He warns against deterministic economic interpretations, emphasising the role of social and religious institutions in influencing these distributions. This evidence can be used to support the thesis that *sceattas* can not be considered currency in the modern sense, and that models based on the idea of an incipient cash economy are unlikely to work. Newman also notes the probable effect of sampling and retrieval bias, and the need to contextualise these distributions by a closer understanding of settlement hierarchy and function, and landscape organisation.

Hamwic *and Hampshire*

Hamwic offers far and away the most extensive data from a single settlement. Major reports on ceramics (Timby 1988), coins (Andrews 1988; Metcalf 1988) and non-ferrous metalwork (Hinton 1996) have been published. Although the animal bones and environmental evidence from *Hamwic* have not yet been definitively published, synoptic reports on the bone assemblages illustrate the quantity of material available (eg Bourdillon 1994).

In contrast few excavations of contemporary sites in Hampshire have been as informative as the work on Brandon and Wicken Bonhunt in East Anglia. Portchester, and to a lesser extent Chalton, Cowdery's Down, and Winchester, have produced middle-Saxon assemblages. Saxon finds have been reported from Faccombe Netherton, the Sombournes, Andover (Old Down Farm), the Meon Valley, and Romsey (F Green, pers comm), but it is not certain that they fall within the period AD 650–850. Further work is needed to establish their potential, as is also the case for material recovered from excavations at Rowner, Emsworth, Hayling Island, Chichester, Pagham, Selsey, and Gunard (*cf* Hodges 1981, 56, fig 6.4).

Hampshire lacks a widespread, easily recognisable, diagnostic ceramic such as Ipswich ware. Fieldwork has consequently been less successful in identifying trends in settlement patterns on the basis of surface finds. The possible exception to this is the Meon Valley Survey. Metal-detected finds form a smaller proportion of finds reported to archaeological curators within the region than is the case in East Anglia (Dobinson and Denison 1995, tables ix, xi). Whether this is a reflection of less intensive detectorist activity, a factor of different approaches to liaison between detectorists and curating bodies, or a consequence of a lower density of such finds in Hampshire is uncertain. The absence of an immediately distinctive and widespread pottery for the period, compared with the apparent paucity of other surface artefact finds, suggests that systematic analysis and comparison of field survey data is currently impractical.

Analytical studies of *Hamwic* and its region have been dominated by ceramic studies. Hodges' (1981) monograph established a paradigm for the significance and interpretation of imported ceramics and of *emporia* more generally. His study of locally produced wares has subsequently been developed by Timby (1988), exploiting the substantial assemblages recorded subsequent to Hodges' publication. The absence of an Ipswich-ware equivalent makes it harder to find and date sites, but in recompense the more varied composition of the assemblages from Hampshire facilitates the study of spatial and temporal diversity. The broad picture is one of a middle-Saxon threshold represented by a shift from chaff-tempered to flint and quartz-tempered fabrics in the 8th century (Hodges 1981, 56). Hodges identifies thirteen sites in Hampshire and West Sussex which had, at that date, produced middle-Saxon pottery (*ibid*, 56, fig 6,4). This total can be augmented by the as yet unexamined material from work noted above at King's Sombourne, Little Sombourne, the Test Valley, Faccombe Netherton, Romsey, and the Meon Valley Survey. Within *Hamwic* itself, recent analysis has recognised the outline of chronological variation, and has gone some way towards isolating probable production areas for local wares (Timby 1988, 111–16). It is possible that chronological and geographical variation is related.

Bourdillon (1988; 1994) has published synoptic reports on the animal bone assemblages. These agree with O'Connor's (1989b) conclusions that the preponderance of aged domestic species and the lack of variety in the meat diet, suggest an administered food supply, rather than the market-led production of animal foodstuffs for the provisioning of the settlement. Bourdillon emphasises the potential of the study of animal bones for drawing conclusions about the character and organisation of the hinterland of *Hamwic*.

Methodological limitations

Formal comparison of site characteristics is compromised by a variety of factors relating to sample size and representativeness, deposit and artefact taphonomy, and variation in the retrieval procedures employed. These can be briefly summarised as follows:

Sample size and representativeness

Leaving aside notions of exactly what, in settlement or landscape terms, an excavated site is a sample of (*cf* Wagstaff 1991), the sizes of excavations varied from a few hundreds or even tens of square metres (eg Wharram Percy, Cottam) to many hectares (Mucking, Southampton, West Heslerton).

With the exception of the 'landscape' excavations at Mucking and West Heslerton, the archaeological investigations represent uncertain fractions of larger settlement complexes. Given the probability of variation across such settlements, comparison between the characteristics of an arbitrarily selected area of one site with a similarly partial sample of another is problematic. It is not possible to draw reliable conclusions from small samples of large sites. Such samples are neither reliable nor valid: they can not be replicated and we do not know what they represent as a sample of the whole.

Deposit taphonomy

Post-depositional processes affecting the contexts from which finds were retrieved vary enormously between sites, from intact stratigraphic sequences (eg Barking, Jarrow, Monkwearmouth, Whitby) and surface middens (eg Brandon), to plough attrition and erosion in varying degrees (eg Mucking, Maxey, Chalton, Cowdery's Down, West Heslerton). These factors have a major impact on the composition of assemblages, particularly with regard to:

- Residuality: on multi-period sites there is a risk that the finds characteristic of certain activities may have been introduced in reworked material from earlier deposits;

- *Mixed ploughzone deposits*: finds within mixed deposits can derive from various phases of occupation. Although the distribution of such artefacts may reflect their original location, the potential to make temporal distinctions between chronologically undiagnostic artefacts is lost. The problem is acute on sites such as Middle Harling and North Elmham (Norfolk), where occupation continues into the 9th–10th centuries and many finds could come from any period between the 7th and 10th centuries;

- *Associations between finds and features*: deposit subsidence and accumulation can introduce archaeological finds to the upper fills of features long after their disuse. At Riby (Lincs), for example, large quantities of middle Saxon material were found in ditches which defined a series of curvilinear enclosures. These 'stock enclosures' are therefore argued to have been of 7th to 8th-century date (Steedman 1994). Although this is a reasonable proposition the published report does not provide sufficient information on deposit taphonomy for it to be established that the finds were not a later introduction;

- *Artefact taphonomy*: survival of some artefact classes is compromised by physical or chemical processes active in the buried environment, and major differences in survival can occur within ploughed and unploughed sites in otherwise similar environments, for example Maxey (Lincs) and Brandon (Suffolk). The survival of animal bone may be severely affected by certain subsoils and agricultural regimes. Inter-site comparisons must take such disparities into account.

- *Retrieval/screening procedures*: crucial components of animal bone assemblages will not be recovered except by sieving. The retrieval of ceramic and metal artefacts is also improved by systematic screening, and the metal component of artefact assemblages can only be described accurately when metal detectors have been employed (Dobinson and Denison 1995, 36–7). The bulk of the artefact assemblage from a site often resides in the ploughsoil. Indeed it has been suggested that 90% of the sub-surface assemblage should be represented in the plough-soil at any one time (quoted in Clark and Schofield 1991, 96). Where this is not comprehensively sampled, the value of comparisons with artefact suites from other sites is compromised. The lower ploughsoil horizon may contain the greater proportion of the surviving material from the ploughzone. This horizon may also retain important information regarding the spatial distribution of artefacts. In terms of inter-site comparison, this horizon may hold as much relevant information as the natural-cut features, but sadly it is frequently machined away.

Conclusions: classification of sites and study regions

Inconsistencies in classification, and disparate approaches to interpretation make comparative overview difficult. Notwithstanding this, and in spite of the problems of taphonomy and sample bias, certain patterns can be established:

- Many sites share a similar range of craft activities (eg copper alloy casting, iron smithing, bone and antler working, glass making) and evidence of consumption (copper alloy and bone objects, imported pottery and glass, *sceatta* coinage) to those found on *emporia* such as *Hamwic*, Ipswich, and Fishergate, York. These sites include known monastic foundations (eg Jarrow, Whitby, Barking Abbey) as well as others of debated function (eg Flixborough, Brandon);
- Many differences can be attributed to shortcomings in sample size and validity and artefact retrieval strategy. Such factors can even affect the retrieval of pottery, especially where it appears in comparatively small quantities. No 7th or 8th-century ceramics are, for example, reported from the excavations at Church Close, Hartlepool (Daniels 1988), although earlier

investigations nearby (Cramp 1976a, 222), recovered seemingly contemporary ceramics in association with buildings similar to those reported from the later excavations. If this is the case with ceramics, how much more can it be said to be true of more technically difficult, smaller scale production employing expensive raw materials? Hinton (1996, 102) may be correct when contrasting the evidence for non-ferrous metalworking at *Hamwic* with the 'hints at York and Dorestad of a distinctively richer element' on the strength of evidence for gold working (as distinct from gilding which is represented at *Hamwic*; *ibid*, 80–1). But the fact that only *c* 4% of the settlement has been excavated using modern archaeological techniques (Brisbane 1988, 101) urges caution in such judgements.

Notwithstanding these considerations, a provisional three-fold classification of 7th to 8th-century sites might be adopted on the basis of the artefacatual/ecofactual evidence for the activities carried out within them. Sites are referred to by the numbers (here in brackets) used above p 96.

- *Sites with evidence for artefact production and discard comparable to those found on* emporia – with evidence for one or more of non-ferrous metalworking, smithing, bone/antler working, and a comparatively high volume and wide range of artefacts including imported items (eg 1, 2, 6, 10, 14, 25, 26, 29, as well as the *emporia*: 9, 22, 32);
- *Sites with evidence for artefact discard comparable to these sites, but without evidence for production* – a comparable range and frequency of artefacts, including imports, but no clear indication that any were manufactured on the site (eg 4, 7, 13, 16, 17, 18, 21, 27);
- *Sites with sparse evidence for artefact discard* – no evidence for craft production, sparse artefact density with imports (if any) limited to functional items such as lava querns (eg 3, 5, 12, ?15, 23, 24, 28, 30, 31).

This is a very provisional classification, particularly for the sites listed in the second category. However, there would appear to be significant differences between the sites listed in the first and third groups. The identification of the recent excavations at Willingham (Cambs) and Yarnton (Oxon) as 'sparse' sites supports the view that the previously excavated sites in this group lack artefacts simply due to retrieval bias; Yarnton, in particular, was screened by the use of metal detectors (G Hey, pers comm). The character of their ceramic and animal bone assemblages also appears smaller and less diverse than those of many of the sites referred to above, although this may be influenced by retrieval factors. An interesting aspect at two of the 'sparse' sites – Cowdery's Down and Yeavering – is the presence of timber buildings using sophisticated carpentry and large quantities of sawn timber planking, which may relate to function in terms of secure storage as well as to elite display.

Maxey (Lincs) is the only one of these sites to present evidence for iron smelting, and the association of such activity with a site poor in artefactual terms is worth noting. Only ambiguous evidence for iron smelting has ever been found in the *emporia* (*Hamwic*), and such primary processing does not seem to be associated with the first two classes described above. The archaeological context of the most thoroughly investigated middle-Saxon iron-smelting complex, Ramsbury (Wilts), is poorly understood, although it has been suggested that it was at an estate centre (Haslam 1980), and may represent a stage in the centralisation and control of production subsequent to that apparent at Maxey.

Discrimination between sites involved in metal artefact production and with extensive access to manufactured commodities can perhaps be achieved through the comparison of animal bone assemblages. *Emporia* appear to be characterised by a meat diet dominated by sheep/goat and cattle staples (O'Connor 1991, 276–87). In contrast the monastic sites of Jarrow and Barking Abbey made more use of pig and fowl respectively (*ibid*, fig 41, 281), whilst Wicken Bonhunt consumed a disproportionate percentage of pigs (Crabtree 1994). Interpretation of data of this sort in terms of access to the habitats of wild species, dedicated estate production, and comparative indices of diversity of food resource is central to understanding the interrelationships between settlements. It is clear that the further refinement of animal bone assemblage characterisation represents an important component of any such study.

Dating is a further consideration. Settlements are usually attributed to the period *c* AD 650–850 on the basis of diagnostic metalwork or ceramics. Assuming differential access to different commodities, and acknowledging that middle-Saxon hand-made ceramics are usually identified on the basis of association with such diagnostic types, it is probable that some 'early Saxon' sites in fact represent middle-Saxon settlements which were not integrated into networks of production and supply. If this is the case, identification of this element of the settlement pattern, primarily concerned with subsistence production, will be difficult. Careful consideration of 'early-Saxon' sites which produce diagnostically middle-Saxon material in small quantities may provide a starting point. This is of particular relevance to debates concerning 7th to 8th-century settlement nucleation and its relationship to increasing population, which has been a favourite explanation for changes in middle-Saxon settlement pattern (Wade 1983, 75; Scull 1993, 78).

A recent overview of cemetery data from Ipswich, London, and *Hamwic* (Scull 2001) identifies shortcomings in our knowledge of burial grounds associated with these settlements, largely due to incomplete excavation. There is too little information for demographic study, but Scull suggests a pattern to late 7th/early 8th-century burial, involving the use of several discrete cemeteries peripheral to each settlement. A similar pattern of multiple peripheral burial grounds is evident at the late 7th-century monastic sites of Ripon (Hall and Whyman 1996, 143, fig 36) and Whitby (Wilmott 1996, 15; the site of St Mary's church to the west of the medieval abbey – *ibid*, fig 2 – may indicate the site of a further early burial ground). The meaning of such arrangements deserve serious consideration. Were the different burial grounds for different kin groups? What is the significance of a change to centralised burial provision at a single location (in both a monastic and secular context), and the implications of apparent similarities between secular and monastic settlements?

Although the period of study has been defined as *c* AD 650–850, it is apparent from a variety of classes of evidence that the early/mid 8th-century witnessed some of the more significant transformations in settlement patterns, production, and distribution. This is suggested by the increase in the production and distribution of *sceatta* coinage (Metcalf 1984), the revised dating of the commencement of the production of Ipswich ware from *c* AD 650 to *c* AD 700 (Blinkhorn 1999), the increasing use of stone in building construction as, for example at Hartlepool (Daniels 1988), Whitby (Rahtz 1976), Winchester (Biddle 1975), Northampton (Williams *et al* 1985), and at many churches, as well as the indications of an early 8th-century origin for the *emporia* at *Hamwic* (Brisbane 1988, 103) and Fishergate, York (Kemp 1996, 66). Bede's *Historia Ecclesiatica* can perhaps be seen as more of a product of change than a report on changes past.

It must be stressed that a more thorough examination of the data is needed to test the provisional classifications proposed above. The uneven availability of data, as well as the need for more comprehensive consideration of taphonomy and retrieval factors, and a closer reading of the contextual aspects of published reports, will have to be addressed.

4.4.4 Research proposals and conclusions

Our review of the evidence from sites of the period *c* AD 650–850 concluded that different classes of settlement can be identified in terms of material 'signature' (subject to post-depositional and retrieval factors). Comparison between settlements in the terms proposed requires that discrepancies in the survival and retrieval of different material classes are accounted for. This component of the study could be pursued further through:

- The detailed investigation of issues of taphonomy and retrieval affecting the sampling of the relevant sites,
- A detailed consideration of the full range of structural, artefactual, ecofactual, and contextual data bearing on issues of production, distribution and consumption,
- The construction of comparative chronologies between sites.

Ipswich and East Anglia

Over 30 excavations within Ipswich have produced significant middle-Saxon assemblages, including all of the major categories of material considered in this study. The other major sites (listed on Table 13) offer assemblages for comparison in one or more of these categories. Although retrieval methods have varied from site to site, comparability at specified levels of definition should nevertheless allow sites to be assessed in terms of their assemblages, using triangular coordinate graphs and multivariate statistical analyses, with particular reference to a number of finds and techniques which we now look at in detail.

Animal bone assemblages

Assemblages should be compared in terms of access to domesticated and wild species, and the representation of skeletal components indicative of specialised butchery practices and/or differential access to specific cuts of meat (see p 38). Intra-settlement comparison at Ipswich and possibly Brandon may allow the identification of zones according to different patterns of livestock utilisation as, for example, production and consumption, as proposed for the National Gallery and Strand sites in London (Rackham 1994b, 131), and differential access to food resources. Indications of the concentration and treatment of particular species and body parts may highlight the nature of processing activities occurring in the settlement and their ultimate products (eg pine marten pelts at Fishergate: O'Connor 1991, 259). Evidence for the replication of similar activities at locations across the site, rather than in large specialised 'zones', may throw light on Scull's model of *emporia* function (1997).

Ceramics

Relative proportions of continental imported wares (both generically and specific types), Ipswich ware, and handmade wares should be compared both within and between sites, as an index of access to, and involvement in, distribution mechanisms of different ceramic types (and their contents). The data from excavated sites can be compared with that from surface retrieval, further discussed below (work on the isolation of imported fabrics may lead to the better identification of such material within rural assemblages.)

Multivariate analysis

This should involve quantification and comparison of the evidence for production and consumption represented by different classes of material, including querns, *sceattas*, copper alloy and other non-ferrous metals (manufacturing evidence and objects), craft production in other materials (eg bone and antler working, weaving). Multivariate analysis of selected criteria may allow the identification of clusters of functions from assemblages within and between settlements, offering a more subtle discriminatory measure than simple presence/absence.

Sceattas

Further detailed study of the distributions of this coinage, possibly supported by compositional analysis, may allow the investigation of possible localised production centres for some of the series (cf Newman).

Handmade ceramics

Compositional investigation of handmade ceramics from middle-Saxon sites is needed to establish groupings and, by extension, modes of production, and possible sources and extents of distribution networks (cf Timby 1988, 110). Comparison between handmade early-Saxon ceramics and their middle-Saxon equivalents within a locality may identify clusters relating to the degree of dispersal or concentration of production, possibly allowing the recognition of particular centres of production, or the widespread distribution of ceramics from a single source. Similarly, compositional analysis of copper alloy artefacts may discriminate between multiple production centres with opportunistic access to metal, and the products of a more restricted number of centralised metal sources, with the possibility of recognising compositional 'signatures'.

Archaeobotanical assemblages

The study of material from Ipswich and Brandon has indicated a clear bias towards 'consumer' assemblages, in contrast to the 'producer' evidence found in small-scale excavations on rural sites such as Hay Green (Norfolk). Both Ipswich and Brandon offer considerable potential to investigate access to different plant resources, including the study of intra-settlement patterning of access to and processing of plant materials (P Murphy, pers comm).

Cemeteries

Comparison of finds from late 7th to early 8th-century cemeteries with those found in other contexts at Ipswich (largely unpublished) may indicate the origin, connections, and associations of some types or styles of artefact in the region. The work of Gabor Thomas on strap ends (a class of artefact which, interestingly, does not appear in grave assemblages) provides a starting point that could be developed in terms of other metal artefacts. The notion of 'prestige goods' has loomed large in explanations for the existence of *emporia*. Cemeteries, as arenas for the expression and negotiation of social identity, are frequent find spots for 'high-status' middle-Saxon artefacts, at least until c AD 730, after which accompanied burials are rare or non-existent (Geake 1997, 125). The fact that the apparent heyday of *emporia* sites, in the mid and late-8th century, seems to coincide with a near cessation of the practice of grave-good deposition may have implications both for the role of *emporia*, and that of personal accoutrement in the expression of social identity. These questions are interconnected, and offer a perspective on differences in the role and physical structure of *emporia* sites, chronologically between the late 7th/early 8th and mid-8th centuries in the case of Ipswich, and geographically in comparisons between Ipswich and *Hamwic* (cf Scull 1997).

Integration of field survey data

East Anglia has a wealth of good field survey data for the period c AD 650–850. Integration of the results of the various surveys (above p 96), and particularly between assemblages derived from survey and excavation, is a primary goal. The potential to compare and contrast sites on the basis of surface 'signatures' should be maximised. Various material classes can be compared with 'control' data from excavated sites.

In order to 'upgrade' field survey data and render it consistent within such an analytical framework, some of the work already carried out requires enhancement. The data standards and retrieval levels proposed in the research design for the Kingdom of East Anglia Project (West and Wade 1983) should be taken as the base line for research, and may themselves require refinement to provide an extra level of detail to address certain questions. Correlating data requires the development of methodologies to assess the level of previous recovery from sites, particularly in the case of metal-detected assemblages. The evidence that sites can be all but exhausted of fresh finds by repeated ploughing and metal detecting (Richards 1999), means that the intensity of previous work on any site needs to be established. Comparison of the character of known surface artefact scatters – particularly in respect of proportions of Ipswich ware, imported wares, handmade wares, copper alloy and other non-ferrous metal artefacts, and coins – will almost certainly require further fieldwork to:

- Systematise intensity of coverage, if possible during optimum conditions (cf Silvester 1988, 12), within and between sites and regions,
- Obtain sufficient quantities of pottery from each surface scatter to allow effective comparison (*ibid*),
- Incorporate within surveys sites that are represented by low densities of middle-Saxon material, not always followed up with fieldwalking at greater resolution when encountered,
- Ensure comparable recovery of metal artefacts from each site by systematic metal detector survey. This would provide an opportunity for establishing 'specific desiderata for the precision of contextual information required from detecting finds' as recommended by the English Heritage/CBA survey (Dobinson and Denison 1995, 62).

The presence of substantial surface quantities of animal bone and industrial debris in association with a number of middle-Saxon sites – as at Hay Green, Norfolk (Silvester 1988, 37), and Wormegay, Norfolk (Andrews 1992, fig 7, 21) – presents interesting methodological problems. Such assemblages are from contexts that would usually be considered unsuitable for systematic analysis, due to the disturbed nature of the horizons in which they are found. The potential usefulness of these data requires assessment, as does the possibility of developing retrieval and quantitative methodologies for use in their analysis. The proposed use of field survey data should therefore involve five stages:

Stage 1: formal assessment and quantification of existing data from systematic field walking and metal detecting,

Stage 2: compilation of 'retrieval history' for each site, including location, quantity, and nature of 'unsystematically' metal-detected material where possible,

Stage 3: augmentation of that data by further retrieval where necessary (eg fieldwalking at greater level of resolution, systematic metal detecting including iron objects, quantified recovery of other types of evidence, eg animal bone),

Stage 4: necessary quantification and recording of augmented existing data,

Stage 5: comparison of known sites and analysis of results in terms of distinct settlement types.

The Kingdom of East Anglia Project envisaged that the project would ultimately advance to 'structured sample excavation of selected sites' (West and Wade 1983, 20). Following the programme of comparative analysis suggested above, research could be developed in one or both of two directions:

1 The detailed investigation of specific type-sites, by non-destructive techniques of evaluation and/or sample excavation as originally proposed in the Kingdom of East Anglia Project,
2 An expansion of fieldwork from known sites into adjacent unexplored areas in order to comprehensively describe middle-Saxon settlement across an entire district. This could be compared, for example, with the area of Suffolk studied within the Kingdom of East Anglia Project (Newman 1992, fig 8, 35). In addition this would allow the investigation of land use in the light of models such as those proposed by Hayes (1991).

In summary, proposals for the investigation of middle-Saxon Ipswich and its hinterland are:

- Comparison of the composition of artefact and animal bone assemblages within (in the case of Ipswich and, possibly, Brandon) and between contemporary sites,
- Investigation of degrees of dispersal/concentration of manufacturing via compositional analysis of ceramics and copper alloy artefacts,
- Establishing comparable data from the substantial number of sites known as surface artefact scatters, and comparing the resultant artefact signatures,
- Comparison of artefact assemblages from both excavations and field survey with those from known funerary contexts, investigating the possibility of recurring combinations of artefacts within graves and cemeteries to identify the origins of artefacts and their regionally specific usage.

Hamwic *and Hampshire*

Comparative study will benefit if the analyses suggested for the East Anglian sites were also carried out on the same classes of materials from excavations in Hampshire. *Hamwic* dominates our knowledge of middle-Saxon settlement archaeology and offers greater scope for intra-site analysis than any comparable site. Comparison of animal bone assemblages (as described above p 40) may identify zones in terms of different patterns of access to food resources, although results to date are not encouraging (Bourdillon 1994, 122). The concentration and specific treatment of particular species and body parts may highlight the nature of processing activities occurring in the settlement (as at the Six Dials site; *ibid*, 122). Demonstrating the replication of similar activities at locations across the site – evident in the *Hamwic* bone data (*ibid*) – rather than in large specialised 'zones', may throw light on the *emporia* models suggested by Scull (1997).

It has already been noted (p 99) that the lack of a dominant regional ceramic tradition equivalent to Ipswich ware suggests a different relationship between *Hamwic* and its hinterland than that between Ipswich and East Anglia. This may also account for the more restricted regional distribution of the possible *Hamwic sceatta* coinage compared to its East Anglian equivalent. The characterisation of clay outcrops within the Hampshire region may identify regional production sources of middle-Saxon ceramics. Building on work that has already been undertaken, ceramic assemblages from excavation and surface survey within the region can be compared (visually, petrologically and compositionally) with the *Hamwic* type series. As has been noted above, the comparison of the degree of diversity of sources of the clay used in chaff-tempered pottery to that employed in its flint and quartz-tempered successors has particular potential. Patterns resulting from these analyses can be compared with those obtained from ongoing work in other regions, notably the East Midlands, significantly an area remote from any of the known *emporia*.

The distribution of the various *sceatta* series coins within Hampshire should be investigated, and their occurrence or absence beyond the region established (*cf* Metcalf 1988). There may be potential to compare the range and extent of various types within and beyond Hampshire with the pattern for East Anglia, where Newman (1998), following Archibald, has suggested localised minting, possibly under monastic auspices. A distinctly different pattern in the Hampshire basin and its environs might augment the clear differences in ceramic provision.

Compositional analysis of copper alloy artefacts from early and middle-Saxon contexts may discriminate between production centres. Multivariate analysis permits the comparison of the evidence for production and consumption as represented by different classes of material, including querns, *sceattas*, copper alloy and other non-ferrous metals.

Work by Helen Geake (1997) has resulted in the production of an up-to-date corpus of grave goods from burials dated between *c* AD 600–850. Comparison of those from Hampshire and West Sussex with assemblages from *Hamwic* and elsewhere may indicate the origin, connections, and associations of some types of artefact in the region. Although Geake's work demonstrated the widespread distribution of most middle-Saxon grave goods across England, and her argument is based on the comparative absence of regionally specific artefact types (*ibid*, 125–6), it may be possible to investigate regional patterning through multivariate comparisons of groups or suites of burial artefacts within and between regions. This takes on particular relevance in the light of the suggestion that distinctive and imported artefacts were utilised in different ways in different regions, reflecting the changing role of 'high-status' objects in differing social contexts.

Although field survey data exists for Hampshire (cf the Meon Valley Survey), and can be incorporated into some of the proposed analyses, it has not been recovered on a scale that justifies attempts to integrate it into analyses to the extent proposed for East Anglia.

In summary, further investigation of the interrelationships between and contrasting roles of different settlements can be pursued using three related approaches:

- Comparing the composition of artefact and animal bone assemblages within (in the case of *Hamwic*) and between contemporary sites. Spatial patterns evident in the disposal of animal bone can also be explored regardless of assemblage composition;

- Investigating the extents of distribution of the different middle-Saxon ceramic types found in *Hamwic* and Hampshire, and degrees of dispersal/concentration of manufacturing via compositional analysis of ceramics, in particular as already noted, in comparing chaff-tempered and the later flint and quartz-tempered fabrics;

- Comparing artefact assemblages from settlements with those from known funerary contexts, and investigating the possibility of recurring combinations of artefacts within graves and cemeteries to investigate origins and regionally specific usage.

4.5 Regionality and medieval landscapes

Jonathan Finch

4.5.1 Background

The debate about the relationship between medieval towns and their rural hinterlands is one forged from an urban vocabulary. Urban areas are described as 'drawing' on their rural hinterlands for necessary resources; the hinterlands react and reorganise to supply the needs and wants of the urban areas; the urban areas sit at the very top of the settlement hierarchy and are distinguished by a developed and sophisticated culture. The hinterlands become, in comparison, utilitarian landscapes of production, where the peasants are condemned to poverty by the oppression of the feudal yoke, and where the subtle undulations of the local agrarian conditions are flattened out in the shadow of the urban centre. This may be a caricature of what is increasingly seen as a highly complex set of relationships, but the dynamic between the two is still essentially defined in terms of the urban area – the view from the city walls. But it is a selective view – a view that rarely notices the opulence of rural medieval churches, the timber-framed rural guild hall, or the complex agricultural strategies apparent in the sinuous hedges that follow the curves of open-field furlongs. Nor does it often mention the degree of poverty within the hierarchical urban community, nor the sprawling suburbs filled with those anxious to avoid the expensive urban taxes or excluded from the 'mysteries' of their trade. Clearly there was much more to the experience of urban and rural life in the medieval period, and a much more complex and fluid relationship between them.

Recent research, however, has begun to question the supremacy of the urban centre as the force of change and progress. No longer seen as 'non-feudal islands in a feudal sea' (Postan 1975, 238–9), urban areas are being interpreted as manifestations of developments within rural society. It is in the rural areas that we now look for proto-capitalism amid the changing structure of rurally based industries, such as textiles and metalworking. Towns can now be seen as landscape elements sustained by the rural economy, since the rural population was by far the larger of the two until the 19th century, and it is the structures of power in the rural areas that, to some extent, determine where, when, and how urban areas

developed. In assessing the importance of rural landscapes in the debate about urban hinterlands, and in particular the significance of regionalism, it is perhaps worthwhile to reorientate the vocabulary. The purpose of recasting the relationship from a rural perspective is that it enables new questions to be posed and so, hopefully, the answers may shed new light, not just on the dynamic relationship between urban and rural areas, but on the rural areas in their own right.

The basic framework for medieval urban development, characterised by expansion and innovation in the 12th and 13th centuries, followed by two centuries of structural stability, but marked by mixed fortunes across the country as a whole, as the economy readjusted to the new socio-economic conditions, seems to be generally agreed upon (Britnell 1981; Dyer 1996a; Masschaele 1994). Within that framework, however, there is still room for considerable debate about the extent to which the role of towns changed. James Masschaele (1997) has argued that the marketing infrastructure had matured to its full extent by the beginning of the 14th century, and that its primary function was to meet the requirements of the 50 major towns. Britnell has, however, argued that this is too static a model, and has suggested instead that the hierarchy of medieval towns was in considerable flux before the late 14th century, but that the number of commercial centres was narrowed thereafter, when the marketing framework was restructured (Britnell 2000). Britnell's model is distinct because it takes account of the rural context for urban change, and, in particular, hints that regional differences in demesne management strategies, the distribution of landless cottars, and the structure of rural industry, may all have played an important role in determining urban development. The different regional responses to the social and economic conditions of the later Middle Ages clearly affected urban development and the significance of the market infrastructure, particularly where industrial development was evident, such as in the textile trade.

Although historians have used records of debt litigation to measure the relationship between the rural and urban spheres and the extent of 'commercialisation' (Britnell 1996; Britnell and Campbell

1995; Dyer 1992), this is a very particular type of trading relationship associated with the main urban markets. It has been demonstrated that a considerable amount of trade continued to be conducted in the rural, rather than urban, areas, and it was conducted directly between producer and consumer. As such it left little or no documentary evidence, and is consequently 'hidden' from the historian, but is an important area for archaeological investigation (Dyer 1992).

The high level of rural trade suggests that supplying the urban market was but one particular facet of rural economies. Although the urban hierarchy is acknowledged to have been in flux, the hinterlands are rarely conceived as anything other than uniform landscapes in the economic shadow of the urban centre. The hinterland is, by definition, conceived as a non-regional landscape type. However, with the exception of London, no medieval urban area was large enough to completely overshadow the character of its broader rural environs. It is perhaps significant that although the term 'hinterland' is borrowed from the German, the German *hinterland* refers to the wide, extensive marketing space that provided a variety of goods beyond the *umland*. It was the *umland* which formed the immediate environs of the town and which supplied the basic demands such as food (Eiden and Irsigler 2000). The gradation in spheres of influence around urban centres is clearly complex and must relate both to the position of the centre in the regional settlement hierarchy, but also to the characteristics of the agricultural region itself.

It is clear to see that the urban hinterlands debate needs to take greater cognisance of the regional diversity of rural landscapes, if we are to understand the forces behind the process of urbanism within the medieval period. Urban areas can no longer be taken to be the leading force for change within medieval society, and must instead be recognised as an integrated element within the wider landscape. Once this has been accepted it is clear that the regional diversity of the rural landscape must be acknowledged as an important factor behind urban development and urban change. Having established how the regional medieval landscape might inform the investigation of urban hinterlands, it is worth considering the significance of regionalism within the current agenda within rural settlement studies.

The most recent initiative has been Roberts and Wrathmell's *Atlas of Rural Settlement* (2000a),

produced as part of English Heritage's Monument Protection Programme, in order to establish a national framework within which the significance of medieval settlement sites could be evaluated. As such it takes its lead from similar mapping initiatives concerned with the natural and with historic landscape characterisation (Countryside Commission and English Nature 1996; Fairclough *et al* 1999). Working from the first edition Ordnance Survey maps of the early 19th century, it is argued, firstly, that the settlement pattern broadly reflects that of the medieval landscape, and, secondly, that it displays a meaningful correlation with other data sets, such as deserted medieval village sites, the presence of woodland in Domesday, and even Anglo-Saxon pagan burials. It identifies three broad provinces within the country: Central, North and West, and South-East. These provinces are characterised by particular landscape elements, such as nucleated villages in the Central Province, and each is divided into smaller sub-provinces that recognise local topography. The correlation with earlier data sets is taken to demonstrate that the three basic provinces were established, and were affecting the development of the landscape, at an early stage.

The project has certainly given a far greater sense of detail, and a more rigorous methodology, to national patterns that had already been identified by various authors who had mapped deserted medieval villages, moated sites, and ancient woodland, for example (Beresford and Hurst 1971; Aberg 1978; Rackham 1990). These zones or provinces have informed the investigation of historic landscapes since the subject emerged in the 1950s and it is difficult to see any substantive differences between the new map and that produced by Joan Thirsk in 1967, using 16th and 17th-century probate inventories (Darby 1951; Thirsk 1967). It is essential to reiterate that, just as urbanism is a process, so too is rural land use, and the danger of projects like the *Atlas*, is that they cannot embody process and change. As Tony Brown and Glenn Foard have argued about the Saxon landscape, 'to try at this stage to draw together all the evidence from a region, let alone from the country as a whole, might well confuse the picture by mixing up different but unrecognised chronologies and landscape types' (1998, 69).

On a local scale, settlements moved up and down the settlement hierarchy and changed their morphological characteristics even within the post-

Enclosure landscape of the 18th and 19th centuries. The structure of land ownership could facilitate or frustrate attempts to restructure the landscape that might, if the conditions prevailed, result in the desertion of a village at a time when the population was stable or even increasing (Wrathmell 1980, 120; Neave 1993, 132). But, on a much wider scale, the different trajectories followed by each agrarian region have radically effected the condition of the archaeological resource. Chris Taylor has gone so far as to characterise the east of the country as the 'zone of destruction' due to the impact of modern arable farming on the archaeological resource, compared to the extent of preservation in the pastoral west (Taylor 1972). The central province is of particular significance, since the boundary between arable and pastoral areas swept across it in the 17th century, preserving a medieval arable-based landscape beneath the turf of pastoralism. This marked differential in post-depositional conditions is rarely acknowledged in synoptic mapping projects, but is reflected in the choice of medieval sites excavated, which is heavily biased to the central and western areas (Williamson 1998).

The intellectual framework within which single site, parochial, or regional projects are situated may have moved on from early attempts to establish the date of village desertion, but they now seem equally fixed upon establishing the origins of the nucleated village. Major landscape and settlement studies such as those in the East Midlands, West Midlands, Wessex, and Somerset, despite acknowledging the importance of encompassing a variety of landscape and settlement types, all eventually focus on the nucleated village and the question of its origins and its relationship to the open-field system.

The preoccupation with nucleated villages is gradually being balanced by important studies of dispersed settlement (Austin 1989; Dyer 1991). If there has been a research bias within dispersed settlement it has been towards the exavation of highland settlement or even seasonal settlement associated with summer grazing. The large areas of lowland dispersed settlement have not yet received the attention they merit despite pioneering studies that have demonstrated their enormous potential (Wade-Martins 1980; Bailey 1989; Warner 1996). Dispersed settlements are no longer characterised as marginal areas of little significance to the medieval economy, but as full and industrious areas practising innovative and reflexive regimes that mixed farming and industry (Lewis *et al* 1997). Those

who champion such landscapes are, however, increasingly vocal and it is apparent that understanding these settlement landscapes not only increases our understanding of diversity within the medieval landscape, but contributes to our understanding of the chronology of landscape development across the country as a whole (Austin 1989; Williamson 1988; Roberts and Wrathmell 1998; Oosthuizen and James 1999).

As suggested above, detailed work on the subprovinces identified by Thirsk and others is where the significance and complexity of medieval landscapes is to be found. Whereas early work concentrated on specific sites usually found in the Central Province, such as Wharram Percy, or the west of the country, more recent investigations of the historic landscape have attempted to place sites within a wider regional context, seeking to include a variety of landscape types and agrarian regimes within their remit. However, this broader approach has yet to fully recognise the significant and variable role of urban areas and their relationship with their rural hinterland.

Archaeology, and in particular small finds analysis, has a key role to play, not only in establishing whether or not these agrarian regions are evident in the material record, but also in establishing the pattern of relationships between the various points within the settlement hierarchy. Although artefacts such as pottery have proved frustratingly inconclusive on the issue of village foundation, artefacts have a much greater role to play in establishing the relationships within and across the medieval landscape.

Several questions can be asked of the archaeological evidence:

- Can regional and sub-regional agrarian regimes be recognised among the assemblages of material culture found in areas of nucleated and dispersed settlement?
- Can different regimes of agriculture be detected amongst ecofactual and artefactual evidence?
- Can the role of urban areas be demonstrated to be distinct in different agrarian regions?
- What distinguishes settlements at different points within the hierarchy of settlement in terms of morphology, housing, production, and trade?

The answers to these questions will obviously vary from region to region and through time but it is important to raise such fundamental issues if the

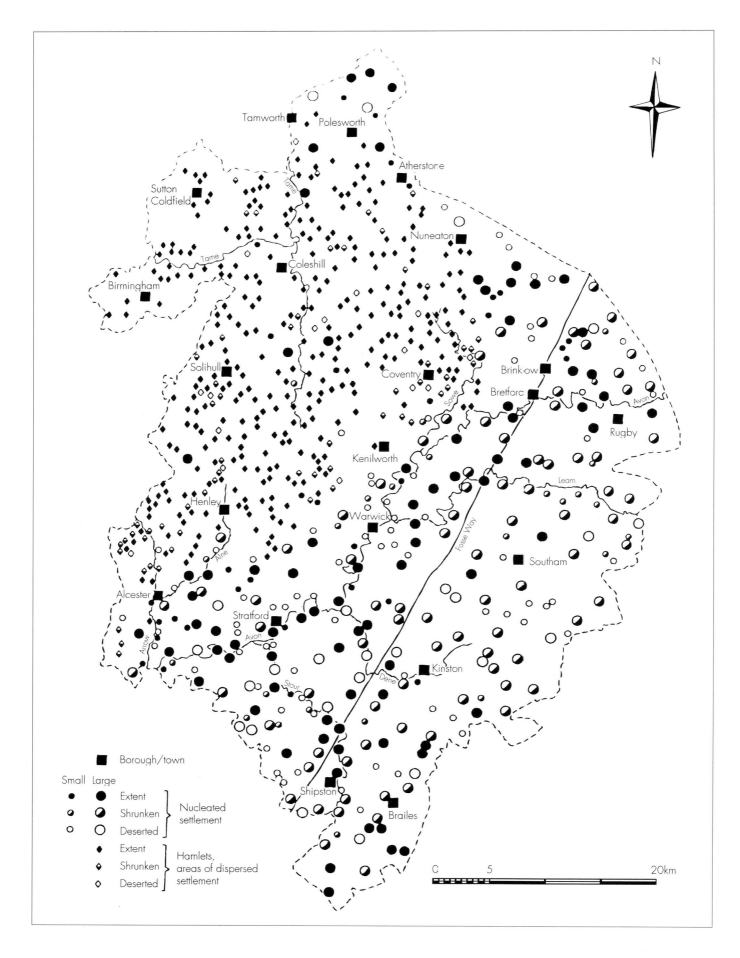

Fig 9 The settlement pattern of Warwickshire c 1300–1500 (after Dyer 1996a)

relationships between rural and urban areas, between settlement economy and society are to be addressed.

4.5.2 Sample areas and review of previous work

Warwickshire

One area which has received considerable attention is Warwickshire, which was quickly identified as a region that straddled a marked boundary between the open arable Feldon landscape in the south-east, characterised by classic nucleated villages, and the more heavily wooded Arden in the north-west where settlement was far more dispersed (Fig 9). The 'bocage' landscape of the Arden in the north-west was characterised by small enclosed fields and a considerable amount of woodland, interspersed with hamlets and isolated farmsteads. In contrast the 'champion' landscape of the Feldon south-east was dominated by arable crops in large open-field systems. The region's attraction to archaeologists stems, in part, from the possibility that there is considerable continuity between the Roman, medieval, and modern landscapes. Surface finds, excavation, and topographical analysis all point to the fact that the south-east was where most early settlement activity was concentrated, leading to the suggestion that that the division seen within the medieval landscape had much earlier antecedents (Hooke 1985, 126; Roberts and Wrathmell 2000b).

Landscape and settlement

The pattern of settlement within Warwickshire has been studied extensively by Roberts (1982; 1985), whilst attention has also been paid to the villages and farmsteads (Hilton 1966; Hooke 1996). The concentration of plough teams and settlements mentioned in Domesday, towards the south and east of the county, compared with the greater presence of woodland in the north-west, suggest that the agrarian division was quite distinct by the 11th century (Darby 1977). Despite the high concentration of deserted villages that have come to light over the last 30 years and extensive work on pre-conquest charter evidence (Hooke 1985), the chronology of settlement nucleation in the Feldon area is still far from clear. What does seem clear is that the area of land under arable cultivation reached to some township boundaries well before the conquest.

Della Hooke (1996) has attempted to map the early medieval estate boundaries and those of the emerging ecclesiastical framework, from documentary sources including charters. Elements of the agricultural landscape such as hedges and field systems have been mapped across large areas of the county, although some parts, such as the honour of Dudley and the Sutton Chase areas have received more intensive study (Hunt 1997; Hodder 1988). Recent work on the medieval woodland of Warwickshire has suggested, however, that far from being stable elements within the landscape, woodland areas have been subject to considerable change over the medieval and post-medieval periods (Wager 1998). The medieval landscape included many different types of woodland management and the distinction between a wooded north-west and a barren south-east is too simplistic.

Patterns of urban settlement and evidence from urban morphology have also been studied in some detail (Dyer 1996a; 1996b; Lilley 1994a; 1994b; 1995; Slater 1980; 1982; Phythian-Adams 1979; Wallsgrove 1992). Chris Dyer's study of the lay subsidies of 1327 has identified 23 towns in medieval Warwickshire, twelve of which are in the Arden and eleven in the Feldon. Dyer has also traced the spheres of urban influence, using manorial court records, pleas of debt, and other commercial sources, but concluded that most contact was usually within a 10km radius (Dyer 1992; 1996a).

Finds assemblages

The pottery of Warwickshire was poorly understood until relatively recently (Mellor 1994), but the Warwickshire Museum has commissioned a pottery type series for the region which should radically improve the platform for future research. There are 162 medieval pottery reports from sites in Warwickshire listed on the Medieval Research Group Pottery database (Woodcock et al, forthcoming). However, different methodologies were adopted in the description and quantification of these assemblages, and their integration will require further work.

Norfolk

The failure of extensive surveys within the Central and Western provinces of the country to answer basic questions about the chronology of settlement change and the origins of the nucleated village, may well stem from the fact that such extensive landscape redevelopment has obscured or removed the more ephemeral evidence for its precursors. There is now a need to adopt alternative approaches in regions which might appear to be less obviously rewarding in terms of traditional forms of evidence. The complex landscape of East Anglia has yet to receive the same concerted effort seen in the Midlands despite being one of the richest and most densely populated medieval regions. There are many intriguing patterns evident in the archaeology that suggest further research would be rewarding. The eastern boundary of the 'Central province', for example, has been repeatedly represented as following the western edge of the fens up into Lincolnshire, when in fact many of the distribution patterns used to corroborate its boundaries suggest that it would be more inclusive to take the boundary south of the fens and through Norfolk. Furthermore, the distribution of Anglo-Scandinavian place-names, deserted medieval villages, and evidence that ridge and furrow was once far more widespread than surviving relicts indicate, all suggest a complex palimpsest of changes, in a region that does not share the clear-cut divisions between highland and lowland topography.

Landscape and settlement

Early 17th-century writers in Norfolk distinguished between two areas of the county that had distinct husbandry regimes, and which broadly correspond with the basic division between soil types in the county. The light, free-draining sandy soils in the north and west of the county, were described as the 'Chiefest Corn-Country' that was 'mostly open and playne ... Corn it beareth very good and in great plenty' (Hood 1938, 67). The area was associated with arable crops fertilised by sheep folded on the land at night, larger units of landholding, and a strong element of social control exercised through the manorial court system. It was contrasted by the plateau of boulder clay in the south and east of the county that was described as being 'wonderful fat, and comparable for goodness with the Woodland in Suffolk' (Hood 1938, 67). In this wood-pasture region, the emphasis was on cattle rearing and dairy farming, often supplemented by a number of by-employments such as linen weaving, tanning, and woodworking (Williamson 1995; Thirsk 1987, 50). The landscape was a chaotic mixture of densely hedged irregular closes, with numerous small groves or copses. Units of landholding were generally

smaller, with a considerable number of lesser gentry in close proximity to each other. In the absence of a single large landowner, whose estate might dominate a number of parishes, the social structure was less pyramidal and social control was typically weaker (Thirsk 1987, 49). The settlement pattern was dispersed throughout the landscape, in contrast to the more nucleated pattern in the north-west.

This simple dichotomy has been given greater detail by a number of historical and archaeological surveys (Thirsk 1987; Holderness 1994; Roberts and Wrathmell 2000a). The distinct economies in the marshland of the fens and breckland areas of the south-west are now recognised, as are the claylands dissected by river valleys and the high southern plateau (Holderness 1994). The medieval economy of the Breckland has already shed considerable light upon the sophisticated land management practiced in the medieval period, and how this related particularly to access to markets (Bailey 1989). The settlement pattern in the north-east of the county was relatively dispersed and there was a complex mixture of landholding. Campbell's work on arable systems in the north east has demonstrated considerable variety in seeding and cropping systems that make this area distinct. Campbell warns against making simple correlation between soil types, technology and productivity, however (Campbell 1981, 1983). The area was the heartland of the county's textile industry, generating a considerable wealth from at least the 13th century (Wade Martins and Williamson 1999, 13–16).

Work on the early landscape of Norfolk, examining the distribution of place-name elements as well as sokemen and freemen from Domesday, suggests that the combination of documentary and landscape evidence may yet lead to a more detailed understanding of the tenurial differences which helped shape very different landscapes within the county (Williamson 1993). Tom Williamson's work on place-name elements such as *ham* and *tun*, for example, has demonstrated how they relate to relationships within the settlement hierarchy, rather than anything to do with chronology (Williamson 1993, 88). Other work on the evidence for open-field systems in Norfolk has also revealed that they were once far more extensive than once thought. Relict earthworks preserved mainly in post-medieval parkland suggest that ridge and furrow was more widespread than the landscape now suggests, whilst work on historic maps has also demonstrated that strip fields, whether ridged or not, once extended across the county (Liddiard 1999; Skipper 1989). All of these studies demonstrate the need to understand both medieval and post-medieval land use, if the pattern and hierarchy of settlements is to be understood. Both dispersed and nucleated settlements are evident in the county. East Anglia boasts the highest number of moated sites in the country, and examples have been excavated at Hempstead and Kelling in Norfolk (Rogerson and Adams 1978). Although deserted medieval villages are not common in Norfolk, examples have been surveyed at Pudding Norton, Roudham, Godwick, Waterden, and Egmere (Cushion *et al* 1982).

The importance of recognising all aspects of the settlement hierarchy, and not just hamlets, villages, and towns, is demonstrated by new work on early monastic and castle foundations in the county. The presence of significant early foci within the landscape, which have previously been labelled as ecclesiastical, is now being recognised as having an important impact on the pattern of settlement, and the sharp distinction between secular and ecclesiastical is being questioned (Pestell 2000). The early ecclesiastical structure in Norfolk has always been obscure with little evidence of the minster model seen so clearly in the West Country.

The relationship between medieval settlement and castles has also been examined in Norfolk, and has brought into question any simplistic relationship between castles and settlement densities. It is usually argued that castles were established close to existing population concentrations in order to subdue, govern, and administer the province. Recently it has been argued that the distribution of castles mirrors the local settlement pattern: isolated in areas of dispersed settlement and associated with villages elsewhere (Creighton 1999). Work in Norfolk, however, suggests that the presence of large numbers of freemen may have impeded or restricted the ambitions of castle builders. Robert Liddiard has argued that the castles of Norfolk are located according to dynastic ambition and ease of establishment, leading to a disproportionate number in the more sparsely populated west of the county (Liddiard 2000). This raises important points about the settlement hierarchy and what exactly the relationships were between the settlement hierarchy and the impact of tenurial relationships.

A regional study of medieval commemoration in Norfolk has demonstrated the impact that quite localised social structures can exercise on patterns of material culture. The pyramidal hierarchy in the north-west of the county was reflected in less competitive strategies of commemoration than were seen amongst the less wealthy, but more numerous lesser gentry in the south-east (Finch 2000). Networks of coastal or river transport clearly effected the distribution of materials throughout the county, just as building materials were brought from different sources in the east and west of the county (Harris 1989). Patterns of trade were also evident, however, with the textile industry promoting links in certain areas with Norwich, London, and the Low Countries. Clearly, urban areas extended their horizons of influence depending on their role and function as well as their size.

Finds assemblages

The publication of the *Norwich Survey* has provided an extremely useful research platform for ceramics in the region (Jennings 1981). Other data has come from the excavations at Castle Acre, for example, although the lack of extensive excavations of rural settlement sites in the county has hampered comparisons between rural and urban assemblages (Milligan 1982; Wade 1997, 52). However, Mellor was able to conclude that the ceramic traditions and their sub-regions are well established for the county (1994, 51). Mellor also noted that the later medieval wares have received less attention than the early examples and that the Saxo-Norman interface as well as Late Medieval Transitional Ware both need more systematic attention (Mellor 1994, 71). Further work is also needed on the relationship between urban and rural areas particularly focusing on production and distribution throughout the region. There is a useful collection of material from the Norwich Survey excavations which would provide a useful platform for any rural/urban comparison, which will soon be supplemented by the Castle Mall excavations (Margeson 1993; Sheppard forthcoming).

4.5.3 Research proposals

The review of medieval regional landscapes has revealed a focus on settlement to the exclusion of land use, production and consumption, or industry. This focus of research has not, therefore, facilitated work on the relationship between rural and urban areas. The recent expansion of interest in regional landscapes should be welcomed, but many of the regional studies still exhibit an overwhelming interest in the origins of the village, without offering any methodological innovations to cut the Gordian knot. There is also an increasing emphasis on mapping, but these tools can only ever describe or rationalise, and never explain or interpret. There is the added danger that they deny process and change within the landscape, particularly the very significant changes in the post-medieval landscape. The sections below outline some areas of research that will help to establish a dialogue between urban and rural medieval studies and, it is hoped, offer new insights in both directions:

Land use

As the studies in Warwickshire have demonstrated, the conventional study of nucleated settlement has yet to deliver new evidence about the chronology of settlement change. The key element must be to understand the use made of the land, since this will provide evidence about levels of subsistence, engagement with the market, and the impact of tenurial conditions on production. Brown and Foard's work on settlement change in Northants has, for the first time, provided evidence that the process of nucleation and the laying out of extensive open fields may not be contemporary, and that the open fields may represent a subsequent and dramatic reorganisation of the community's agricultural system (Brown and Foard 1998). Careful analysis of the landscape elements and of minor excavations and interventions within extant medieval villages may help to build up a clearer picture of these changes. Environmental evidence provides key data in this area and although it is increasingly being integrated with other artefacts and finds it rarely appears to be used alongside documentary evidence. It is only by looking at land use and communities together, that the development of settlement can be understood.

Regional specialisation

Having established a broader framework within which to investigate medieval rural settlement, regional 'signatures' amongst the artefactual and ecofactual evidence may become apparent. Although it is assumed that regional specialisms developed in the 16th and 17th centuries from biases evident in the medieval regimes, it has not yet proved possible to verify such claims. The accumulation of data from building forms, farming structures, agricultural technology, and ecofacts, should

build towards profiles of medieval regional landscapes. Significant advances in agricultural innovation may well have resulted from the bringing together of various developments in innovative ways or situations rather than a single dramatic technical innovation (Astill 1998, 171; Campbell 1997).

Centres of production and consumption

The settlement hierarchy is still rather crudely conceived in terms of the relationship between villages/rural and towns/urban. A far greater understanding of the full range of settlement types is needed, and should include large elite structures such as castles as well as religious institutions. Two features are of particular significance. First is the role of the middle range of settlement types, large or planned villages which, although never fully 'urban', take on some formal market functions and may have been deliberately promoted as such through the granting of rights or liberties. The second point is the distribution of skilled trades such as blacksmiths and millers. The extent of manorial or community control over these trades could be a key element in economic structures and the role of certain places, either manorial complexes or larger settlements.

Sustenance

Again closely linked to land use, technology, and innovation, the changes in diet and priorities in living conditions reflect many factors of medieval economy and society. It not only heralds significant changes in the production of individual households and communities, it may also signal a more active participation in exchange and markets. Major changes have been evident in the late medieval diet for some time, but the full ramifications of those changes in terms of the rural/urban dynamic have yet to be fully explored. It is also significant that the diet of the elite was differentiated from that of others in a number of ways. Most obviously, vast tracts of land were put aside for hunting, which was in itself highly charged with social and religious symbolism. Power was also demonstrated by overcoming the seasonality that marked the diet of the majority.

The strength of the medieval period is the enormous variety of evidence available with which to address these and many other issues. The range is further extended by the wealth of documentary evidence, which can be used in conjunction with the material remains. Pottery is obviously extremely common within medieval excavations and the progress which has been made within the two sample areas demonstrates the body of data with which archaeologists can work. Recent studies have also realised the potential of comparative work conducted on rural and urban assemblages, demonstrating that it is possible to identify distinctions between the two (Brown 1997; Courtney 1997a). The full ramifications of this, and similar studies, draws us into more detailed studies of other areas such as the use of space in rural and urban buildings. The plan forms of rural and urban buildings have long been paralleled (Pantin 1962–3; Schofield 1995) but there is still work to do on room use and social organisation within them. One key aspect of this discussion must be defining who is using the rural and urban buildings. The fact that elite families and religious institutions both maintained rural and urban residences, or in the latter's case, guest houses, must be taken into account when dealing with building traditions in the rural and urban arenas. Other artefacts such as glass are increasingly well documented and studied, and as prestige items offer important insights into lifestyle, standards of living, and use of domestic space (Tyson 2000). Other common artefacts including metalwork offer considerable potential for future work. Common to both urban and rural sites, the processes of manufacture, use, and reuse of metalwork offer opportunities to examine local styles of production and exchange. Great potential is also offered by advances in the analysis of slags and bloomery finds associated with the production of ironwork. Rare earth elements provide distinctive signatures that can be used to suggest provenance (G McDonnell, pers comm). Finally, environmental evidence has been extensively used in urban areas where its preservation is more common, but its potential for understanding the relationship between urban and rural areas has been hampered by its less frequent use on rural sites.

An archaeology of inhabitation

These broad categories are far from exhausting the full extent of possibilities and yet the relationship between rural and urban areas is central to them all. Many issues, such as the relationship between rural and urban building types, fall within them although they may have merited a section of their own. They are intended to provide a more focused platform for research into the relationship between rural and urban areas, that promotes integration and thematic research, and that highlights the vital role of the rich archaeological resource.

One of the greatest disappointments with new initiatives such as synoptic mapping programmes stems from the fact that an archaeological approach to the landscape has failed to prioritise the material nature of social relations. There is a profound sense of dislocation in acronyms and symbols: the sylvan home of Hardy's *Woodlanders* is labelled CWEXW5. In contrast, the domestic realism of the probate inventories used by Thirsk and Spufford, draws the pots and pans, the cheese frames, and the bedsteads into the rhythm of the farming year (Thirsk 1987; Spufford 1974). The archaeology of regional landscapes in the historic period must address the nature of life within them. The morphology of the settlements, the field systems, roadways, and domestic and farm buildings, are all the product of social relations embedded within the landscape. The archaeology of settlements alone will not bring us any nearer understanding the development of the medieval landscape nor medieval society. The emphasis must be upon the archaeology of inhabitation – a wider brief that examines the material remains of production, exchange and consumption at all three points and within a variety of landscape regions. It is the patterns of production and consumption, as well as the social conditions, which may well define the ability and desire of individuals and communities to participate within the rural/urban relationship.

4.6 Towns and the environment

Rebecca Roseff and Dominic Perring

4.6.1 Background

Towns have large appetites. Urban lifestyles consume resources that are difficult to replace and provoke environmental change across a broad landscape. Environmental quality is also an important issue within the towns themselves, where deteriorating conditions have often characterised growing cities. Influenced by political concerns the issue of sustainable development remains at the forefront of current environmental thinking.

Sustainability has been described as 'development that meets the needs of the present without compromising the ability of future generations to meet their own needs' (WCED 1987). Defined thus, most past urban development within England can be described as sustainable: where there have been episodes of failure and decay these can be attributed to social and economic forces unrelated to the environmental burdens imposed by the urban process. The theme of this chapter is therefore not so much about whether or not towns can be sustained, but about the long-term relationship between towns and environmental change.

The debate over sustainable development has, however, promoted a substantial body of research. This has given particular attention to ways of measuring levels of urban impact. These centre on the definition and measurement of urban ecological footprints, which represents an estimation of the land area necessary to sustain the resource consumption and waste discharge of a particular population (Wackernagel and Rees 1996, 5). Sustainability indicators have also been much in vogue, and involve check lists of features that can be used to mark whether or not a defined population is developing in ways that are perceived, by those who prepare these lists, as being more or less sustainable (DoE 1996; LGMB 1994).

Descriptive studies of these aspects of the relationship between urban populations and the territories that support them have been undertaken for a series of modern cities. What is remarkable about this work is an almost complete lack of reference to the past. Yet the need for an historical perspective is imperative: without an established base line, trends cannot be measured. Archaeology can make a significant contribution to research by providing measures of past ecological change and by locating such change in the context of changing patterns of production and consumption. The archaeological record permits a longitudinal study of ecological change in response to processes of urbanisation. It can provide the time depth needed to understand the genesis of current urban ecosystems, and to measure the long-term effects of urban change on diverse classes of habitat.

There are two complementary directions that study can take. At a crude level material inputs and outputs can be modelled in order to provide archaeological descriptions of past urban ecological footprints. Such approaches will highlight areas of similarity and dissimilarity between different periods of urban development, and place modern descriptions of ecological impacts and sustainability criteria within an historical context. It is also possible to describe more dynamic models of past ecosystems from this evidence, based around the reconstruction of energy flows into and out of the town. Measurable elements used in contemporary studies of ecosystems include energy, nutrients, productivity, population, succession, diversity, stability, and degree of modification (Simmons 1996, 20). Not all of these factors are easily open to archaeological study, but the data certainly exists from which we can describe some of the principal features of past energy flows. Certain types of change, such as an increase in the reuse of materials or a redirection in patterns of supply, can represent mitigation and response to environmental change. Evidence for such changes can be sought in the archaeological record and used as markers of stress within models of ecological change.

The obvious subject for study is London itself. For most of its history this has been England's largest and most important town, with its greatest ecological footprint (Joplin and Girardet 1996). This city also boasts some of the richest archives of documentary sources, and has witnessed intense programmes of archaeological research in both town and country. For these reasons a survey of London's changing impact on the regional environment is proposed. Modelling is necessarily rendered more complex by the exceptional importance of international trade to London's economy, but no urban trajectory can properly be described without looking at evidence for such trade and such complications add to the interest of the study. This is an opportunity to address some of the questions raised in chapter 2 of this report about how the English countryside has been transformed by the urban process (Q10–11). It will allow an assessment of the extent to which towns have both depleted natural resources and stimulated (or responded to the stimulus of) improved agricultural productivity.

The object is twofold:

- To model the direction and volume of flow of different materials into and out of London and to use these to describe energy flows. Such modelling will be based on estimates of the quantities of resources required by the city. This will require some estimation of individual and collective needs, of patterns of reuse, and of transport costs and constraints;
- To identify patterns of anthropogenically induced change within the landscape, both in terms of changing patterns of countryside management and in terms of changes to urban and rural ecosystems.

This study would effectively address the question 'How did the growth of London alter the surrounding countryside, and how did London respond to external forces?' (McAdam *et al* 2000, 20).

4.6.2 Sample areas and databases

The City of London has been studied in considerable archaeological detail. The close sampling of many hundreds of sites provides a detailed record of patterns of consumption and local environmental change from the foundation of the city *c* AD 50 down to the present day (Schofield and Maloney 1998; Shepherd 1998). London's waterfront sites are particularly valuable. These present a sequence of tightly dated rubbish assemblages deriving from the urban occupation. They also preserve strata associated with the operation of the Thames and its tributary rivers, allowing for studies of changing water regimes. Perhaps most informatively they were often built of large structural timbers, and dendrochronological evidence offers an important resource for the study of both forestry management and local climate change.

Greater London also incorporates a series of different rural landscapes that have been overtaken by

the growing city. Development led archaeological excavations and surveys in such areas mean that they have also been studied in rewarding detail. The Museum of London therefore holds an impressive archive of samples and records relating to both urban consumption and rural environmental change in the face of urban growth. The potential of the environmental material has been the subject of a recent review by Rackham and Sidell (2000), according to whom:

> Greater London is unparalleled in Britain for the diversity of environments preserving its archaeological remains … No other city boasts this diversity of topography and range of preserved materials (although there are similarities at York), and no other region can claim a similar intensity of habitation throughout the archaeological record. The nature of evidence available for analysis includes firstly the soils and sediments themselves … Biological remains have been preserved within these and other depositional environments by waterlogging, charring and mineralisation, and range from diatoms, pollen, seeds and trees to ostracods, molluscs, foraminifera, insects and bones.

Greater London defines an arbitrary study area. There is no compelling reason to argue that this region should be studied in its entirety, or that study should stop at its borders. Greater London does, however, include elements of most of the different local landscapes on which the Roman and medieval city depended. It has also been given some degree of coherence as a subject of study by the sporadic application of common approaches to archaeological sampling within the region. The London Archaeological Archive contains over 120,000 boxes of material, including pottery, building materials, registered finds, palaeobotanical and faunal remains, and paper records, from 4000 archaeological interventions. This is an awesome resource. Three sources of sample can be exploited in future research:

- *Samples recovered and processed in previous archaeological investigations.* There are several hundred relevant archive reports and databases. Sample quality varies, but large collections of animal bones exist for London for all periods and the animal bone database includes records of several hundred thousand bones. Although there are a number of published reports (87 are listed in Hall and Tomlinson 1997), no work of overall synthesis has been published. Sieving for seeds and fish bones is standard procedure. Although the synthesis of this information will provide an important starting point, the samples were not taken with this project in mind and 'natural' environments (as opposed to cultural/economic waste) are under-represented. The scale of under-representation and sample bias will need to be assessed, and allowed for in the modelling of the data;

- *Samples collected but not yet processed or analysed*. Unprocessed samples held by the Museum of London currently include: 100+ waterlogged plant macrobotanic samples, 50+ soil monoliths (including diatom and pollen); 100+ fish bone, and many tonnes of animal bone. These often have better potential than the material that has already been studied because the samples can be processed specifically to test models proposed. Any research programme built on the use of these samples will also need to involve a review of the extent to which samples have deteriorated in quality whilst in storage;

- *Purposive sampling on redevelopment sites in target landscapes*. Ongoing archaeological fieldwork within the Greater London area, conducted within the context of the development process, allows for further purposive sampling of target landscapes and periods for which the currently available sample is inadequate.

A selective strategy will be required in order to use these samples to best effect. This will involve the detailed study of a series of representative locales within the landscape, rather than an exhaustive review of all available material.

4.6.3 Review of previous work

Sustainability studies

Since the 1980s there has been considerable debate on sustainability issues and studies of material flows within cities and the urban environment (eg Breheny 1992; Stren *et al* 1992). Studies typically take a holistic view owing much to systems theory (as Boyden *et al* 1981; Boyden 1992, 163). This involves separating the city ecosystem into its component parts, and modelling flows, inputs, and outputs. From such studies it is possible to establish profiles for different types of ecological footprint. Measurement of ecological footprints starts from the assumption that every category of energy,

material consumption, and waste discharge requires the productive or absorptive capacity of a finite area of land or water. If the area required for consumption and waste by a defined population are added up, the total area represents the land requirements (or 'ecological footprint') of that population. Such accounting gives a representation of the land requirements and potential impact of settlements of all types. For example it has been estimated that present day London draws on the produce of an area equivalent to 125 times its surface area to feed, clothe, and house the urban population. At the same time the city exports a volume of waste products (carbon dioxide, dust, refuse, sewage), that can have an equivalent scale of impact (Joplin and Girardet 1996, 10). These exports are in part a product of cultural choices about the definition of what constitutes waste, and reflect also on strategies adopted for the absorption and reuse of such products.

Archaeological studies of urban impact have generally taken place within the field of site catchment analysis (Clark 1952; Vita-Finzi and Higgs 1970). This has been developed to encompass energy-flow models: where the amount of energy contained in food, and the amount needed to produce the food is calculated and projected to take account of a year's need and a defined population (Speth and Speilmann 1983; Binford 1983). Butzer (1982) has expanded this approach through his studies of archaeology as human ecology. Most agree that the material parts of a city ecosystem – the non-biotic and biotic – can be recognised and analysed, but many hold that it is impossible to measure the influence of culture on such systems (Soderstrom 1993). Thomas (1991), for example, argues that it is social behaviour that brings about permanent and irreversible effects upon the future and drives change, not resources. Further criticism of site catchment analyses revolves around difficulties in defining the area of study. Because of these methodological and theoretical difficulties, there have been few detailed studies into how much land was needed to support past settlements, and what techniques (technical, social, and cultural) were used to ensure supply.

Two archaeological studies of settlement 'sustainability' merit brief attention. Fletcher (1995; 1999) has attempted to describe the factors that can limit settlement growth, with particular reference to the constraints imposed by social behaviour. He believes that there are limits to the population densities that can be achieved without crossing critical stress thresholds, and that there are similarly limits to the area that any given town can grow to occupy before communication problems become too acute to permit effective social interaction. These limitations to achievable densities and scales can, however, be overcome through investment and innovation. He suggests that episodes of urban growth above and beyond earlier limits are made possible by technological and social changes, themselves usually consequent on shifts in modes of production. In this model, therefore, the main factors that promote and constrain urban growth are those of human social behaviour, rather than economic or ecological. This deterministic model arguably underestimates the importance of other social and cultural variables, but is in any case concerned with only one question: 'how big can towns get?'

A much more broadly based approach to the issue of urban impact is represented by the work of the Ystad Project (Berglund 1992). This inter-disciplinary project has looked at a region in southern Sweden over an 8000-year time scale, with the aim of finding the causes behind changes in society and landscape. Research has addressed the relationship between the ecosystem, production, and consumption on the one hand and population pressure, social structure, economy, and technology on the other. Many other regional landscape surveys have tackled similar issues, but such surveys have tended to look at long-term processes of change in which the details of the dialogue between town and country are not addressed. Further research is warranted.

The landscape of the London region

Archaeological research within the London region has tended to concentrate on the biological evidence from the larger urban centres (City of London, Southwark, and Westminster). Vegetation change across the broader landscape is surprisingly poorly understood, even for the historic period (McAdam et al 2000, 25). There is a comparative lack of radiocarbon-dated pollen sequences and more samples are needed to extend spatial and temporal range. Documentary and cartographic sources are increasingly valuable for the later periods, but even these can mislead. Patterns of change evident in the pollen record show gradual deforestation with the rise of agricultural systems, but some regeneration in the Saxon period. But changes occur at different

dates and intensities across the region, and more work is needed on the differences between the different types of geological landscape present. Change in woodland management in response to increased demand has, however, been described in some detail from the evidence of timber supply to London (Murphy 1995; Goodburn 1994). GIS-driven terrain modelling would provide a useful base for any such research, and would additionally support the predictive functionality of the Greater London Sites and Monuments Record.

Patterns of soil erosion have received sporadic attention (eg Boardman 1990; Needham and Macklin 1992), but there is no recent synthesis of evidence from the London hinterland. Loss of soil fertility through erosion and/or nutrient status may have led to lower yields and resulted from increased pressure on the resource, and merits further attention. Similarly crop fertility has been measured by weed assemblages associated with grain (M Jones 1988), although there are interpretational difficulties in provenancing assemblages and defining representative samples.

Urban supply

Most models of ecological footprints depend to a large extent on the evidence of urban consumption of essentials such as water, food, energy (fuel, traction, etc), building material and clothing. Several studies have described aspects of the ways in which medieval London was supplied. Alongside Dyer's (eg 1996a) research on estate provisioning, the Centre for Metropolitan History has undertaken important work on the supply of food and fuel (Galloway et al 1996; Murphy and Galloway 1992). The following summary of the state of recent research concentrates on the work that has been done on modelling some of the principal inputs and outputs. This is not a comprehensive review of a subject that has indirectly generated a vast literature (as, for instance, in the supply of ceramics).

Food

It has been noted that despite the obvious nature of the question 'how was London fed?' this remains one of the most difficult to answer (McAdam et al 2000, 20). London's demands were widely felt. Dairying and perishable horticulture were carried out closest to the city, followed by fuel production, whilst arable and pasture lay furthest from the

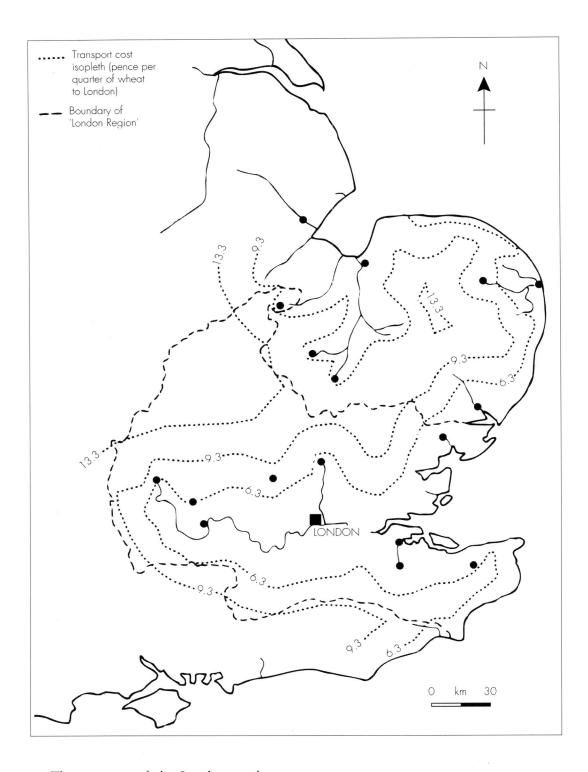

urban core. The presence of the London market encouraged estates to specialise in wheat, where soils were suitable, although transport costs limited the spread of cash crops.

The Feeding the City project explored the impact of 14th-century London on regional agriculture, using a variety of manorial accounts including Inquisitions Post Mortem (Campbell *et al* 1992). The project reviewed the evidence of both urban consumption (the demand for food)

Fig 10 The cost of carrying wheat to London from within southern England *c* 1300. Even simple, single commodity, cost-driven models of an urban hinterland generate complex and discontinuous patterns of relationship (after Campbell *et al* 1992)

and rural production (the supply of grain). The research has suggested some revised estimates to the size of London's population, now thought to have been about 80,000 or more in AD 1300 (Keene 1995, 12). Where only land transport was available supplies of grain appear to have been drawn from within a twenty mile radius from the city, but water transport allowed the exploitation of sources of grain from sources up to 60 miles distant (Fig 10). These calculations concern demesne sales only. Peasant production, perhaps two thirds of the total, is unaccounted for in this model and may have been less influenced by transportation costs (Langdon 1995). The Feeding the City project also reviewed changes in land use and farming regime, on the basis of the documented extent of pasture, arable, meadow, and park. The study confirms that arable and pasture were mixed, reflecting the reliance of arable farming on manure and traction derived from livestock.

No broad-based survey of livestock management within the region has been undertaken. There is a growing body of anecdotal information on the exploitation of wild sources of foods, as through fisheries, deer parks, warrens, and so on, but no synthesis of the data has been attempted.

Fuel

The Feeding the City Project was extended to consider fuel supply in the late 13th and early 14th centuries (Galloway et al 1996), drawing also on the assessment of woodland yields developed by Rackham (1982; 1990). Manorial accounts indicate that London exerted a major influence on woodland management. Some manors around London specialised in fuel supply, and large urban estates relied heavily on their own lands for fuel (eg Westminster Abbey). Forestry management served to generate supplies of both fuel and building timber. There was a close connection between these areas of supply, indeed redundant structural timbers provided an important source of fuel. The built environment generally contains large stores of such potential fuel.

Straw, spoiled animal fodder, wood, charcoal, and coal were all used as fuel in medieval towns (Schofield and Vince 1994, 114). Some household accounts enable annual fuel consumption to be calculated, and a broader assessment of fuel requirements can build from a calculation of the fuel needed to process an average per capita grain requirement for bread and ale. Estimates must take account of considerable variations. For instance the demand for fuel in cold years is potentially double of that in hot ones (Manley 1974). The total fuel consumption of the ten counties of the London region may have been 1,035,000 tons in 1300, falling to 649,000 tons in 1400 (due to the population fall), 21%–23% of which was used for baking and brewing. Some requirements were met by coal, so this is a maximum figure. London lies in a wooded area, and could have been self sufficient in fuel, with some surplus for export.

Documentary sources show that coal was coming to London from the 13th century, in particular for use in limekilns at a time when wood was becoming expensive. The supply of coal was developed from around 1550, at which time many of the extensive woods of Middlesex succumbed to clearance for grazing, tillage, or horticulture. By 1600 coal had just replaced wood as a general fuel for London, when per capita consumption was 0.75 tons per annum, the dry wood equivalent of which is 1.76 tons. There is an evident trend towards increased volumes of coal dust in later medieval deposits, but archaeological reports have yet to describe and measure this pattern.

Building material

Several architectural surveys permit a detailed assessment of the quantities of supplies involved in supporting London's building trade (eg Schofield 1995; Perring 2002). A methodology is suggested by the work undertaken by Shirley on the estimates of quantities involved in the construction of the Roman fort at Inchtuthil (2001). Several studies have also explored the demands of medieval timber structures (Raglan 1963; Rackham 1972).

Timber was widely exploited as a building material. Timbers recovered from archaeological contexts in London are routinely recorded for both structural detail and information on woodland management. The exploitation of both managed woodland and wildwood sources can be traced from the early Roman period (Goodburn 1995). In the 10th and 11th century, timber from very large, straight-grained oaks were particularly common in London. Such wood grows in dense woodland, where competition restricts lower branches and the timber probably came either from wildwood, or overgrown, Roman-managed woodland. Large straight trees are not found in later periods. It is suggested that the wildwood disappeared around this time and timber came predominantly from pollarded trees (Goodburn 1992). At broadly the same time there is evidence that coppicing cycles were reduced, which again would allow the standards within the coppice to branch at a lower level.

The management of underwood in London was characterised by short cropping cycles (seven years), though by the later 14th century it had lengthened to a mode of eight years. The shorter coppicing cycles may have been due to a greater need for fuel. The most extensive woods around London were royal or ecclesiastical, although lesser stretches were also in lay hands. Woodland was perceived as a commercial product yielding an annual crop for sale. The economic significance of forestry is suggested by the fact that English timber was traded with Flanders. During the later medieval period much cleft-oak board was imported from the Baltic and Germany, and in the early post-medieval period softwood began to be imported in large quantities.

Studies of stone supply in the London region depend on outdated studies (eg Jope 1964; Williams 1971), although some detailed studies of particular building projects and classes of material are available (eg Rook *et al* 1984; Pritchard 1988; Tatton-Brown 1991; Maloney 1983; Hill *et al* 1980). Building stone from archaeological excavations is usually only kept if it is worked, and few reports contain macroscopic photographs and petrological descriptions of stone (eg de Domingo 1994). Building stone is difficult to provenance, for while petrological analysis can relate finds to their geological source, this will usually leave open the question of which individual quarry was exploited. The study of stone in London is also hampered by the lack of a reference collection. The reuse of building material is common to most periods, indeed it is suggested that in the Anglo-Saxon period all building stone was reused (Parsons 1990). The Greater London Sites and Monuments Record is compiling a survey of quarries drawing on Local Authority landfill sites, map analysis, the 'Stow' survey, and other documentary sources. Most such quarries were of post-medieval date, and excavated for brickearth, sand, and gravel. Additionally there are several national surveys of quarries (eg Ashbee 1996; Instone 1996; Richardson and Trueman in prep.; Salzman 1952).

Other manufactured goods

Clothing is perhaps the most evidently essential of the manufactured imports required by the urban community. Consumer fashion and the use of dress to describe status and identity has invariably played a vital part in establishing levels of demand and in structuring patterns of supply. Historical studies of the cloth trade in the medieval period can be more useful than the archaeological data (eg Lloyd 1977; Carus-Wilson 1944; Power 1941; Harte and Ponting 1983) and much is known about wool production, manufacture, and distribution of cloth, at least for the medieval period. Historical evidence shows that cloth manufacture is a complex process with its technology constantly developing and changing, and this affected the amount and type of cloth that could be produced (Edrei 1983). More is known about wool cloth than linen, hair cloth, or mixed fibre, because it is both better documented and preserved in archaeological deposits.

A wide range of other household goods is well represented in the archaeological record (pottery, small finds, glass, etc). London was also a producer and exporter of such items.

Water

The modern hydrology of the Thames basin has been studied in detail (IoH 1997), and several studies have examined how London's water supply may have differed in the past. Roman London was primarily supplied by wells, springs, and rivers found within the settlement itself, in some cases feeding local aqueducts (Wilmott 1982; 1983; Wacher 1995, 101). London was self-sufficient in water although many of the local sources, such as the Walbrook stream, were soon polluted. Saxon and early medieval London drew on similar sources, but, later in the medieval period, increased demand encouraged the exploitation of more distant sources. Monastic houses pioneered the construction of conduits. In the 1230s, for example, the newly arrived Greyfriars established their own water supply from outside the city. In 1237 the city bought land containing wells or springs at Tyburn and brought it via lead pipes to a great conduit in Cheap, which in 1378 was extended to Cornhill. By 1350 some houses possibly had an individual supply, but water was usually carried from conduits by waterbearers. Archaeological evidence supplements these sources, and some private houses had rainwater cisterns, and many wells (Schofield 1984, 79, 97).

Waste disposal

Rubbish disposal

Urban rubbish can be difficult to dispose of (Keene

1982; Dyer 1989), although towns have generally supported communities of scavengers able to find value in many forms of waste. Past legislation and litigation witness an intermittent concern with the control of waste disposal and sewage. Drawing on archaeological and historical sources, Brothwell (1982) has proposed estimates of pre-industrial waste output. Processing industries, notably butchery, are particularly well represented in rubbish assemblages.

Cultural and economic factors are both brought to bear in changing attitudes to waste. Hygiene has often been a problem. The ova of intestinal parasites found in cess pits illustrate the endemic infestation of medieval urban populations. The location and distribution of cess pits (as at Milk Street and Watling Court in the city of London) suggest that cross-contamination with wells was commonplace. High parasite ova counts from Saxon occupation levels at Watling Court in London demonstrate that human excreta was present in significant quantities in the domestic environment – indeed the conditions were such as to guarantee reinfection (Schofield *et al* 1990). Problems with faecal contamination of floors were markedly less evident in the later medieval period (from the 11th century onwards). A decline in the range and numbers of species in insect assemblages also suggest that houses were cleaner in later periods (Kenward and Allison 1994b).

O'Connor (2000) has shown how complex food webs could develop where refuse was not cleared from the urban area (a particular characteristic of the early medieval town). Organic refuse provided an energy store that could sustain dense faunal populations. Larger predators, such as cats and hawks, were found at the top of a food chain involving smaller predatory vertebrates and invertebrates, which in turn fed on the detritivores and scavengers that fed on the dead organic matter supplied in garbage.

Soil pollution

Soils are geochemical sinks for contaminants and provide a geoarchaeological record of human activity. The burning of coal, smelting of iron, and metalworking in general, have contributed a heavy load of trace metal contaminants to the environment. Studies of modern distributions of heavy metals are well advanced (eg Kelly and Thornton 1996), and mass spectrometry has regularly been used to identify mineral enrichment of agricultural

soils (eg Entwhistle *et al* 1998). Such approaches and techniques can be applied to the archaeological study of known industrial sites.

River pollution

It is relatively easy to study water quality from the archaeological evidence, from a variety of palaeoecological sources such as changes in freshwater mollusc assemblages in riverside sediments and diatom analysis. Diatoms measure salinity and pollution, and a methodology has been developed for London (Juggins 1988). About six studies have been completed within the region, including a long, well-dated sequence from Westminster.

Changing patterns in the consumption of fish have also been used as a measure of river pollution. At York, fish present in the 8th to 9th-century diet were typical of well-oxygenated rivers, but from the 11th century marine fish replaced the more sensitive species (A Jones 1988; O'Connor 1991). The implication is that water quality had declined. This was a period when several aspects of urban environmental quality witnessed improvement, and it is possible that towns became more efficient at exporting pollution downstream. This problem is best illustrated by Boyd's (1981) study of later medieval estuarine sediments from the river Fleet in London. Flora and fauna in the streambed witness nutrient enrichment caused by sewage pollution during the first part of the 14th century. Pollution had subsequently destroyed most aquatic life and left a reduced assemblage. The likely cause of the change was the presence of a wharf upstream used by London's meat market, where entrails and waste were thrown into the stream.

Outwash sediments can also contain other markers of changing aquatic environments, as where they contain trace chemicals, or biological molecules that can be used to identify algae (Thomas 1993). The main requirement is to obtain samples from tightly dated contexts, an achievable objective where sediments are buried by historically or dendrochronologically dated episodes of reclamation and canalisation. London is particularly well served by such contexts, although their purposive sampling is not undertaken as a matter or course.

Air pollution

Brimblecombe (1982) has modelled atmospheric change in medieval London on the basis of estimated population sizes and documented changes in the character of fuel use. This study is based on crude models of urban change and there are historical and archaeological data that need also to be taken into account. Analysis of marble shows a correlation between the length of atmospheric exposure and sulphur dioxide penetration (Braun and Wilson 1970). A coordinated sampling programme might be able to chart different patterns of sulphur dioxide penetration throughout the medieval period as a test of the models developed on the basis of the historical and archaeological data. Coal dust and charcoal can also be recovered from lake and marine sediments as a further test of the progress of atmospheric pollution. Domestic air pollution is also one of the likely causes of the evidence for sinusitis that has been traced in Anglo-Saxon burials (Wells 1977).

4.6.4 Research proposals

Two research objectives were set out at the start of this chapter. We suggested that it should be possible to model London's changing ecological footprint, based on the evidence of the demands and outputs of the metropolis. At the same time the impact of such demands on the surrounding landscape can be described, both in terms of agrarian production and in terms of the ways in which ecosystems changed and developed in response to urbanisation. Our theme here is the progressive modification of local environmental systems consequent on the imposition of an urban environment. Although the study of the landscape itself requires further purposive sampling, this can be structured to take place within the context of the ongoing archaeological investigation that occurs within the context of local redevelopment. Most other aspects of research can be conducted on the basis of the available synthetic studies and samples, although some more detailed examination of the available archive (an assessment of potential) should precede the implementation of a full programme of research.

Modelling of inputs and outputs

The direction and volume of flows of different materials in and out of the city can be estimated and measured. As Simmons has observed (1996, 25), 'the study of energy flow through human-controlled systems is clearly capable of yielding results of both academic interest and practical value. Complex interactions involving the materials of both ecology and economics can be modelled'. But, as Simmons also points out, the quantification of the data for a good energy analysis is difficult, and problems attach to the dynamic and changing nature of such systems.

Different models will need to be constructed to illustrate the suggested workings of the different component parts of the supply system. In the first instance attention can be structured against the measurable elements described in ecosystem modelling. These broadly defined systems (energy, nutrients, etc) will need to be subdivided into a series of smaller component systems. Therefore, for example, the modelling of energy supply should build on the separate study of discrete flows involved in the demand for food, fuel, traction, and so on. Each of these elements of energy supply can in turn be studied on the basis of the different classes of archaeological and historical data available. Thus inputs and outputs involved in baking and brewing will be modelled separately from those associated with estuarine fishing. Many different small-scale models will need to be built, and there will be a series of complex exchanges between them.

Not all elements of supply are equally susceptible to study, and several elements of the modelling will necessarily rely on ethnographic parallels. Some factors best suited to archaeological evidence will be found by analysing the requirements of individual household units and multiplying upwards to find the whole city supply. House construction is an example of this, after the manner of Rackham (1972). Other factors, better suited to historical evidence, ethnographic parallels, and experimental archaeology evidence, will be established by taking the whole city supply and reducing down to the individual unit. Grain and fuel supply are good examples of this, after the manner of Campbell *et al* (1993) and Galloway *et al* (1996). The process of constructing such models will, however, ask new questions of the archaeological evidence.

Once constructed in terms of material flows, such models can then be converted to represent net energy flows and stores. Therefore, for example, fuel can also be represented as calorific value less the energy utilised in its management, collection, and transport. The material flow model can be understood in classical economic terms, whilst the energy flow model offers an analysis comparable to those used in modern ecological economics.

Modelling will be further complicated by the fact

that the different elements of supply all operated within an integrated landscape of production and consumption. Exchanges between the different models will also need to be mapped. For instance models of the supply of beef have to take account of the way in which cattle could be stored, representing wealth, and 'consumed' as draught animals within systems of cereal production. Such factors can be left as unknowns until the main material flows have been modelled, at which point it should be possible to estimate limits for the integrating variables. It must also be remembered in such measurement that there were 'stores' in the system, for instance a proportion of timber building material would eventually serve as fuel.

Modelling of ecological change

The impact of the progressive urbanisation of the London region can be measured in terms of both changing patterns of urban consumption and in the evidence of environmental impacts on the rural landscape. We need to see if change took place evenly across the landscape, or if there are geographical patterns (Rackham and Sidell 2000, 26).

The changing nature of settlement environments can also be revealed in the pathologies of human populations (drawing on the evidence for diet, pollution, occupational injury, general morbidity, etc). Research may also find it useful to compare human populations with other species resident within the urban area (cats, dogs, rats, fowl, etc). It is likely that common trends in the pathology and morbidity of different species will share a common cause in the local environment. Where environmental remains are particularly well preserved there is also scope for the modelling of ecological change within urban ecosystems. The impact of urbanisation can be clearly evident in the changing character of the local flora and fauna (as de Moulins 1990), although the reworking of urban deposits makes it difficult to find intact assemblages suitable for comparative study.

The analysis of pollen, ostracods, molluscs, diatoms, pollen, plant macrofossils, insects, skeletal remains of vertebrates, and invertebrates, permits a detailed reconstruction of past animal and plant populations from a variety of habitats and archaeological landscapes, and the location of change within the context of documented phases of urban development. The suites of species present at different stages of urban development can be identified,

and characterised by ecological attributes and mode of dispersal. This would determine the effect of the changing urban environment upon the local flora and fauna, and in particular provide information on the arrival and spread of alien and introduced species in urban habitats, and how these relate to the native species present. The hemeroby (ie degree of unnaturalness) of species groups can also be identified in theoretical models, and tested against archaeological assemblages and the contemporary record. The results can be compared with present-day indices of hemeroby to determine whether common attributes of hemerobic species (such as ruderality) are constant, or whether there has been change through time in the character of the urban ecosystem.

The relative importance of local environmental change (fragmentation and change of local landscapes due to the impact of urban development and industrial change), can be measured within the context of broader trends (climatoligical, species introductions, change of urban context in which local landscapes occur, etc). Modelling can be concentrated on target archaeological landscapes selected to illustrate a range of different habitats, in areas where past industrial and urban interventions are well documented and where archaeological samples are easily obtained. The best data will generally derive from riverside contexts along the Thames and its tributaries (Wandle, Fleet, Walbrook, Lea, etc). Models should be structured to address questions that would be asked of modern ecosystems, but will need to take account of the character of the archaeological record. For instance all but the smallest mammals are unlikely to be sufficiently well represented in the sample base to be useful in modelling, whereas insects are likely to provide more rewarding data for analysis. A critical list of species and processes would need to be established at an early stage of research. This would need to concentrate attention on those species likely to be preserved, abundant,and responsive to change.

The models will explore the upstream and downstream ecosystems of the landscapes, with sufficient pre to post-urbanisation temporal reach to provide contextual information. Model parameters might therefore be differently adapted for each target landscape, such that a sample base can be established to adequately trace the effects of urbanisation and industrialisation. Archaeological samples can be used to measure the relative incidence of critical species within the target landscapes. Emphasis should be placed on diachronic samples, especially from alluvial contexts and riverside reclamations where changing environments are best studied. Studies can address change to synanthropic types within certain plant, insect, and faunal communities.

In this chapter we have discussed the potential of two related types of system modelling that could be applied in the study of London's ecological impact. Because of the complexity of the subject it has not been possible to give detailed attention to each of the elements that will merit separate modelling. Future research into these issues would benefit from a research cycle involving the following stages:

- The outline and theoretical modelling of material flows within the component parts of London's supply system (fuel supply, hunting, quarrying, etc). This would be used to identify the various sub systems that can be studied, and to define and source a range of measurable parameters to be used in the detailed modelling process;

- The identification of representative landscapes within the region where ecosystems can be reconstructed from the evidence actually or potentially available;
- A detailed assessment of the quality and potential of samples and archives held by the London Archaeological Archive against their potential to contribute to the modelling of the material flows and local ecosystems identified as worth investigating;
- A review of the sampling strategies applied in the course of ongoing fieldwork in the Greater London area with a view to building a framework that would facilitate future data collection against the research interests described here;
- The detailed modelling of the material flows, and their conversion into energy flows;
- The integration of the separately modelled elements in order to describe London's changing ecological footprint;
- The description of the relative importance of macro and micro environmental change based on the ecosystem modelling described above.

CHAPTER FIVE

Conclusions and recommendations

5.1 Curatorial practice and the use of the archaeological resource

This review, by seeking to build research from the disparate results of ongoing fieldwork, puts some aspects of current archaeological practice to proof. Any attempt at comparative study, any form of regional review which crosses the boundaries traditionally drawn around areas of archaeological study, is constrained by the availability and quality of data. These constraints can sometimes seem to be of frightening proportion but the problems need not be insuperable.

Most archaeological work in England is regulated by archaeologists working for local or strategic planning authorities (ie County and District Archaeologists). Specifications and briefs advanced by such archaeologists are usually structured within the context of agreed regional approaches that incorporate some areas of standardised procedure. Such standards provide a base line for the professional conduct of most archaeological work.

Where supported by reference to agreed research frameworks, these regulatory controls can be used to exact agreement to adhere to a proper sampling and analytical methodology by both sponsors and agents of archaeological investigation. If excavation is deemed an appropriate response to the proposed destruction of remains in a redevelopment programme, this is because a sufficiently high level of archaeological study is proposed to mitigate the loss of the archaeological resource. It is therefore legitimate to hope that finds can be recovered and measured in a fashion that will facilitate research of the character proposed here. Indeed one of the main purposes of this report is to make it easier for

archaeological contractors and curators, operating within commercial and planning constraints, to build justifications for more ambitious sampling strategies than might otherwise be possible.

The study of complex networks of sites asks difficult questions of current archaeological practice. It continues to be the case that Sites and Monuments Records have difficulties in handling the level of demand placed on them. In preparing this report we were disappointed by the limitations of some of the SMR records consulted. The implications are worrying for research, since several regional archaeological databases can not be used to their full potential. This is an area that has already been identified as one where further investment would be of use (English Heritage 1995), and this view can be reiterated here.

Competitive tendering allows developers to obtain prompt attention to the problems of specific sites, and, although there is some dissatisfaction within the archaeological community about the way in which competition is structured, these are problems that the profession should be able to address. It will always be difficult, however, to exploit the opportunities presented by developer-funded work to advance the broader studies of settlement landscapes that are the object of most archaeological research and are the particular concern of this review. Developers and their archaeological contractors will usually, and justly, consider their responsibility to run no further than the boundaries of the site that needs excavation. If this problem is not to become a permanent bar to more ambitious research the following approaches should be considered:

- Consistent approaches to data collection and description should be developed against specific research platforms, and agreed through the application of briefs within the context of agreed regional research priorities (for which see further below). The use of 'recovery levels' would provide the flexibility required to ensure that exemptions can be allowed where the character of the archaeology so justifies, and to allow for more adventurous departures from standard practice where this is warranted;
- Pottery type series and other classificatory systems remain a priority for further work and

should be structured to establish common and agreed descriptions. Some reassessment of existing collections may be justified;

- Much archaeological data is inaccessible, and it remains the case that excavations are not structured to encourage a wider use of the information obtained. The better dissemination of digital data has always been desirable and is now practical;
- Specific areas of research can be enabled by structures described above, but require the detailed attention of dedicated researchers. Several of the topics described here are suitable for graduate research and in all areas there is scope for widening the research community involved.

5.2 Methodological recommendations

Study of variation

No aspect of archaeology commands such a vast literature as the study of variation. This underpins everything from pottery seriation to the principles of stratigraphic excavation. Every field of specialist archaeological research has its own body of literature dedicated to the problems of describing difference. It is therefore frustrating to find that very little attention has been given to the broader problems of characterising differences between whole settlements and entire assemblages. If the deceptively simple question 'how does this site differ materially from its nearest neighbours?' were asked more frequently, our methodologies might improve accordingly. The process would be helped if our definitions of neighbourliness were extended to address spatial, temporal, and social confines.

Some form of base-line description of what constitutes a site assemblage would be a valuable aid to this endeavour, although the problems of achieving this are not to be underestimated: there are so many variables and so much data to take into account. Ideally such a description would draw on divergent sets of information derived from different fields of archaeological study. The potential of multivariate analysis has been referred to at several points in this review (as p 64), but there are difficulties in establishing quantitative measures that allow comparison between different artefact classes. The variables need definition in a way that facilitates valid comparison. Some excavations now record the volume of earth excavated from each context. This simple

approach might offer a useful way forward, but the practice is not widespread. Appropriate measures of all classes of artefact and material (as p 63) can be described relative to a base measure of the volume of spoil excavated. These descriptions would in turn permit a comparative measurement of all aspects of the site assemblage (coin, small finds, building material, animal bone, pottery, etc).

In this way a site that generates surprisingly few finds of any type, perhaps reflecting local patterns of rubbish disposal, can be distinguished from one where only select materials are under-represented, where local differences in supply or use might instead be in evidence. Such measurement can be used to explore inter and intra-site differences, and is central to the study of rubbish disposal practices and the reworking of material (Evans and Millett 1992).

Sampling and quantification of assemblages

It would ease the task of comparative and synthetic study if there was greater consistency in the approaches routinely adopted in the recovery and description of finds assemblages. The issue of standardisation is, however, a difficult one. The growth of commercial archaeology has seen a progressive codification of procedure, one of the main purposes of which has been to establish a level playing field within which competing contractors can prepare estimates of costs against a fixed specification. Ian Hodder (1999, 205–07) has persuasively argued that these universalising tendencies militate against open and inclusive approaches to the study of the past. Whilst regulatory constraints can be used to provide a degree of quality control in situations where market forces might otherwise limit horizons, it is also bound to stifle innovation. It would be worrying if field archaeology were to be tempted into a 'one size fits all' approach to the recording and recovery of data. Systems of quantification appropriate for the study of one aspect of contrast will not be equally appropriate for others. Methodologies should be structured against explicitly described research targets, not applied in unthinking habit.

But the research opportunities described in this report would benefit from a more considered approach to the ways in which archaeological finds are recovered and described. There are clear research benefits to agreed regional sampling strategies, provided there is a clear and demonstrable link between research objectives and the methods recommended. A strong case can be made for the more widespread adoption of the following sampling approaches (most of which are already widely adopted), in the construction of such research programmes:

- Common reference could be made to an agreed range of 'recovery levels', building on those proposed by Carver (1987, 130). The use of sample levels should be structured with a view to achieving greater comparability between finds assemblages in target landscapes. Retrieval histories should in any case be documented in full. Descriptions of the sample level attained can be included within national and regional databases (SMRs, etc), in order to help researchers assess the character and potential of available assemblages;

- Sieving of control samples should be the default approach on archaeological excavations that generate finds assemblages. Standard approaches to such sampling and retrieval (range and volume of sample, sieve mesh sizes, etc), can be established on the basis of the character of the sampling exercise (as related to the 'recovery level');

- The quantification methods available should be applied more widely and more ambitiously (again 'recovery levels' can be used to establish types of archaeological exercise where such quantification need not be a requirement), and

extended to all pertinent classes of material (as for instance, to facilitate the comparison of samian with other classes of ceramics);

- Where detailed recovery is possible and a proper level of investment in analysis can be justified, bone is perhaps best described by minimum animal units (MAU, above p 41) and pottery by estimated vessel equivalents (EVES, above p 49);

- Carcass part analysis, butchery, ageing, and sexing are all vital to the study of variability within the faunal assemblages. Pottery studies rely, above all, on agreed and commonly described pottery type series; and the recommendations of Fulford and Huddlestone (1991) are strongly endorsed;

- The controlled recovery of finds from topsoil and plough horizons should be conducted on relevant artefact scatters, since for some classes of site this is where the bulk of the evidence will be found;

- Metal detectors should be used as a matter of course in archaeological fieldwork to improve recovery of metal artefacts.

More work can be recommended in several areas. Some larger assemblages recovered from previous excavations, where these are supported by an adequate quality of documentation and where the methods of recovery were not inappropriately selective, have much to contribute to the issues discussed here. It is not clear where the funds for the reassessment of published work may be found, but there are instances where the re-evaluation of good assemblages would be a more cost-effective way of advancing research than investing in new excavation.

The classification and provenancing of 'undiagnostic' classes of coarse and greywares is central to studies of local and regional patterns of exchange, whilst contextual studies of ceramics would better establish which forms relate to particular uses. It is also important to consider the use life of ceramics on site, particularly of forms for which close dates of manufacture are available.

The effect of post-depositional processes on artefact assemblages has a critical impact. It is exceptionally difficult to deal with the consequences of reworking and residuality on multi-period sites (ie in almost all urban areas), whilst the effects of ploughing and decay have altered the composition of finds on most rural sites. Research into the identification of residuality amongst faunal remains is still experimental. Little has changed since a Council for British Archaeology working party described this as an important area of research (Thomas 1983), and further work on the issue is urgently needed.

5.3 Informing research strategies

Theoretical models drawn from historical geography are of limited use to the archaeological research discussed here, although some (eg central place theory) have generated a very considerable archaeological literature. Most definitions of hinterlands are ill suited to archaeological study: there are too many overlapping fields of influence to take into consideration and many of these elude spatial definition. The complex landscape of past settlement is instead best defined as a series of peaks of consumption, the patterns of which evidence underlying social and economic structures, and permit study of the changing approaches to power and its replication through the manipulation of resource. This is a more exciting subject for social research, where archaeology has a leading role to play.

Academic study can address the comparative analysis of networks of interrelated sites, in which archaeological finds represent the most important single source of information but where a wide range of other sources of information has value. The emphasis given to period and place in the definition of individual central places and their hinterlands is a necessary point of departure, but becomes peripheral to the broader study of the social transitions that have created our urban landscapes, and of the impact that such changes have had on the world that we inhabit. The further development of the methodological tools that archaeology already has to hand, allied to a clear sense of research purpose, has the potential to radically change the nature of the archaeological contribution to the urban debate.

Almost all English settlement landscapes have the potential to contribute to one or more of the research themes described in this report, and it is hoped that some of the points raised in this review will be drawn upon to support local programmes of research and in the management of the archaeological resource.

One of the objectives of this report has been to identify areas where there are research benefits to be obtained from archaeological work, and this will necessarily establish a test of conservation policy. The fact that a case for research can be established does not mean that the needs of conservation can be ignored, but it introduces a balance of potential benefit. There will be occasions when clearly directed research, supported adventitiously by programmes of developer-funded works, might find justification in this review.

Although specific subjects and regions have been given particular emphasis, this is by way of example. Several landscapes and themes neglected here have equivalent potential. Regardless of where such work should best be conducted, a strong case can be made for the intensive study of preferred areas or subjects. The Wroxeter Hinterland Project, as but one example of many, has demonstrated the value of defining and concentrating attention on a specific landscape. The project has given focus not only to the different archaeological issues of the region, but has been used as a vehicle for developing archaeological methodology and promoting a wider interest in the past. Archaeology needs such projects.

Without directed programmes of study the archaeological information obtained from the progress of development-led projects and casual interest is bound to be patchy. For instance, even in the richest and best-documented landscapes, there are vital components that await study, and could do so indefinitely without the impetus of an applied programme of research. A case in point is the Roman countryside around Colchester, which is poorly served by villa excavations. By way of contrast no end of villas have been studied in the territory of Verulamium, where study is instead hampered by the need for further work on urban assemblages. It is only by reviewing the potential of archaeological landscapes in this way that these *lacunae* can be seen in context and given full weight. A stronger case can now be made for the detailed excavation of carefully selected villa sites in Essex, and in Hertfordshire towards the reassessment of the Wheeler and Frere archives and assemblages. These two exercises would considerably improve our ability to describe the Roman landscapes of south-east Britain and to understand the social and economic forces that shaped them. Similar arguments are presented here for work that could be undertaken on the early medieval environs of Southampton and Ipswich, and several other exciting areas of study are summarised elsewhere in this report.

Projects structured around networks of sites have the advantage of being able to engage the interests of a wider community and the processes of drawing comparisons and contrasts are a more challenging test of archaeological methods and theory. It is largely because of this potential that English Heritage has seen this as a suitable area of strategic research and contributed towards the work described here.

This report gives occasional emphasis to the better studied areas of south-east England; a consequence of the concern with the major changes that have occurred in this region and of the quality of data available here. The material poverty of some other regions is, however, an important subject for investigation in its own right. Such areas are likely to require much more sampling in order to permit characterisation, yet the intensity of present-day development in some of these under-represented regions is also lower. In such instances there may be some case for encouraging independently funded programmes of work in order to improve the basis of the sample.

One point that emerges clearly from both this study and the regional framework documents that have appeared (eg Glazebrook 1997) is that low-status sites have poorly served archaeological research. The past history of research has involved mining richer archaeological seams for higher status finds and structures, and we are left in comparative ignorance about the settlements of the vast majority of the population: the rural poor. This is an area of research that is benefiting from the more egalitarian approach to site selection that flows from the prescriptions of PPG 16 (DoE 1990). Poor settlements that were once considered uninteresting, and could not distract attention from flagship projects on higher status sites, are now routinely investigated. The results of such excavations are awkwardly difficult to obtain and there are still many instances where opportunities for research revealed at the evaluation stage have yet to be followed up.

Another concern is the lack of tightly dated frameworks within which analysis can take place. Episodes such as the Boudiccan revolt of AD 60 are of rare and exceptional importance, since they allow direct comparison between contemporary assemblages at different locales. Any site with a clear dating framework, especially where the dated horizons do not involve reworking of earlier archaeological levels, is doubly valuable (for which reason forts and castles have particular promise). In the assessments of site potential and importance this factor is not always given adequate weight. Since dated horizons tend to be those associated with buildings referred to in historical or epigraphic sources they are most unlikely to occur on low-status sites, and so where they do their importance is inestimable.

There are many other recommendations scattered throughout this report. Many of these are well represented elsewhere in the archaeological literature, and need not be rehearsed at length here. It is worth reasserting the fact, however, that most of the approaches and studies described here can be applied beyond the boundaries of England, and that there is a wealth of research taking place elsewhere that deserves to be given higher prominence in our regional debate. All of the systems and processes described here have frontiers that extend much further and wider.

Bibliography

Abel, W, 1980 *Agricultural fluctuations in Europe from the thirteenth to the twentieth centuries*, London

Aberg, A (ed), 1978 *Medieval moated sites,* CBA Res Rep 17, London

Abrams, P, 1978 Towns and economic growth: some theories and problems, in Abrams & Wrigley 1978, 1-33

Abrams, P, & Wrigley, E A, (eds), 1978, *Towns and societies, essays in economic history and historical sociology,* Cambridge

Addyman, P V, 1964 A dark-age settlement at Maxey, Northants, *Medieval Archaeol,* 8, 20–73

Addyman, P V, & Leigh, D, 1973 The Anglo-Saxon village at Chalton, Hampshire: second interim report, *Medieval Archaeol,* 17, 1–25

Albarella, U, 1997 The Roman mammal and bird bones excavated in 1994 from Great Holts Farm, Boreham, Essex, English Heritage AML report 9/97, London

Albarella, U, & Davis, S J M, 1996 Mammals and birds from Launceston Castle, Cornwall: decline in status and the rise of agriculture, *Circaea,* 12,1 (for 1994), 1–156

Alcock, L, 1992 Message from the dark side of the moon: western and northern Britain in the age of Sutton Hoo, in Carver 1992, 205–16

Allason-Jones, L, 2001 Material culture and identity, in James & Millett 2001, 19–25

Allen, J R L, & Fulford, M G, 1996 The Distribution of south-east Dorset Black burnished category I pottery in South-West Britain, *Britannia,* 27, 223–81

Allen, J R L, & Fulford, M G, 1999 Fort building and military supply along Britain's Eastern Channel and North Sea coasts: the later second and third centuries, *Britannia,* 30, 163–84

Andrews, P (ed), 1988 *Southampton finds 1: the coins and pottery from Hamwic,* Southampton

Andrews, P, 1992 Middle Saxon Norfolk: evidence for settlement, 650–850, *Ann Norfol Archaeol and Hist Research Group,* 1, 13–28

Armit, I, Champion, T C, Creighton, J, Gwilt, A, Haselgrove, C C, Hill, J D, Hunter, F & Woodward, A, 2000 *Understanding the British Iron Age; an agenda for action,* Cambridge

Armitage, P L, 1982 Studies on the remains of domestic livestock from Roman, medieval and early modern London: objectives and methods, in Hall & Kenward 1982, 94–106

Arnold, C, 1988 *An archaeology of the early Anglo-Saxon Kingdoms,* London

Arnold, D E, Neff, H, & Bishop, R L, 1991 Compositional analysis and 'sources' of pottery: an ethnoarchaeological approach, *American Anthropol,* 93, 70–90

Ashbee, J, 1996 MPP stone quarrying industry: step 1, unpub Lancaster Univ Archaeol Unit report

Astill, G G, 1994 Archaeological theory and the origins of English towns – a review, *Archaeologia Polona,* 32, 27–71

Astill, G G, 1998 Medieval and later: composing an agenda' in J Bayley (ed) *Science in Archaeology. An agenda for the future,* London, 169–77

Astill, G G, & Grant, A, (eds), 1988 *The countryside of medieval England,* Oxford

Aston, M A, 1986 Post-Roman central places in Somerset, in Grant 1986, 49–77

Aston, M A, & Lewis, C (eds), 1994 *The medieval landscape of Wessex,* Oxford

Atkinson, M, & Preston, S J, 1998 The late Iron Age and Roman settlement at Elms Farm, Heybridge, Essex, excavations 1993–5: an interim report, *Britannia* 29, 85–110

Austin, D, 1989 The excavation of dispersed settlements in medieval Britain, in M Aston, D Austin & C Dyer (eds) *The rural settlements of medieval England,* Oxford, 231–46

Ayers, B S, 1997 Anglo-Saxon, medieval and post-medieval urban', in Glazebrook 1997, 59–66

Bahn, P, & Flenley, V, 1992 *Easter Island. Earth island,* London

Bailey, M, 1989 *A marginal economy? East Anglian Breckland in the later Middle Ages,* Cambridge

Baker, J, & Brothwell, D, 1980 *Animal diseases in archaeology,* London

Barber, B, & Bowsher, J, 2000 *The eastern cemetery of Roman London. Excavations 1983–1990,* Museum of London Monograph 4, Lavenham

Barford, P M, 2002 *Excavations at Little Oakley,* Essex,

1951–78: Roman villa and Saxon settlement, East Anglian Archaeol, 98, Chelmsford

Barnish, S J B, 1989 The transformation of classical cities and the Pirenne debate, *J Roman Archaeol*, 2, 385–400

Barrett, J, 1997 Theorising Roman archaeology, in Meadows *et al* 1996, 1–7

Barrow, C J, 1995 *Developing the environment. Problems and management*, Harlow

Bass, W M, 1987 *Human Osteology*, Columbia

Bassett, S (ed), 1989 *The origins of Anglo-Saxon kingdoms*, Leicester

Bassett, S (ed), 1992 *Death in towns: urban responses to the dying and the dead, 100–1600*, Leicester

Baxter, M J, 1994 *Exploratory multivariate analysis in archaeology*, Edinburgh

Bayley, J, 1991 Anglo-Saxon non-ferrous metalworking: a survey, *World Archaeol*, 23.1, 115–130

Bedwin, O, 1985 Excavations at Mount House, Braintree 1984, *Essex Archaeol Hist*, 16 (1984–5), 28–37

Bekker-Nielsen, T, 1989 *The geography of power: studies in the urbanization of Roman North-West Europe*, BAR Int Ser 477, Oxford

Benfield, S, & Garrod, S, 1992 Two recently discovered Roman buildings at Colchester, *Essex Archaeol Hist*, 23, 25–38

Beresford, G, 1987 *Goltho: the development of an early medieval manor, c. 850 – 1150*, English Heritage Archaeol Rep 4, London

Beresford, M W, 1967 *New towns of the Middle Ages*, Leicester

Beresford, M W, 1981 English medieval boroughs: a handlist: revisions, 1973–1981, *Urban Hist Yearbook*, 59–65

Beresford, M W, 1988 *New towns of the Middle Ages: town plantation in England, Wales and Gascony* (2nd edn), Gloucester

Beresford, M W, & Finberg, H P R, 1973 *English medieval boroughs: a handlist*, Newton Abbott

Beresford, M W, & Hurst, J G (eds), 1971 *Deserted medieval villages*, London

Berg, D S, 1999 The mammal bones, in C Philo & S Wrathmell (eds), *Roman Castleford. Volume II, excavations 1974–85. The structural and environmental evidence*, Sheffield, 223–79

Berglund, B E, 1992 Landscape reconstruction in Southern Sweden, in Pollard 1992, 25–37

Berry, A C, & Berry, R J, 1967 Epigeneric variation in the human cranium, *J Anatomy*, 4 (2), 361–79

Biddle, M, 1975 Excavations at Winchester 1971. Tenth and final interim report, *Antiq J*, 55, 96–126, 295–337

Biddle, M, 1976 The towns, in Wilson 1976, 99–150

Biddle, M, 1990 *Artefacts from medieval Winchester. Part II Object and economy in medieval Winchester*, Winchester Studies 7, Oxford

Biddle, M, & Hill, D, 1971 Late Saxon planned towns, *Antiq J*, 51, 70–85

Binford, L R, 1983 *In pursuit of the past*, London

Binford, L R, & Bertram, J B, 1977 Bone frequencies - and attritional processes, in L R Binford (ed), *For theory building in archaeology*, Academic Press, 77–153

Bintliffe, J, & Hamerow, H, (eds), 1995 *Europe between late antiquity and the Middle Ages*, Oxford

Birss, R, 1982 The potters behind the potsherds, *Essex Archaeol News*, 78, 4–5

Blackburn, M A S, 1993 Coin finds and coin circulation in Lindsey, *c.* 600–900, in A Vince (ed), *Pre-Viking Lindsey*, Lincoln, 80–90

Blackburn, M A S, & Lyon, S, 1986 Regional die production on Cnut's *quatrefoil* issue, in M A S Blackburn (ed), *Anglo-Saxon monetary history: essays in memory of Michael Dolley*, Leicester, 223–72

Blagg, T F C, & King, A C, (eds), 1984 *Military and civilian in Roman Britain*, BAR Brit Ser 136, Oxford

Blair, J, 1988 Minster churches in the landscape, in Hooke 1988b, 35–58

Blinkhorn, P W, 1999 Of cabbages and kings: production, trade and consumption in Middle Saxon England, in M Anderton (ed), *Anglo-Saxon trading centres: beyond the emporia*, Sheffield, 4–20

Blinkhorn, P W, forthcoming, *The Ipswich ware project: ceramics, trade and society in Middle Saxon England*, Medieval Pottery Res Group Special Paper

Boardman, J, 1990 *Soil erosion in Britain: costs, attitudes and policies. Education network for environment and development*, Falmer

Boivin, N, & French, C A I, 1999 New questions and answers in the micromorphology of the occupation deposits at the Souks site, Beirut, *Berytus*, 43 (1997–98), 181–210

Bond, J M, & O'Connor, T P, 1999 *Bones from medieval deposits at 16–22 Coppergate and other sites in York*, The Archaeology of York 15/5, York

Boon, G C, 1974 Counterfeit coins in Roman Britain, in Casey & Reece 1974, 95–172

Boserup, E, 1983, The impact of scarcity and plenty on development, *J Interdisciplinary Hist*, 14, 185–209

Bourdillon, J, 1988 Countryside and town: animal resources of Anglo-Saxon Southampton, in Hooke 1988b, 177–95

Bourdillon, J, 1994 The animal provisioning of Saxon Southampton, in Rackham 1994c, 120–5

Bowman, A K, & Thomas, J D, 1994 *The Vindolanda writing-tablets (Tabulae Vindolandenses II)*, London

Boyd, P, 1981 The micropalaentology and palaeoecology of medieval estuarine sediments from the Fleet and Thames in London, in J Neale & J Brasier (eds) *Microfossils from the recent and fossil shelf seas*, Chichester, 274–92

Boyden, S, 1992 *Biohistory: The interplay between human society and the biosphere, past and present*, Man and the Biosphere Series 8, Paris

Boyden, S, Millar, K, Newcombe, B, & O'Neill, B, 1981 *The ecology of a city and its people. The case of Hong Kong*, London

Bradley, R, 1984 *The social foundations of prehistoric Britain*, London

Brain, C K, 1967 Hottentot food remains and their bearing on the interpretation of fossil animal bone assemblages, *Scientific papers of the Namib Desert Research Institute*, 32, 1–11

Branigan, K, 1987 *The Catuvellauni*, Stroud

Branigan, K, & Miles, D (eds), 1989 *The economies of Romano-British villas*, Sheffield

Brasier, M D, 1986 Excavations at 147 Lexden Road, Colchester, *Essex Archaeol Hist*, 16 (1984–1985), 145–9

Braudel, F, 1972 *The Mediterranean and the Mediterranean world in the Age of Philip II*, London and New York

Braudel, F, 1977 *Capitalism and material culture, Vol 1*, Baltimore MD

Braun, R, & Wilson M, 1970 Removal of atmospheric sulphur by building stones, *Atmosphere and Environment*, 4, 371–8

Breheny, M J (ed), 1992 *Sustainable development and urban form*, London

Brickstock, R J, 1987 *Copies of the* Fel Temp Reparatio *coinage in Britain; a study of their chronology and archaeological significance*, BAR Brit Ser 176, Oxford

Brimblecombe, P, 1982 Early urban climate and atmosphere, in Hall & Kenward 1982, 10–25

Brisbane, M, 1988 *Hamwic* Saxon Southampton: an 8th century port and production centre, in Hodges & Hobley 1988, 101–8

Britnell, R H, 1981 The proliferation of markets in England 1200–1349, *Econ Hist Rev* 2nd Ser 33, 209–21

Britnell, R H, 1995 Commercialisation and economic development in England 1000–1300, in Britnell & Campbell 1995, 7–27

Britnell, R H, 1996 *The commercialisation of English society 1000–1500* (2nd edn), Manchester/New York

Britnell, R H, 2000 Urban demand in the English economy, 1300–1600, in Galloway 2000, 1–22

Britnell, R H, & Campbell, B M S (eds), 1995 *A commercialising economy. England 1086 to c 1300*, Manchester

Brooks, H, & Bedwin, O, 1989 *Archaeology at the airport. The Stansted archaeological project 1985–1989*, Chelmsford

Brooks, H, & Wallis, S, 1991 Recent archaeological work in Great Chesterford', *Essex Archaeol Hist*, 22, 38–45

Brooks, S T, & Suchey, J M, 1990 Skeletal age determination based on the os pubis: a comparison of the Acsadi-Nemeskeri and Suchey-Brooks methods, *Human Evolution* 5, 227–38

Brothwell, D R, 1981 *Digging up bones: the excavation, treatment and study of human skeletal remains* (3rd edn), London

Brothwell, D, 1982 Linking urban man with his urban environment', in Hall & Kenward 1982, 126–9

Brothwell, D R, 1994 On the possibility of urban-rural contrasts in human population palaeobiology, in Hall & Kenward 1994, 129–36

Brothwell, D R, Dobney, K, & Ervynck, A, 1996 On the causes of perforations in archaeological domestic cattle skulls, *Int J Osteoarchaeology*, 6, 471–87

Brown, A E (ed), 1995 *Roman small towns in Eastern England and beyond*, Oxbow Monograph 52, Oxford

Brown, D H, 1997 Pots from houses, *Medieval Ceram* 21, 83–94

Brown, N, 1999 *The Archaeology of Ardleigh, Essex:*

excavations 1955–1980, East Anglian Archaeol, 90, Chelmsford

Brown, T, & Foard, G, 1998 The Saxon landscape: a regional perspective, in Everson & Williamson 1998, 67–94

Bryant, S, 1997 Iron Age, in Glazebrook 1997, 23–34

Buckley, D G (ed), 1978 *Archaeology in Essex to AD 1500*, CBA Res Rep 34, London

Buckley, D G, 1997 Introduction, in Glazebrook 1997, 1–4

Burnham, B C, & Wacher, J, 1990 *The small towns of Roman Britain*, London

Burnham, B C, Collis, J, Dobinson, C, Haselgrove, C, & Jones, M, 2001 Themes for urban research, c. 100 BC to AD 200', in James & Millett 2001, 67–76

Bush, H, & Zvelebil, M (eds) *Health in past societies. Biocultural interpretations of human skeletal remains in archaeological contexts*, BAR Int Ser 567, Oxford

Butzer, K W, 1982 *Archaeology as human ecology*, Cambridge

Cadman, G E, 1983 Raunds: an excavation summary, *Medieval Archaeol*, 27,107–22

Calvo, V R, 1995 Produccion artesanal, viticultura y propiedad rural en la Hispania Tarraconense, *Gerión*, 13, 305–34

Cambridge, E, & Rollason, D, 1995 Debate: the pastoral organization of the Anglo-Saxon Church: a review of the 'minster hypothesis', *Early Medieval Europe*, 4.1, 87–104

Campbell, B M S, 1981 Commonfield origins – the regional dimension, in T Rowley (ed), *The origins of open filed agriculture*, London, 112–30

Campbell, B M S, 1983 Arable productivity in medieval England: some evidence from Norfolk, *Journal of Economic History* 43, 379–404

Campbell, B M S, 1997 Economic rent and the intensification of English agriculture, 1086–1350, in G Astill and J Langdon (eds), *Medieval Farming and technology. The impact of agricultural change in northwest Europe*, London, 225–50

Campbell, B M S, Galloway, J A, & Murphy, M, 1992 Rural land-use in the metropolitan hinterland, 1270–1339: the evidence of Inquisitiones Post Mortem, *Agricultural Hist Rev* 40, 1–22

Campbell, B M S, Galloway, J A, Keene, D, & Murphy, M, 1993 *A medieval capital and its grain supply: agrarian production and distribution in the London region c 1300*, Hist Geog Res Ser 30, London

Campbell, G, 1994 The preliminary archaeobotanical results from Anglo-Saxon West Cotton and Raunds, in Rackham 1994c, 65–82

Carandini, A, 1980 Il vigneto e la villa del fondo di Settefinestre nel Cosano: un caso di produzione agricola per il mercato transmarino, in J H D'Arms & E C Kopff (eds), *The seaborne commerce of ancient Rome: studies in archaeology and history*, Memoirs of the American Academy at Rome 36, Rome, 1–10

Carr, R D, Tester, A, & Murphy, P, 1988 The Middle Saxon settlement at Staunch Meadow, Brandon, *Antiquity*, 62, 371–7

Carter, G A, 1998 *Excavations at the Orsett 'Cock'*

enclosure, Essex, 1976, East Anglian Archaeol 86, Chelmsford

Carter, H, 1972 The study of urban geography, London

Carus-Wilson, E M, 1944 The English cloth industry in the late 12th and early 13th century', Econ Hist Rev, 14, I, 32–50

Carver, M O H, 1985 Theory and practice in urban pottery seriation, J Archaeol Sci, 12 5, 353–66

Carver, M O H, 1987 Underneath English towns, London

Carver, M O H, 1989 Kingship and material culture in early Anglo-Saxon East Anglia, in Bassett 1989, 141–58

Carver, M O H (ed), 1992 The Age of Sutton Hoo. The seventh century in north-western Europe, Woodbridge

Carver, M O H, 1993a Arguments in stone: archaeological research and the European town in the first millennium, Oxbow Monograph 29, Oxford

Carver, M O H (ed), 1993b In search of cult: essays presented to Philip Rahtz, Woodbridge

Casey, P J, 1984 Roman coinage of the fourth century in Scotland, in R Miket & C Burgess (eds), Between and beyond the walls: essays...in honour of George Jobey, Edinburgh, 295–304

Casey, P J, 1995 Roman coins, in M O H Carver (ed), Excavations at York Minster Vol I: from Roman fortress to Norman cathedral, London, 394–413

Casey, P J, & Reece, R, (eds), 1974 Coins and the archaeologist, BAR Brit Ser 4, Oxford

Casteel, R W, 1978 Faunal assemblages and the 'weigemethode' or weight method, J Field Archaeol 5, 71–7

Castells, M, 1977 The urban question: a Marxist approach, London

Chaplin, R E, 1971 The study of animal bones from archaeological sites, New York

Charles-Edwards, T, 1972 Kinship, status and the origins of the hide, Past and Present, 56, 3–33

Cherry, J F, 1984 The emergence of the state in the prehistoric Aegean, Proc Cambridge Philological Soc, 210. 30, 18–48

Childe, V G, 1956 Piecing together the past, London

Christaller, W, 1966 Central Places in Southern Germany, (trans C W Baskin), Englewood Cliffs NJ

Christie, N, & Loseby, S T, (eds), 1996 Towns in transition. Urban evolution in late antiquity and the early Middle Ages, Aldershot

Clark, J G D, 1952 Prehistoric Europe: the economic basis, London

Clark, R H, & Schofield, A G, 1991 By experiment and calibration: an integrated approach to the archaeology of the ploughsoil, in Schofield 1991, 93–105

Clarke, C P, 1988a Late Iron Age enclosures at Kelvedon: excavations at the Doucecroft site 1985–86, Essex Archaeol History, 19, 15–39

Clarke, C P, 1988b Roman Coggeshall: excavations 1984–85, Essex Archaeol Hist, 19, 47–90

Clarke, C P, 1998, Excavations to the south of Chignall Roman villa, Essex, 1977–81, Chelmsford

Clarke, F, et al, 1998, Romano-British Settlement at Little London Chigwell, West Essex Archaeol Group

Clarke, H, & Ambrosiani, B, 1995 Towns in the Viking Age (2nd edn), London

Clarke, S, 1999 Contact, architectural symbolism and the negotiation of cultural identity in the military zone, in P Bakder, C Forcey, S Jundi, & R Witcher (eds), TRAC 1998: Proceedings of the eighth annual Theoretical Roman Archaeology Conference, Leicester 1998, Oxford, 36–45

Cleere, H, 1974 The Roman iron industry of the Weald and its connection with the Classis Britannica, Archaeol J, 131, 171–99

Clutton-Brock, J, & Grigson, C, (eds), 1984 Animals and Archaeology: 4. Husbandry in Europe, BAR Int Ser 227, Oxford

Collins, A E, 1996 Great Chesterford. The origins of a Roman civitas. Excavation and research in the Great Chesterford region 1965–1985, unpub Essex County Council report

Collis, J, Allen, J, Burnham, B, Hamerow, H, McDonnell, G, & Vince A, nd, Towns and innovation, in Urban Themes, AD 1000–1600, unpub CBA report, 7–10

Condron, F, 1997 Iron production in Leicestershire, Northamptonshire and Rutland in antiquity, Trans Leicestershire Archaeol Hist Soc, 71, 1–20

Conheeney, J, 2000 Inhumation burials, in Barber & Bowsher 2000, 277–96

Connor, A, & Robinson, B, 1997 Excavation of Anglo-Saxon settlement at High Street, Willingham, Cambs, Cambs County Council Fieldwork Summary

Cool, H E M, 1994 The quantification of Roman vessel glass assemblages, English Heritage AML report, London

Cool, H E M, Lloyd Morgan, G, & Hooley, A D, 1995 Finds from the fortress, The archaeology of York 17.10, York

Cornell, T J, & Lomas, K (eds), 1995 Urban society in Roman Italy, London

Costin, C L, 1991 Craft specialisation: issues in defining, documenting and explaining the organisation of production, Archaeol Method Theory, 3, 1–56

Countryside Commission and English Nature, 1996 The Character of England: landscape, wildlife and natural features, Cheltenham

Courtney, P, 1997a Ceramics and the history of consumption: pitfalls and prospects, Medieval Ceram 21, 95–108

Courtney, P, 1997b The tyranny of constructs: some thoughts on periodisation and culture change, in Gaimster & Stamper 1997, 9–24

Courtney, P, forthcoming Raunds and its region, in S Parry (ed), The Raunds Survey

Coutts, C M, 1991 Pottery and the emporia: imported pottery in Middle Saxon England with particular reference to Ipswich, unpub PhD thesis Univ Sheffield

Cox, M, 2000 Assessment of parturition, in Cox & Mays 2000, 131–42

Cox, M, & Mays, S, (eds), 2000 Human osteology in archaeology and forensic science, London

Crabtree, P J, 1994 Animal exploitation in East Anglian villages, in Rackham 1994c, 40–54

Crabtree, P J, 1996 Production and consumption in an

early complex society: animal use in Middle Saxon East Anglia, *World Archaeol*, 28(1), 58–75

Cramp, R J, 1969 Excavations at the Saxon monastic sites of Wearmouth and Jarrow, Co Durham; an interim report, *Medieval Archaeol*, 13, 21–66

Cramp, R J, 1976a Monastic sites, in Wilson 1976, 201–52

Cramp, R J, 1976b Analysis of the finds register and location plan of Whitby Abbey, in Wilson 1976, 453–7

Cramp, R J, & Miket, R, 1982, *Catalogue of the Anglo-Saxon and Viking antiquities in the Museum of Antiquities, Newcastle Upon Tyne*, Newcastle Upon Tyne

Creighton, J, 2000 *Coins and power in late Iron Age Britain*, Cambridge

Creighton, O, 1999 Early castles and rural settlement patterns: insights from Yorkshire and the East Midlands, *Medieval Settlement Res Group Annu Rep* 14, 29–33

Crossan, C, Smoothy, M D, & Wallace, C, 1990 Salvage recording of Iron Age and Roman remains at Ickleton Road, Great Chesterford, Essex, *Essex Archaeol Hist*, 21, 11–18

Crummy, N, 1983 *The Roman small finds from excavations in Colchester 1971–9*, Colchester Archaeol Rep 2, Colchester

Crummy, N (ed), 1987 *The coins from excavations in Colchester 1971–9*, Colchester Archaeol Rep 4, Colchester

Crummy, N, Crummy, P, & Crossan, C, 1993 *Excavations of Roman and later cemeteries, churches and monastic sites in Colchester, 1971–88*, Colchester Archaeol Rep 9, Colchester

Crummy, P, 1981 *Aspects of Anglo-Saxon and Norman Colchester*, Colchester Archaeol Rep 1, CBA Res Rep 39, London

Crummy, P, 1984 *Excavations at Lion Walk, Balkerne Lane, and Middleborough, Colchester, Essex*, Colchester Archaeol Report 3, Colchester

Crummy, P, 1992, *Excavations at Culver Street, the Gilberd School and other sites in Colchester 1971–85*, Colchester Archaeol Rep 6, Colchester

Crummy, P, 1995 Camulodunum – a review, in Hawkes & Crummy 1995, 169–70

Crummy, P, 1997, *Colchester*, Colchester

Cunliffe, B W, 1976, *Excavations at Portchester Castle II: Saxon*, London

Cunliffe, B W, 1985 Aspects of urbanization in northern Europe, in Grew & Hobley 1985, 1–5

Cunliffe, B W, 1988, *Greeks Romans and barbarians. Spheres of interaction*, London

Cunliffe, B W, 1993, *Wessex to AD 1000*, London

Cunliffe, B W & Davenport, P, 1985 *The temple of Sulis Minerva at Bath: Vol. 1, the site*, Oxford

Cunliffe, B W, & Munby, J, 1985, *Excavations at Portchester Castle. Vol. IV: medieval, the Inner Bailey*, London

Cushion, B, Davison, A, Fenner, G, Goldsmith, R, Knight, J, Virgoe, N, Wade, K, & Wade-Martins, P, 1982 Some deserted village sites in Norfolk, *East Anglian Archaeol* 14, 40–101

Daniels, R, 1988 The Anglo-Saxon monastery at Church Close, Hartlepool, Cleveland, *Archaeol J*, 145, 158–210

Dannell, G B, & Wild, J P, 1987 *Longthorpe II. The military works-depot: an episode in landscape history*, Britannia Monograph 8, London

Dark, K R, 1994 *Civitas to kingdom*, London & New York

Dark, K R, & Dark, P, 1997 *The landscape of Roman Britain*, Stroud

Darby, H C, 1951 *An historical geography of England before 1800*, Cambridge

Darby, H C, 1977 *Domesday England*, Cambridge

Darling, M J, Gurney, D A, & Green, C, 1993 *Caister-on-Sea excavations by Charles Green, 1951–55*, East Anglian Archaeol 60, Chelmsford

Darvill, T, & McWhirr, A, 1984 Brick and tile production in Roman Britain: models of economic organization, *World Archaeol*, 15.3, 239–61

Davey, P J, & Hodges, R (eds), 1983 *Medieval ceramics and trade: the production and distribution of later medieval pottery in North-West Europe*, Sheffield

Davies, J A, 1986 The Meare Heath, Somerset, hoard and the coinage of barbarous radiates, *Numis Chron*, 146, 107–18

Davies, J A, 1988 Barbarous radiates: a study of the irregular Roman coinage of the 270s/280s, unpub PhD thesis Univ Reading

Davies, J A, 1992 Barbarous radiate hoards: the interpretation of coin deposits in late third century Roman Britain, *Oxford J Archaeol*, 11.2, 211–24

Davies, J A, & Gregory, A, 1991 Coinage from a *civitas*, *Britannia*, 22, 65–102

Davis, K, 1991 Population and resources: fact and interpretation, in K Davis & M S Bernstam (eds), *Resources, environment and population: present knowledge, future options*, New York & Oxford, 1–24

Davis, S J M, 1986 *The archaeology of animals*, Batsford

Davison, A, 1988 *Six deserted villages in Norfolk*, East Anglian Archaeol 44, Chelmsford

Davison, A, 1990 *The evolution of settlement in three parishes in South-East Norfolk*, East Anglian Archaeol 49, Chelmsford

de Domingo, C, 1994 The provenance of some building stones in St Mary Spital by geological methods, *London Archaeol*, 7.9, 240–3

de Moulins, D, 1990 Environmental analysis, in C Maloney, *The Upper Walbrook Valley in the Roman period*, The Archaeology of Roman London 1, CBA Res Rep 69, London, 85–115

Dearn, M J, 1991 The economy of the Roman south Pennines, with particular reference to the lead extraction industry in its national context, unpub PhD thesis Univ Sheffield

Dickson, C A, 1987 The identification of cereals from ancient bran fragments, *Circaea*, 4, 95–102

Dobinson, C, & Denison, S, 1995 *Metal detecting and archaeology in England*, London and York

Dobney, K, & Goodman, G, 1991 Epidemiological studies of dental enamel hypoplasias in Mexico and Bradford: their relevance to archaeological skeletal studies, in Bush & Zvelebil 1991, 81–100

Dobney, K M, Jacques, S D, & Irving, B G, 1996 *Of butchers and breeds. Report on vertebrate remains from various sites in the City of Lincoln*, Lincoln Archaeological Studies 5, Lincoln

Dobney, K, Kenward, H, Ottoway, P & Donel, L, 1998 Down but not out: biological evidence for complex economic organization in Lincoln in the late 4th century, *Antiquity*, 72, 417–24

Dobney, K M & Reilly, K, 1988 A method for recording archaeological animal bones: the use of diagnostic zones, *Circaea*, 5, 79–96

DoE (Department of the Environment), 1990 Planning Policy Guidance note 16, *Archaeology and Planning*, London

DoE (Department of the Environment), 1996 *Indicators of Sustainable Development for the United Kingdom*, London

Dolley, R H M, 1976 The coins, in Wilson 1976, 349–72

Drake, J, 1990 *Castle Hill Roman Villa*, East Anglian Archaeol, Chelmsford

Draper, J, 1985 *Excavations by Mr H P Cooper on the Roman Site at Hill Farm,Gestingthorpe, Essex*, East Anglian Archaeol, 25, Chelmsford

Draper, J, 1988 Excavations at Great Chesterford, Essex, 1953–5, *Proc Cambridge Antiq Soc*, 75 (for 1986), 3–42

Drury, P J, 1972 The Romano-British settlement at Chelmsford, Essex: Caesaromagus. Preliminary report, *Essex Archaeol Hist*, 4, 3–29

Drury, P J (ed), 1976 Braintree: excavations and research, 1971–76, *Essex Archaeol Hist*, 8, 1–143

Drury, P J, 1978a *Excavations at Little Waltham, 1970–71*, CBA Res Rep 26, London

Drury, P J, 1978b The early and middle phases of the Iron Age in Essex, in Buckley 1978, 47–54

Drury, P J, 1988 *The mansio and other sites in the south-eastern sector of Caesaromagus*, Chelmsford Archaeol Trust Rep 3, and CBA Res Rep 66, Chelmsford

Drury, P J & Rodwell, W.J, 1973 Excavations at Gun Hill, West Tilbury, *Essex Archaeol Hist*, 5, 48–112

Ducos, P, 1984 La contribution de l'archéozoologie a l'éstimation des quantités de nourriture: évaluation du nombre initial d'individus, in J Clutton-Brock & C Grigson (eds.), *Animals and archaeology: 3. Early herders and their flocks*, BAR Int Ser 202, Oxford, 13–24

Dunnett, B R K, 1971 Excavations in Colchester, 1964–8, *Essex Archaeol Hist*, 3.1. 1ff

Dyer, C, 1989 *Standards of living in the later Middle Ages: social change in England c. 1200–1520*, Cambridge

Dyer, C, 1991 *Hanbury: settlement and society in a woodland landscape*, Leicester

Dyer, C, 1992 The hidden trade of the Middle Ages: evidence from the West Midlands of England, *J Hist Geogr*, 18, 141–57

Dyer, C, 1996a Market towns and the countryside in late medieval England, *Canadian J Hist*, 31, 18–34

Dyer, C, 1996b Rural settlements in medieval Warwickshire, *Birmingham Warwickshire Archaeol Soc*, 100, 117–33

Earle, T (ed), 1991 *Chiefdoms: power, economy and ideology*, Cambridge

Eastham, A, 1997 The potential of bird remains for environmental reconstruction, *Int J Osteoarchaeology* 7, 422–9

Ecclestone, J, & Havis, R, 1996 Late Iron Age and Roman occupation at Hatfield Peverel: excavations at Sandford Quarry 1994, *Essex Archaeol Hist*, 27, 13–21

Eddy, M R, 1982 *Kelvedon: the origins and development of a Roman small town*, Essex County Council Occas Pap, 3, Chelmsford

Eddy, M R, 1995 Kelvedon and the fort myth in the development of Roman small towns in Essex, in Brown 1995, 119–28

Edrei, W, 1983 The productivity of weaving in late medieval Flanders, in Harte & Ponting 1983, 108–20

Eiden, H, & Irsigler, F, 2000 Environs and hinterlands: Cologne and Nuremberg in the later Middle Ages, in Galloway 2000, 43–58

Ellis, N C, 1981 The Roman ironworks from Kelvedon, unpub BA dissertation, Univ Leicester

Engels, D W, 1990 *Roman Corinth*, Chicago

English Heritage, 1991 *Exploring our past*, London

English Heritage, 1995 *Review of the implementation of PPG 16, archaeology and planning*, unpub report

Entwhistle, J A, Abrahams, P W, & Dodgshon R A, 1998 Multi-element analysis of soils from Scottish historical sites. Interpreting land-use history through the physical and geochemical analysis of soil, *J Archaeol Sci*, 25, 53–68

Esmonde-Cleary, A S, 1989 *The ending of Roman Britain*, London

Essex County Council (A Garwood), 1996 Roman Great Chesterford. Gazetteer of unpublished sites, unpub Essex County Council report

Evans, J, 1985 Aspects of later Roman pottery assemblages in Northern Britain, unpub PhD thesis, Univ Bradford

Evans, J, 1988 All Yorkshire is divided into three parts; social aspects of later Roman pottery distribution in Yorkshire, in J Price and P R Wilson (eds), *Recent research in Roman Yorkshire*, BAR Brit Ser 193, Oxford, 323–38

Evans, J, 1990 From the end of Roman Britain to the 'Celtic west', *Oxford J Archaeol*, 9, 91–103

Evans, J, 1993 Pottery function and finewares in the Roman north, *J Roman Pottery Stud*, 6, 95–118

Evans, J, 1995 Roman finds assemblages, towards an integrated approach?, in P Rush (ed), *Theoretical Roman Archaeology Conference*, 33–58

Evans, J, 2001 Material approaches to the identification of different Romano-British site types, in James & Millett 2001, 26–35

Evans, J and Millett, M, 1992 Residuality revisited, *Oxford J Archaeol*, 11.2, 225–4

Everson, P, & Williamson, T, (eds), 1998 *The archaeology of landscape: studies presented to Christopher Taylor*, Manchester

Fairclough, G, Lambrick, G, & McNab, A (eds), 1999 *Yesterday's world, tomorrow's landscape. The English*

Heritage historic landscape project 1992–94, London

Farwell, D E and Molleson, T I, 1993 *Poundbury, vol 2: the cemeteries*, Dorset Natur Hist Archaeol Soc Monograph 11, Dorchester

Faulkner, N, 1994 Later Roman Colchester, *Oxford J Archaeol*, 13, 93–120

Faull, M L, 1984 *Studies in late Anglo-Saxon settlement*, Oxford

Fawn, A J, Evans, K A, McMaster, I, & Davies, G M R, 1990 *The Red Hills of Essex. Salt-making in antiquity*, Colchester

Fenwick, V, 1984 *Insula de Burgh*: Excavations at Burrow Hill, Butley, Suffolk, 1978–1981, in S Chadwick Hawkes, J Campbell, & D Brown, *Anglo-Saxon Stud Archaeol Hist*, 3, 35–54

Ferembach, D, Schideztsky, I, & Stloutkal, M, 1980 Recommendations for age and sex diagnosis of skeletons, *J Human Evolution*, 9, 517–49

Fieller, N R J, & Turner, A, 1982 Number estimation in vertebrate samples, *J Archaeol Sci*, 9, 49–62

Finch, J, 2000 *Church monuments in Norfolk before 1850: an archaeology of commemoration*, BAR Brit Ser 317, Oxford

Finley, M I, 1985 *The ancient economy* (2nd edn), London

Finnegan, M, 1978 Non-metric variation of the infracranial skeleton, *J Anatomy*, 125 (1), 23–37

Fletcher, R, 1995 *Limits to settlement growth*, Cambridge

Fletcher, R, 1999 Appraising the urban future: an archaeological time perspective, in T Murray (ed) *Time and archaeology*, London & New York, 88–108

Foster, J, 1986 *The Lexden tumulus: a re-appraisal of an Iron Age burial from Colchester, Essex*, BAR Brit Ser 156, Oxford

Fox, R L, 1996 Ancient hunting: from Homer to Polybius, in Shipley & Salmon 1996, 119–53

France, N E, & Gobel, B M, 1985 The Romano-British temple at Harlow, Essex, unpub West Essex Archaeological Group report

Frayn, J M, 1993 *Markets and fairs in Roman Italy*, Oxford

Frend, W.H C, 1992 Pagans, Christians, and 'the Barbarian Conspiracy' of AD 367 in Roman Britain, *Britannia*, 23, 121–31

Frere, S S, 1983 *Verulamium excavations 2*, Rep Res Comm Soc Antiq London, 41, London

Frere, S S, 1987 *Britannia: a history of Roman Britain* (3rd edn), London

Fulford, M G, 1975, *New Forest Roman pottery*, BAR Brit Ser 17, Oxford

Fulford, M G, 1982 Town and country in Roman Britain – a parasitical relationship?, in D Miles (ed), *The Romano-British Countryside: Studies in Rural Settlement and Economy*, BAR Brit Ser 103, Oxford, 403–19

Fulford, M G, & Huddleston, K, 1991 *The current state of Romano-British pottery studies. A review for English Heritage*, English Heritage Occas Pap, 1, London

Fulford, M G, & Timby, J, 2000 *Silchester: excavations on the site of the forum-basilica, 1977, 1980–86*, Britannia Monograph 15, London

Gaffney, V, White, R H, & Buteux, S T E, forthcoming *Wroxeter, the Cornovii, and the urban process. Final report on the work of the Wroxeter Hinterland Project and Wroxeter Hinterlands Survey, 1994–1999*

Gaimster, D, & Stamper, P (eds), 1997 *The age of transition: the archaeology of English culture 1400–1600*, Soc Medieval Archaeol Monograph, 15; Oxbow Monograph 98

Galloway, J A (ed), 2000 *Trade, urban hinterlands and market integration c. 1300–1600*, Centre for Metropolitan History Working Papers Series 3, London

Galloway, J A, Keene, D, & Murphy, M, 1996 Fuelling the city: production and distribution of firewood and fuel in London's region, 1290–1300, *Econ Hist Rev*, 49.3, 449–72

Gautier, A, 1984 'How do I count you, let me count the ways?', in Clutton-Brock & Grigson 1984, 237–52

Geake, H M, 1997 *The use of grave goods in conversion-period England, c. 600–c. 850*, BAR Brit Ser 261, Oxford

Gilbert, A S, & Singer, B H, 1982 Re-assessing zooarchaeological quantification, *World Archaeol*, 14, 21–40

Gilbert, O L, 1991 *The ecology of urban habitats* (2nd edn), London

Gilchrist, R, & Morris, R K, 1993 Monasteries as settlements: religion, society and economy AD 600–1050, in Carver 1993b, 113–18

Gillingham, J, 1984 The early middle ages (1066–1290), in J Gillingham & R A Griffiths, *The Middle Ages*, Oxford, 1–72

Gimpel, J, 1976 *The medieval machine; the industrial revolution of the Middle Ages*, New York

Glasscock, R E (ed), 1975 *The lay subsidy of 1334*, London

Glazebrook, J (ed), 1997 *Research and archaeology: a framework for the eastern counties, 1. Resource assessment*, East Anglian Archaeol Occas Pap, 3, Norwich

Going, C J, 1987 *The mansio and other sites in the south-eastern sector of Caesaromagus: the Roman pottery*, CBA Res Rep 62, London

Going, C J, 1992 Economic 'long waves' in the Roman period? A reconnaissance of the Romano-British ceramic evidence, *Oxford J Archaeol*, 111, 93–117

Going, C J, 1997 Roman, in Glazebrook 1997, 35–46

Goldberg, P J P, 1992 *Women, work and life cycle in a medieval economy. Women in York and Yorkshire c. 1300–1520*, Oxford

Goodburn, D, 1992 Woods and woodland: carpenters and carpentry, in G Milne (ed), *Timber building technique in London c. 900–1400*, London & Middlesex Archaeol Soc Spec Pap, 15, 106–31

Goodburn, D, 1994 Trees underground: new insights into trees and woodmanship in south east England AD 800–1300, *Botanical J Scotland*, 46.4, 658–62

Goodburn, D, 1995 From tree to town, in T Brigham, D Goodburn, & I Tyers, with J Dillon, A Roman timber building on the Southwark waterfront, London, *Archaeol J*, 152, 33–59

Grant, A, 1982 The use of tooth wear as a guide to the age of domestic ungulates, in Wilson *et al* 1982, 91–108

Grant, A, 1984 Animal husbandry, in B Cunliffe, *Danebury, an Iron Age Hillfort in Hampshire*, CBA Res Rep 52, 496–548

Grant, A, 1989 Animal bones in Roman Britain, in Todd 1989b, 135–46

Grant, E (ed), 1986 *Central places, archaeology and history*, Sheffield

Grauer, A, 1991 Patterns of life and death: the palaeodemography of medieval York, in Bush & Zvelebil 1991, 67–80

Grayson, D K, 1984 *Quantitative zooarchaeology*, London

Green, F J, 1982 Problems of interpreting differentially preserved plant remains from excavations of medieval urban sites, in Hall & Kenward 1982, 40–6

Green, F J, & Lockyear, G, 1994 Seeds, sherds and samples: site formation processes at the Waitrose site, Romsey, in Luff & Rowley-Conwy 1994, 91–104

Gregson, D, 1989 The villa as private property, in Branigan & Miles 1989, 21–33

Greig, J R A, 1982 The interpretation of pollen spectra from urban archaeological deposits, in Hall & Kenward 1982, 47–65

Greig, J R A, 1988 Traditional cornfield weeds – where are they now?, *Plants Today*, Nov-Dec 1988, 183–91

Grew, F, & Hobley, B (eds), 1985 *Roman urban topography in Britain and the Western Empire*, CBA Res Rep 59, London

Griffiths, K E, 1989 Marketing of Roman pottery in second-century Northamptonshire and the Milton Keynes area', *J Roman Pottery Stud*, 2, 66–76

Groenman-van Waateringe, W, 1982 The menu of different classes in Dutch medieval society, in Hall & Kenward 1982, 147–69

Guest, P, 1998 Discussion of the distribution of the coins in and around the town, in N Holbrook (ed), *Cirencester: the Roman town defences, public buildings and shops*, Cirencester Excavations 5, 262–8

Hall, A R, & Tomlinson, P, 1997 *The environmental archaeology database bibliography*, English Heritage AM Lab Report 6/96, London

Hall, A R, & Kenward, H K (eds), 1982 *Environmental archaeology in the urban context*, CBA Res Rep 43, London

Hall, A R, & Kenward, H K, (eds), 1994 *Urban-rural connexions: perspectives from environmental archaeology*, Oxbow Monograph 47, Oxford

Hall, D H, & Coles, J M, 1994 *Fenland survey: an essay in landscape and persistence*, London

Hall, D N, 1988 The late Saxon countryside: villages and their fields, in Hooke 1988b, 99–122

Hall, P (ed), 1966 *Von Thünen's Isolated State: an English edition of Der Isolierte Staat by Johann Heinrich von Thünen* (trans C M Wartenburg), London

Hall, R A, & Whyman, M C, 1996 Settlement and monasticism at Ripon, North Yorkshire in the seventh to eleventh centuries, *Medieval Archaeol*, 40, 62–150

Hally, D J, 1983 Use alteration of pottery vessel surfaces: an important source of evidence in the identification of vessel function, *North American Archaeol*, 4, 3–26

Halstead, P, Hodder, I, & Jones, G, 1978 Behavioural archaeology and refuse patterns: a case study, *Norwegian Archaeol Rev*, 11.2, 118–31

Hamerow, H, 1991 Settlement mobility and the 'Middle Saxon Shift': rural settlements and settlement patterns in Anglo-Saxon England, *Anglo-Saxon England*, 20, 1–17

Hamerow, H, 1993 *Excavations at Mucking. Vol 2. The Anglo-Saxon settlement*, London

Hammerson, M, 1980 Romano-British copies of the coinage of AD 330–341, unpub M Phil thesis, Univ London

Hanson, W S, 1997 Forces of change and methods of control', in Mattingly 1997b, 67–80

Harries, J, 1992 Christianity and the city in Gaul, in J Rich (ed), *The City in late Antiquity*, London, 77–98

Harris, A, 1989 Late 11th and 12th century church architecture of the Lower Yare Valley, Norfolk', unpub M Phil dissertation, Univ East Anglia

Harris, W V, 1999 Demography, geography and the sources of Roman slaves, *J Roman Stud*, 89, 62–75

Hart, C, 1992 *The Danelaw*, London

Harte, N B, & Ponting, K G, (eds), 1983 *Cloth and clothing in medieval Europe*, London

Harvey, D, 1988 *Social justice and the city*, Oxford

Haselgrove, C C, 1982 Wealth, prestige and power: the dynamics of Late Iron Age political centralisation in south-east England, in Renfrew & Shennan 1982, 79–88

Haselgrove, C C, 1987 *Iron Age coinage in south-east England: the archaeological context*, BAR Brit Ser 174, Oxford

Haslam, J, 1980 A middle Saxon iron-smelting site at Ramsbury, Wilts, *Medieval Archaeol*, 24, 1–68

Havis, R, 1993 Roman Braintree: excavations 1984–1990, *Essex Archaeol Hist*, 24, 22–68

Hawkes, C F C, & Crummy, P, 1995 *Camulodunum 2. The Iron Age dykes*, Colchester Archaeol Rep, 11, Colchester

Hawkes, C F C, & Hull, M R, 1947 *Camulodunum. First report on the excavations at Colchester 1930–1939*, London

Hayes, P P, 1988 Roman to Saxon in the South Lincolnshire fens, *Antiquity*, 62, 321–6

Hayes, P P, 1991 Models for the distribution of pottery around former agricultural settlements, in Schofield 1991, 81–93

Heidinga, H A, 1987 *Medieval settlement and economy north of the Lower Rhine*, Assen/Maastricht

Heighway, C M, (ed), 1972 *The erosion of history*, London

Hendy, M F, 1988 From public to private: the western barbarian coinages as a mirror of the disintegration of late Roman state structures, *Viator* 19, 29–78

Heron, C & Pollard, A M, 1987 The analysis of natural resinous material from Roman amphorae, in E A Slater & J O Tate (eds), *Science and Archaeology*, BAR Brit Ser 196, Oxford, 429–47

Hertfordshire County Council, 1997 An archaeology strategy for Hertfordshire, unpublished Hertfordshire County Council (Environment Department) report

Hesse, B, & Wapnish, P, 1985 *Animal bone archaeology*, Washington

Hey, G 1997 Recent radiocarbon results and the final phasing of the Yarnton Saxon site, unpub Oxford Archaeol Unit report

Higham, N J, 1992 *Rome, Britain and the Anglo-Saxons*, London

Hill, C, Millett, M, & Blagg T, 1980 *The Roman riverside wall and monumental arch in London*, London & Middlesex Archaeol Soc Spec Pap, 3, London

Hill, J D, 2001 Romanisation, gender and class: recent approaches to identity in Britain and their possible consequences, in James & Millett 2001, 12–18

Hillier, B, & Hanson, J, 1984 *The social logic of space*, Cambridge

Hillman, G, 1981 Reconstructing crop husbandry practices from charred remains of crops, in Mercer 1981, 123–62

Hillson, S, 1996 *Dental anthropology*, Cambridge

Hilton, R H, 1966 *A medieval society: the west midlands at the end of the thirteenth century*, Cambridge

Hilton, R H, 1984 Small town society in England before the Black Death', *Past and Present*, 105, 53–78

Hilton, R H, 1992 *English and French towns in feudal society: a comparative study*, Cambridge University Press, Cambridge

Hines, J, 1984 *The Scandinavian character of Anglian England in the pre-Viking period*, BAR Brit Ser 124, Oxford

Hines, J, 1994 The becoming of the English: identity, material culture and language in early Anglo-Saxon England', in W Filmer-Sankey & D Griffiths (eds), *Anglo-Saxon Stud Archaeol History* 7, 49–60

Hingley, R, 1989 *Rural settlement in Roman Britain*, London

Hingley, R, 1997 Resistance and domination: social change in Roman Britain, in Mattingly 1997b, 81–102

Hinton, D A, 1986 Coins and commercial centres in Anglo-Saxon England, in M A S Blackburn (ed), *Anglo-Saxon monetary history*, Leicester, 11–26

Hinton, D A, 1996 *Southampton finds 2: the gold, silver and other non-ferrous alloy objects from Hamwic*, Stroud

Hobley, A S, 1995 An examination of Roman bronze coin distributions in the western Empire, unpub PhD thesis, Univ London

Hodder, I (ed), 1989 *The meanings of things*, London

Hodder, I, 1999 *The archaeological process: an introduction*, Malden

Hodder, I, 1979 Pottery distribution; service and tribal areas, in Millett 1979b, 7–24

Hodder, I, 1982 *Wendens Ambo. The excavation of an Iron Age and Romano-British settlement*, The archaeology of the M11, vol 2, Passmore Edwards Museum, London

Hodder, I, & Millett, M, 1980 Romano-British villas and towns: a systematic analysis, *World Archaeol*, 12, 69–76

Hodder, M, 1988 The development of some aspects of settlement and land use in Sutton Chase, unpub PhD thesis, Univ Birmingham

Hodges, R, 1981 *The Hamwih pottery: the local and imported wares from 30 years' excavations at Middle Saxon Southampton and their European context*, CBA Res Rep 37, London

Hodges, R, 1989 *Dark age economics* (2nd edn), London

Hodges, R, 1996 Dream cities: emporia and the end of the Dark Ages, in Christie & Loseby 1996, 289–305

Hodges, R, & Hobley, B, 1988 *The rebirth of towns in the west, AD 700 – 1050*, CBA Res Rep 68, London

Hodges, R, & Whitehouse, D, 1983 *Mohammed, Charlemagne and the origins of Europe: archaeology and the Pirenne thesis*, London

Hohenberg, P M, & Lees, L H, 1985 *The making of urban Europe 1000–1950*, Cambridge, Mass, and London

Holderness, J, 1994 Farming regions, in P Wade-Martins & J Everett (eds) *An historical atlas of Norfolk* (2nd edn), Hunstanton, 102–3

Holmes, J M, 1981 Report on the animal bones from the resonance chambers of the Whitefriars Church, Coventry, in C Woodfield Finds from the Free Grammar School at the Whitefriars, Coventry c. 1545–c. 1557/58, *Post-Medieval Archaeol*, 15, 81–159

Holt, R, & Rosser, G, 1990 *The medieval town: a reader in English urban history*, London & New York

Hood, C (ed), 1938 *The chorography of Norfolk: an historicall and chorographicall description of Norfolck*, Norwich

Hooke, D, 1985a Village development in the West Midlands, in Hooke 1985b, 125–54

Hooke, D, 1985b *Medieval Villages: a review of current work*, Oxford Univ Comm Archaeol Monogr, 5, Oxford

Hooke, D, 1988a Regional variation in southern and central England in the Anglo-Saxon period and its relationship to land units and settlement, in Hooke 1988b, 123–51

Hooke, D, 1988b *Anglo Saxon settlements*, London

Hooke, D, 1996 Reconstructing Anglo-Saxon landscapes in Warwickshire, *Birmingham Warwickshire Archaeol Soc*, 100, 99–117

Hooke, D, & Burnell, S (eds), 1995 *Landscape and settlement in Britain, AD 400–1066*, Exeter

Hope-Taylor, B, 1977 *Yeavering. An Anglo-British centre of early Northumbria*, London

Hopkins, K, 1978 Economic growth and towns in classical antiquity, in Abrams & Wrigley 1978, 35–79

Hopkins, K, 1980 Taxes and trade in the Roman Empire, *J Roman Stud*, 70, 101–25

Howgego, C, 1994 Coin circulation and the integration of the Roman economy, *J Roman Archaeol*, 7, 5–21

Huggins, P J, 1978 Excavation of a Belgic and Romano-British farm with Middle Saxon cemetery and churches at Nazeingbury, Essex, 1975–6, *Essex Archaeol Hist*, 10, 29–117

Hunn, J, 1995 The Romano-British landscape of the Chiltern dipslope. A study of settlement around Verulamium, in R Holgate (ed), *Chiltern archaeology – recent work: A handbook for the next decade*, Dunstable, 76–91

Hunt, J, 1997 *Lordship and the landscape: a documentary and archaeological study of the Honor of Dudley*, *c.1066–1322*, BAR Brit Ser 264, Oxford

Huntley, J P, & Stallibras, S, 1995 *Plant and vertebrate remains from archaeological sites in Northern England*, Architect Archaeol Soc Durham Northumberland Res Rep, 4, 48–9

Hurst, H, 1999 (ed) *The coloniae of Roman Britain: new studies and a review*, J Roman Archaeol Monogr Ser, 36

Hurst, H R, & Roskams, S P, 1984 *Excavations at Carthage: the British mission, v*ol 1, Sheffield

Ijzereef, F G, 1989 Social differentiation from animal bone studies, in Serjeantson & Waldron 1989, 41–54

Instone, E, 1996 MPP stone quarrying industry: step 1 report, unpub Lancaster Univ Archaeol Unit report

IoH: Institute of Hydrology, 1997 *Hydrological data UK 1996 yearbook*, Wallingford

Isserlin, R M J, 1995 Roman Coggeshall II: excavations at 'The Lawns', 1989–93, *Essex Archaeol Hist*, 26, 82–104

James, S, 2001 Soldiers and civilians: identity and interaction in Roman Britain, in James & Millett 2001, 77–89

James, S, & Millett, M, (eds), 2001 *Britons and Romans: advancing an archaeological agenda*, CBA Res Rep 125, York.

Jennings, S, 1981 *Eighteen centuries of pottery from Norwich*, East Anglian Archaeol, 13, Norwich

John, E, 1960 *Land tenure in early England: a discussion of some problems*, Leicester

John, T (ed), 1981 *Medieval Coventry: a city divided?*, Coventry

Johns, C, & Bland, R, 1994 The Hoxne late Roman treasure, *Britannia*, 25, 165–74

Johnson, M, 1993 The Saxon monastery at Whitby: past, present and future, in Carver 1993b, 85–9

Johnson, M, 1996 *An archaeology of capitalism*, Oxford

Johnson, S, 1983 *Burgh Castle: excavations by Charles Green, 1958–61*, East Anglian Archaeol, 20, Chelmsford

Jones, A K G, 1988 Provisional notes on fish remains from archaeological deposits at York, in P J Murphy & C A I French (eds), *The exploitation of wetlands*, BAR Int Ser 186, Oxford, 113–27

Jones, B & Mattingly, D, 1990 *Atlas of Roman Britain*, London

Jones, M K, 1981 The development of crop husbandry', in M K Jones & G Dimbleby (eds), *The environment of man: the Iron Age to the Anglo-Saxon period*, BAR Brit Ser 87, Oxford, 95–127

Jones, M K, 1988 The phytosociology of early arable weed communities, with special reference to southern Britain, in *Festschrift: Udelgard Korber-Grohne. Der prahistorische Mensch und sein Umwelt*, Stuttgart, 43–51

Jones, M K, 1989 Agriculture in Roman Britain: the dynamics of change, in Todd 1989b, 127–34

Jones, M K, 1992 Food remains, food webs and ecosystems, in Pollard 1992, 209–219

Jones, M U, 1973 An ancient landscape palimpsest at Mucking, *Essex Archaeol Hist*, 5, 6–12

Jones, M U, & Rodwell, W J, 1973 The Romano-British

pottery kilns at Mucking, *Essex Archaeol Hist, 5*, 13–47

Jones, R T, Sly, J, Simpson, D, Rackham, J, & Locker, A, 1986 The terrestrial vertebrate remains from excavations at the Castle, Barnard Castle, English Heritage AM Lab Rep

Jones, S, 1994 Archaeology and ethnicity: constructing identities in the past and the present', unpub PhD thesis, Univ Southampton

Jones, S, 1997 *The archaeology of ethnicity*, London

Jope, E M, 1964 The Saxon building-stone industry in Southern and Midland England, *Medieval Archaeo*, 8, 91–118

Joplin, J, & Girardet, H, 1996 *Creating a sustainable London*, London

Juggins, S, 1988 A diatom/salinity transfer function for the Thames Estuary and its application to waterfront archaeology, unpub PhD thesis, Univ London

Keene, D, 1982 Rubbish in medieval towns, in Hall & Kenward 1982, 26–30

Keene, D, 1995 London in the early Middle Ages 600–1300, *London J*, 20.2, 9–21

Kelly J, & Thornton, I, 1996 Urban geochemistry: a study of the influence of anthropogenic activity on the heavy metal content of soils in traditionally industrial and non-industrial areas of Britain, *Applied Geochemstry*, 11, 363–70

Kemble, J, 2001 *Prehistoric and Roman Essex*, Stroud

Kemp, R L, 1996 *Anglian settlement at 46–54 Fishergate*, The Archaeology of York 7/1, York

Kennedy, K A R, 1998 Markers of occupational stress: conspectus and prognosis of research, *Int J Osteoarchaeology*, 8, 305–10

Kenward, H K, 1978 *The analysis of archaeological insect assemblages: a new approach*, The Archaeology of York 19/1, York

Kenward, H K, & Allison, E P, 1994a A preliminary view of the insect assemblages from the early Christian rath site at Deer Park Farms, Northern Ireland, in Rackham 1994c, 89–107

Kenward, H K, & Allison, E P, 1994b Rural origins of the urban insect fauna, in Hall & Kenward 1994, 55–77

Kenward, H K, & Hall, A R, 1995 *Biological evidence from 16–22 Coppergate*, The Archaeology of York 14/7, York

Kenward, H K, & Williams D, 1979 *Biological evidence from the Roman warehouses in Coney Street*, The Archaeology of York 14/2, York

Kenyon, R F E, 1993 The copying of bronze coins of Claudius I in Roman Britain, unpub PhD thesis, Univ London

King, A C, 1984 Animal bones and the dietary identity of military and civilian groups in Roman Britain, Germany and Gaul', in Blagg and King 1984, 187–218

King, A C, 1989 Villas and animal bones, in Branigan and Miles 1989, 5–9

King, A C, 1991 Food production and consumption – meat, in R F J Jones (ed), *Roman Britain: recent trends*, Sheffield, 15–20

Kipling, R, 1994 Winchester and Wessex, unpub PhD dissertation, Univ Leicester

Klein, R G, and Cruz-Uribe, K, 1984 *The analysis of animal bones from archaeological sites*, Chicago

Krantz, G S, 1968 A new method of counting mammal bones, *American J Archaeol*, 72, 286–8

Kubasiewicz, M, 1956 O metodyce badan wykipaliskowych szczatkow kostnych sqierzecych, *Materialy Zachodnio-Pomorskie*, 235–44

LaMotta, V M, and Schiffer, M B, 1999 Formation processes of household floor assemblages, in P M Allison (ed), *The archaeology of household activities*, Routledge, 19–29

Lambrick, G, 1992 The development of late prehistoric and Roman farming on the Thames gravels, in M G Fulford and E Nichols (eds) *Developing landscapes of Lowland Britain. The archaeology of the British gravels: a review*, London, 78–106

Langdon, J, 1995 City and countryside in medieval England, *Econ Hist Rev*, 43.1, 67–72

Lapidary Working Party, 1987 *Recording worked stones: a practical guide*, London

Laurence, R, 1994 *Roman Pompeii: space and society*, London

Lauwerier, R C G M, 1988 *Animals in Roman times in the Dutch Eastern River area*, Nederlandse Oudheden 12 – Project Oostelijk Rivierengebeid 1, Amersfoort

Lavender, N J, 1993 A 'principia' at Boreham, near Chelmsford, Essex: excavations 1990, *Essex Archaeol Hist*, 24, 1–21

Lavender, N J, 1996 A Roman site at the New Source Works, Castle Hedingham: excavations 1992, *Essex Archaeol Hist*, 27, 22–34

Lawson, A, 1983 *The archaeology of Witton, near North Walsham*, East Anglian Archaeol, 18, Chelmsford

Leahy, K, forthcoming Middle Anglo-Saxon metalwork from South Newbald and the 'productive site' phenomenon in Yorkshire

Legge, A J, 1981 Aspects of cattle husbandry, in Mercer 1981, 169–81

Levitan, B, 1993 The animal bones, in A Woodward and P Leach, *The Uley Shrines: excavation of a ritual complex on West Hill, Uley, Gloucestershire: 1978–79*, English Heritage Archaeol Rep, 17, London, 257–301

Lewis, C, Mitchell-Fox, P, & Dyer, C, 1997 *Village, hamlet and field; changing medieval settlements in central England*, Manchester

Lewis, M, & Roberts, C, 1997 Growing pains: the interpretation of stress indicators, *Int J Osteoarchaeology*, 7, 581–6

LGMB: Local Government Management Board, 1996 *Habitat II: a position statement by UK local government*, Luton

Liddiard, R, 1999 The distribution of ridge and furrow in East Anglia: ploughing practice and subsequent land use, *Agr Hist Rev*, 47, 1–6

Liddiard, R, 2000 Population density and Norman castle building: some evidence from East Anglia, *Landscape Hist*, 22, 37–46

Lie, R W, 1980 Minimum number of individuals from osteological samples, *Norwegian Archaeol Rev*, 13, 24–30

Lilley, K D, 1994a A Warwickshire medieval borough: Brinklow and the contribution of town-plan analysis, *Birmingham Warwickshire Archaeol Society*, 98 (for 1993–94), 51–60

Lilley, K D, 1994b Coventry's topographical development: the impact of the priory, in G Demidowicz (ed), *Coventry's first cathedral papers from the 1993 anniversary symposium*, Stamford, 72–96

Lilley, K D, 1995 Medieval Coventry: a study in town-plan analysis, unpub PhD thesis, Univ Birmingham

Lloyd, T H, 1977 *The English wool trade in the Middle Ages*, Cambridge

Loughlin, N, 1977 Dales ware: a contribution to the study of Roman coarse pottery, in D P S Peacock (ed), *Pottery and early commerce: characterisation and trade in Roman and later ceramics*, London, 85–146

Loveluck, C P 1997 Flixborough – the character and economy of a high status Middle Saxon settlement in northern England, unpub paper delivered to the conference *Medieval Europe 1997, Brugge*

Loveluck, C P, 2001 Wealth, waste and conspicuous consumption. Flixborough and its importance for Middle and Late Saxon rural settlement studies, in H Hamerow & A MacGregor (eds), *Image and power in the archaeology of early medieval Britain*, Oxford, 79–130

Luff, R, 1982 *A zooarchaeological study of the Roman north-western provinces*, BAR Int Ser 137, Oxford

Luff, R, 1993, *Animal bones from excavations in Colchester, 197–85*, Colchester

Luff, R, 1998 The faunal remains, in Clarke 1998, 122–4

Luff, R, & Rowley-Conwy, P, (eds), 1994 *Whither environmental archaeology?* Oxbow monograph 38, Oxford

Lyman, R L, 1994 *Vertebrate taphonomy*, Cambridge

Lyne, M A B, & Jefferies, R S, 1979 *The Alice Holt/Farnham Roman pottery industry*, CBA Res Rep 30, London

MacFarlane, A, 1978 *The origins of English individualism*, Oxford

Mackreth, D F, 1987 Roman public buildings, in J Schofield & R Leech (eds), *Urban archaeology in Britain*, CBA Res Rep 61, London, 133–46

Macphail, R I, 1994 The reworking of urban stratigraphy by human and natural processes, in Hall & Kenward 1994, 13–44

Mainman, A J, 1993 *Pottery from 46–54 Fishergate*, The Archaeology of York 16/6, York

Maloney, J, 1983 Recent work on London's defences, in J Maloney & B Hobley (eds), *Roman urban defences in the west*, CBA Res Rep 51, London, 96–117

Maltby, J M, 1982 The variability of faunal samples and their effects on ageing data, in Wilson *et al* 1982, 81–90

Maltby, J M, 1984 Animal bones and the Romano-British economy, in Clutton-Brock & Grigson 1984, 125–38

Maltby, J M, 1989 Urban-rural variations in the butchering of cattle in Romano-British Hampshire, in Serjeantson & Waldron 1989, 75–106

Maltby, J M, 1994 The meat supply in Roman Dorchester and Winchester, in Hall & Kenward 1994, 85–102

Manley, G, 1974 Central England temperatures: monthly

means 1659–1973, *Quarterly J Royal Meteorological Soc*, 100, 289–405

Margeson, S, 1993 *Norwich households: the medieval and post-medieval finds from Norwich Survey Excavations 1971–1978*, East Anglian Archaeol, 58, Chelmsford

Martin, E, 1988 Burgh: the Iron Age and Roman earthwork, *East Anglian Archaeol*, 40, Chelmsford

Martin, T S, 1996 A group of finds from the vicinity of the 'Noah's Ark' Roman villa at Brightlingsea, Essex; *Essex Archaeol Hist*, 27, 311–19

Martin, T S, 2000 The late Iron Age and Roman pottery, in M Medlycott Prehistoric, Roman and post-medieval material from Harlow *Essex Archaeol Hist*, 27, 311–19

Martin, T S, & Wallace, C R, nd, Roman pottery and the historic towns of Essex', unpub report Essex County Council Archaeol unit

Masschaele, J, 1994 The multiplicity of medieval markets reconsidered, *J Hist Geog*, 20, 255–71

Masschaele, J, 1997 *Peasants, merchants and markets: inland trade in medieval England 1150–1350*, New York

Mather, A S, & Chapman, K, 1995 *Environmental resources*, Harlow

Mattingly, D J, 1988 Oil export? A comparison of Libyan, Spanish and Tunisian olive-oil production in the Roman Empire, *J Roman Archaeol*, 1, 33–56

Mattingly, D J, 1997a Beyond belief? Drawing a line beneath the consumer city, in Parkins 1997, 210–18

Mattingly, D J (ed), 1997b *Dialogues in Roman imperialism. Power, discourse, and discrepant experience in the Roman Empire*, J Roman Archaeol Supp, 23, Portsmouth, Rhode Island

Mattingly, H B, & Dolby, M J, 1982 The Sprotborough hoard, *Numis Chron*, 144, 21–33

Mays, S A, 1991 The medieval Blackfriars from the Blackfriars friary, Ipswich, Suffolk (excavated 1983–1985), English Heritage AM Lab Rep, 16/91

Mays, S A, 1997 A perspective on human osteoarchaeology in Britain, *Int J Osteoarchaeology*, 7, 600–4

Mays, S A, 1998 *The archaeology of human bones*, London & New York

Mays, S A, 2000a Biodistance studies using craniometric variation in British archaeological skeletal material, in Cox & Mays 2000, 277–88

Mays, S A, 2000b New directions in the analysis of stable isotopes in excavated bones and teeth, in Cox & Mays 2000, 425–38

Mays, S A, & Cox, M, 2000 Sex determination in skeletal remains, in Cox & Mays 2000, 117–30

McAdam, E, Swain, H, & Tomber, R, 2000 Research priorities for London archaeology AD 2000, unpub Museum of London report

McCarthy, M R, & Brooks, C M, 1988, *Medieval pottery in Britain, AD 900–1600*, Leicester

McCormick, F, 1983 Dairying and beef production in early Christian Ireland: the faunal evidence, in T Reeves-Smyth & F Hammond (eds), *Landscape archaeology in Ireland*, BAR Brit Ser 116, Oxford, 253–67

McIntosh, M K, 1986 *Autonomy and community: the royal manor of Havering, 1200–1500*, Cambridge

McKern, T W, & Stewart, T D, 1957 *Skeletal age changes in young American males*, Technical Rep Headquarters Quatermaster Research and Development Command, Natwick, Massachusetts

McKinley, J I, 2000 Cremation burials, in Barber & Bowsher 2000, 264–76

McWhirr, A, 1986 *Houses in Roman Cirencester*, Cirencester Excavations, 3, Gloucester

Meadows, K, Lemke, C, & Heron, J, (eds), 1996 *TRAC 96 Proc Sixth Annual Theoretical Archaeology Conference Sheffield 1996*, Oxford

Meadows, R H, 1980 Animal bones: problems for the archaeologist together with some possible solutions, *Paleorient* 6, 65–77

Medlycott, M, 1994 Iron Age and Roman material from Birchanger, near Bishops Stortford: excavations at Woodside industrial park, *Essex Archaeol Hist* 25, 28–45

Meheux, K, 1994 The pattern of villas in the Severn Valley: illusion and change, *the Inst Archaeol Pap*, 5, 71–101

Meindl, R S, & Lovejoy, C O, 1985 Ectocranial suture closure: a revised method for the determination of skeletal age at death based on the lateral anterior sutures, *American J Physical Anthropol*, 68, 57–66

Mellor, M, 1994 *Mediæval ceramic studies in England. A review for English Heritage*, London

Mercer, R (ed), 1981 *Farming practice in British prehistory*, Edinburgh University Press

Merrifield, R, 1983 *London, city of the Romans*, London

Metcalf, D M, 1974 Monetary expansion and recession: interpreting the distribution patterns of 7th and 8th century coins, in Casey & Reece 1974, 230–53

Metcalf, D M, 1980 Continuity and change in English monetary history, *c.* 973 – 1086, pt 1, *British Numis J*, 50, 20–49

Metcalf, D M, 1984 Monetary circulation in southern England in the first half of the eighth century, in D H Hill & D M Metcalf (eds), *Sceattas in England and on the continent: the seventh Oxford symposium on coinage and monetary history*, BAR Brit Ser 128, Oxford, 27–69

Metcalf, D M, 1998 The monetary economy of ninth-century England south of the Humber: a topographical analysis, in M A S Blackburn & D N Dumville (eds), *Kings, currency and alliances: Southern England in the 9th century*, Woodbridge, 167–97

Metcalf, M, 1988 The coins, in Andrews 1988, 17–59

Middleton, P, 1979 Army supply in Roman Gaul: an hypothesis for Roman Britain, in B C Burnham & H B Johnson (eds) *Invasion and response: the case of Roman Britain*, BAR Brit Ser 73, Oxford, 81–97

Millar, C, 1974 The Roman settlement of Harlow, Essex, unpub BA dissertation, Univ Leicester

Miller, E, & Hatcher, J, 1978 *Medieval England. Towns, commerce and crafts 1086 – 1348*, London

Miller, T E, 1989 Excavations at Great Chesterford churchyard, Essex, 1986, *Proceedings of the Cam-*

bridgeshire Antiquarian Society 77 (for 1988), 109–18

Miller, T E, 1996 The Romano-British temple precinct at Great Chesterford, Essex, *Proc Cambridge Antiq Soc*, 84 (for 1995), 15–58

Millett, M, 1979a An approach to the functional interpretation of pottery, in Millett 1979b, 35–48

Millett, M (ed), 1979b *Pottery and the archaeologist*, Inst Archaeol Occ Pub, 4, London

Millett, M, 1984 Forts and the origins of towns: cause or effect?, in Blagg & King (eds) 1984, 65–75

Millett, M, 1990 *The Romanization of Britain: an essay in archaeological interpretation*, Cambridge

Millett, M, 1991 Roman towns and their territories: an archaeological perspective, in Rich & Wallace-Hadrill 1991, 169–89

Millett, M, 2001 Approaches to urban societies', in James & Millett 2001, 60–6

Millett, M, & Graham, D, 1986 *Excavation on the Roman-British small town at Neatham, Hants, 1969–79*, Hampshire Fld Club Archaeol Soc Monogr, 3, Gloucester

Millett, M, & James, S, 1983 Excavations at Cowdery's Down, Hampshire, 1978–81, *Archaeol J*, 140, 151–279

Millett, M, Orton, C, Roskams, S, & Evans, J, nd, Residuality, in *Urban themes, AD 1000–1600*, unpub CBA report, 4–6

Milligan, B, 1982 Pottery, in J G Coad & A D F Streeten (eds), Excavations in Castle Acre, Norfolk 1972–7, *Archaeol J*, 139, 199–227

Milne, G, & Richards, J D, 1992 *Two Anglo-Saxon buildings and associated finds*, York Univ Archaeol Pub, 9, York

Milne, G, & Wardle, A, 1995 Early Roman development at Leadenhall Court, London and related research, *Trans London Middlesex Archaeol Soc*, 44, 23–169

Milton, B H, 1986 Excavations in Braintree 1980 and 1984, *Essex Archaeol Hist*, 17, 82–95

Mirza, M N, & Dungworth, D B, 1995 The potential misuse of genetic analyses and the social construction of 'race' and 'ethnicity', *Oxford J Archaeol*, 14.3, 345–54

Moffett, L, 1994 Charred cereals from some ovens/kilns in late Saxon Stafford and the evidence for the pre-*burh* economy, in Rackham 1994c, 55–64

Molleson, T I, 1988 Urban bones: the skeletal evidence for environmental change, *Actes 3 Journées Anthropol Notes, Mono Techniques*, 24, 143–58

Molleson, T I, 1993 The human remains, in Farwell & Molleson 1993, 142–215

Molleson, T I, & Cox, M, 1993 *The Spitalfields project. Vol 2 the anthropology. The middling sort*, CBA Res Rep 86, York

Moorhouse, S, 1978 Documentary evidence for the uses of medieval pottery; an interim statement, *Medieval Ceram*, 2, 3–21

Moreno-Garcia, M, Orton, C, & Rackham, D J, 1996 A new statistical tool for comparing animal bone assemblages, *J Archaeol Sci* 23, 437–53

Morris, A E J, 1979 *History of urban form*, London

Morris, R, 1989 *Churches in the landscape*, London

Morton, A D (ed), 1992 *Excavations at* Hamwic, *Vol 1: excavations 1946–83*, CBA Res Rep 84, York

Mumford, L, 1961 *The city in history*, Harmondsworth

Murphy, M, 1995 *The fuel supply of medieval London 1300–1400*, J British Institute Paris Special Edn

Murphy, M, & Galloway, J A, 1992 Marketing animals and animal products in London's hinterland circa 1300, *Anthropozoologica* 16, 93–100

Murphy, P, 1994 The Anglo-Saxon landscape and rural economy: some results from sites in East Anglia and Essex, in Rackham 1994c, 23–39

Murphy, P, 1997 *Plant macrofossils from a late Roman farm, Great Holts Farm, Boreham, Essex*, English Heritage AM Lab report 7/97

Neal, D S, Wardle, A, & Hunn, J, 1990 *Excavations of the Iron Age, Roman and medieval settlement at Gorhambury, St Albans*, English Heritage Archaeol Rep, 14, London

Neave, S, 1993 Rural settlement contraction in the East Riding of Yorkshire between the mid-seventeenth and mid-eighteenth centuries, *Agr Hist Rev*, 41, 124–36

Needham, S, & Macklin, M, (eds), 1992 *Archaeology under alluvium: papers presented at the British Museum conference, January 1991*, Oxford

Newman, J, 1992 The late Roman and Anglo-Saxon settlement in the Sandlings of Suffolk, in Carver 1992, 25–38

Newman, J, 1995 Metal detector finds and fieldwork on Anglo-Saxon sites in Suffolk, in D Griffiths (ed), *Anglo-Saxon Stud Archaeol Hist*, 8, Oxford, 87–93

Niblett, B R K, 1985 *Sheepen: an early Roman industrial site at Camulodunum*, CBA Res Rep 57, London

Niblett, B R K, & Thompson, I, forthcoming *Alban's buried towns: an assessment of St Albans archaeology up to AD 1600*, London

Noddle, B, 1978 The animal bones, in Wade Martins 1978, 375–411

O'Connor, T P, 1982 *Animal bones from Flaxengate, Lincoln c. 870–1500*, The archaeology of Lincoln 18.1, London

O'Connor, T P, 1982b The archaeozoological interpretation of morphometric variability in British sheep limb bones, unpublished PhD Thesis, University of London

O'Connor, T P, 1984 *Selected groups of bones from Skeldergate and Walmgate*, The Archaeology of York 15/1, York

O'Connor, T P, 1989a Deciding priorities with urban bones: York as a case study, in Serjeantson & Waldron 1989, 189–200

O'Connor, T P, 1989b What shall we have for dinner? Food remains from urban sites, in Serjeantson & Waldron 1989, 13–23

O'Connor, T P, 1991 *Bones from 46–54 Fishergate*, The Archaeology of York 15/4, York

O'Connor, T P, 1993 Process and terminology in mammal carcass reduction, *Int J Osteoarchaeology*, 3, 63–7

O'Connor, T P, 1994 8th–11th century economy and environment in York, in Rackham 1994c, 136–47

O'Connor, T P, 1996 A critical overview of archaeological

animal bone studies, *World Archaeol*, 28(1), 5–19

O'Connor, T P, 2000 Human refuse as a major ecological factor in medieval urban vertebrate communities, in G Bailey, R Charles, & N Winder (eds), *Human ecodynamics*, Oxford

Olivier, A, 1995 *Archaeology review 1994–1995*, London

Olivier, A, 1996 *Frameworks for our past: a review of research frameworks, strategies and perception*, London

Oosthuizen, S, & James, N, 1999 The south-west Cambridgeshire project: interim report 1998–9, *Medieval Settlement Research Group Annual Report*, 14, 17–25

Oota, H, Saitou, N, Matsushita, T, & Ueda S, 1995 A genetic study of 2,000 year old human remains from Japan using mitochondrial DNA sequences, *American J Physical Anthropol*, 98, 133–45

Ordnance Survey, 1991 *Map of Roman Britain* (3rd edn), Southampton

Ortner, D J, & Putschar, W G J, 1981 *Identification of pathological conditions in human skeletal remains*, Washington DC

Orton, C R, 1996 Dem dry bones, in J L Bird, M Hassall, & H L Sheldon (eds), *Interpreting Roman London: studies in honour of Hugh Chapman*, London, 199–208

Orton, C R, & Orton, J, 1975 It's later than you think: a statistical look at an archaeological problem, *London Archaeol*, 2.11, 285–7

Orton, C R, & Tyers, P A, 1992 Counting broken objects: the statistics of ceramic assemblages, in Pollard 1992, 163–84

Orton, C R, Tyers, P A, & Vince, A, 1993 *Pottery in archaeology*, Cambridge

Palliser, D, 1997 English medieval cities and towns, *J Urban Hist*, 474–87

Pantin, W A, 1962–3 The merchants' houses and warehouses of King's Lynn, *Medieval Archaeol*, 6–7, 173–81

Parkins, H (ed), 1997 *Roman urbanism: beyond the consumer city*, London & New York

Parsons, D, 1990 Review and prospect: the stone industry in Roman, Anglo-Saxon and medieval England, in D Parsons (ed) *Stone quarrying and building in England AD43–1525*, Sussex, 1–16

Payne, S, 1972 On the interpretation of bone samples from archaeological sites, in E S Higgs (ed), *Papers in economic prehistory*, Cambridge, 65–81

Payne, S, 1973 Kill-off patterns in sheep and goats: the mandibles from Asvan Kale, *Anatolian Studies*, 23, 281–303

Peacock, D P S, 1969 A contribution to the study of Glastonbury ware from south-western Britain, *Antiq J*, 49, 41–61

Perkins, D, 1973 A critique on the methods of quantifying faunal remains from archaeological sites, in J Matolcsi (ed), *Domestikationsforschung unde Geschichte der Haustiere*, Budapest, 367–69

Perring, D, 1991a *Roman London*, London

Perring, D, 1991b Spatial organization and social change in Roman towns, in Rich & Wallace-Haddrill 1991, 273–93

Perring, D, 2002 *The Roman house in Britain*, London

Pestell, T, 2000 Monastic foundation strategies in the early Norman diocese of Norwich, *Anglo-Norman Studies*, 23, 199–229

Petit, J-P, Mangin, M, & Brunella, P (eds), 1994 *Les agglomérations secondaires; La Gaule Belgique, les Germanies et l'occident romain*, Paris

Phythian-Adams, C, 1979 *Desolation of a city. Coventry and the urban crisis of the late Middle Ages*, Cambridge

Phythian-Adams, C, 1987 *Re-thinking English local history*, Leicester

Pirenne, H, 1925 *Medieval cities: their origins and the rebirth of trade*, Princeton

Pirie, E J E, 1987 Phases and groups within the styca coinage of Northumbria, in D M Metcalf (ed), *Coinage in ninth-century Northumbria*, BAR Brit Ser 180, 103–47

Pollard, A M (ed), 1992 *New developments in archaeological science*, Proc British Academy 77, Oxford

Pollard, R, 1990 Quantification: towards a standard practice, *J Roman Pottery Stud* 3, 75–9

Pomel, M G, 1984 A study of later Roman pottery groups in Southern Britain: fabrics, forms and chronology, unpub M Phil thesis, Univ London

Ponting, M, 1994 Folles and forgeries: an appraisal of the composition of Roman copper alloy coinage, unpub PhD thesis, Univ London

Ponting, M, & Zeepvat, R J, 1994 The coin blanks and pellets, in R J Zeepvat, A Roman coin manufacturing hoard from Magiovinum, Fenny Stratford, Bucks, *Britannia* 25, 5–15: an economic history of Britain in the Middle Ages

Postan, M, 1975 *The medieval economy and society*, Harmondsworth

Power, E, 1941 *The wool trade in English medieval history*, Oxford

Powlesland, D 1998 The West Heslerton assessment, *Internet Archaeology*, 5

Price, J, & Cottam, S, 1998 *Romano-British glass vessels: a handbook*, York

Priddy, D & Buckley, D G, 1987 *Excavations at Woodham Walter and an assessment of Essex enclosures*, East Anglian Archaeol, 33, Chelmsford

Pritchard, F A, 1988 Ornamental stonework from Roman London, *Britannia* 19, 169–89

Pryor, F, French, L, Crowther, D, Gurney, D, Simpson, G, & Taylor, M, 1985 *The Fenland project No 1: Archaeology and environment in the Lower Welland Valley*, East Anglian Archaeol, 27, Cambridge

Purcell, N, 1995 The Roman villa and the landscape of production', in Cornell & Lomas 1995, 151–80

Rackham, D J, 1981 The animal remains, in B Harbottle & B A Ellison, An excavation in the Castle Ditch, Newcastle upon Tyne, 1974–6, *Archaeologia Aeliana* 5. 9, 75–250

Rackham, D J, 1983 Faunal sample to subsistence economy: some problems in reconstruction, in M Jones (ed), *Integrating the subsistence economy*, BAR Int Ser 181, Oxford, 251–78

Rackham, D J, 1986a A comparison of methods of age

determination from the mandibular dentition of an archaeological sample of cattle, in E Cruwys & R A Foley (eds), *Teeth and archaeology*, BAR Int Ser 291, Oxford, 149–68

Rackham, D J, 1986b Assessing the relative frequencies of species by the application of a stochastic model to a zooarchaeological database, in L Wijngaarden-Bakker (ed), Database management and Zooarchaeology, *J European Study Group of Physical, Chemical, Biological and Mathematical techniques applied to Archaeology*, Research Volume 40, 00–00

Rackham, D J, 1987 Practicality and realism in archaeozoological analysis and reconstruction, in C F Gaffney & V C Gaffney, *Pragmatic archaeology. Theory in crisis*, BAR Brit Ser 167, Oxford 47–70

Rackham, D J, 1994a *Animal bones*, London

Rackham, D J, 1994b Economy and environment in Saxon London, in Rackham 1994c, 126–35

Rackham, D J (ed), 1994c *Environment and economy in Anglo-Saxon England,* CBA Res Rep 89, York

Rackham, D J, 1996 Chapter 12, in C D Morris, C E Batey, & D J Rackham, *Freswick Links, Caithness. Excavations and survey 1980–1984*, Stroud

Rackham, J, & Sidell, J, 2000 London's landscapes: the changing environment, in *The archaeology of Greater London* (Museum of London), Lavenham, 11–28

Rackham, O, 1972 Grundle House: on the quantities of timber in certain East Anglian buildings in relation to local supply, *Vernacular Architect*, 3, 3–9

Rackham, O, 1982 The growing and transport of timber and underwood, in S McGrail (ed), *Woodworking techniques before 1500*, BAR Int Ser 129, Oxford, 199–218

Rackham, O, 1990 *Trees and woodland in the British landscape* (2nd edn), London

Rackham, O, 1996 Ecology and pseudo-ecology: the example of ancient Greece, in Shipley & Salmon 1996, 16–43

Raglan, Lord, 1963 The origin of vernacular architecture, in I L L Foster & L Alcock (eds), *Culture and environment. Essays in honour of Sir Cyril Fox*, London, 373–89

Rahtz, P A, 1973 Monasteries as settlements, *Scott Archaeol Forum*, 5, 125–35

Rahtz, P A, 1976 The building plan of Whitby Abbey, in Wilson 1976, 459–62

Redman, C L, 1979 Description and inference with the late medieval pottery from Qsar es-Seghir, Morocco, *Medieval Ceram*, 3, 63–80

Reece, R, 1974a Clustering of coin finds in Britain, France and Italy, in Casey & Reece 1974, 64–77

Reece, R, 1974b Numerical aspects of Roman coin hoards in Britain, in Casey & Reece 1974, 78–95

Reece, R, 1980 Town and country; the end of Roman Britain, *World Archaeol*, 12/1, 77–92

Reece, R, 1987 *Coinage in Roman Britain*, London

Reece, R, 1989 Coins and villas, in Branigan & Miles 1989, 34–41

Reece, R, 1991 *Roman coins from 140 sites in Britain*, Cirencester

Reece, R, 1993 British sites and their Roman coins, *Antiquity*, 67, 863–9

Reece, R, 1995 Site-finds in Roman Britain, *Britannia*, 26, 179–206

Reece, R, & Crummy, N, 1987 *The coins from excavations 1971–9*, Colchester Archaeol Rep, 4, Colchester

Renfrew, C, 1974 Space, time and polity, in M Rowlands & J Friedman (eds), *The evolution of social systems*, London, 89–114

Renfrew, C, & Shennan, S (eds), 1982 *Ranking, resource and exchange: aspects of the archaeology of early European society*, Cambridge

Reynolds, S, 1977 *Introduction to the history of English medieval towns*, Oxford

Reynolds, S, 1994 *Fiefs and vassals. The medieval evidence reinterpreted*, Oxford

Rich, J, & Wallace-Hadrill, A, (eds), 1991 *City and country in the ancient world*, London

Richards, J D 1996 Putting the site in its setting: GIS and the search for Anglo-Saxon settlements in Northumbria, in H Kamermans & K Fennema (eds), *Interfacing the past*: CAA95, Analecta Praehistorica Leidensa 28, Leiden, 377–86

Richards, J D, 1999 What's so special about 'productive sites'?, in T Dickinson & D Griffiths (eds), *The making of kingdoms*, Anglo-Saxon Stud Archaeol History, 10, Oxford

Richardson, S, & Trueman, M, in prep, *MPP stone quarrying industry: step 3*, Lancaster Univ Archaeol Unit report

Rigby, S H, 1993 *Medieval Grimsby: growth and decline*, Hull

Ringrose, T J, 1993 Bone counts and statistics: a critique, *J Archaeol Sci*, 20, 121–57

Rivet, A L F, 1964 *Town and country in Roman Britain* (2nd edn), Hutchinson University Library, London

Roberts, B K, 1982 Village forms in Warwickshire: a preliminary discussion, in Slater & Jarvis 1982, 125–47

Roberts, B K, 1985 Village patterns and forms: some models for discussion, in Hooke 1985b, 7–25

Roberts, B K, & Wrathmell, S, 1998 Dispersed settlement in England: a national view, in Everson & Williamson 1998, 95–116

Roberts, B K, & Wrathmell, S, 2000a *An atlas of rural settlement in England*, London

Roberts, B K, & Wrathmell, S, 2000b Mapping rural settlement: problems and perspectives, in J A Atkinson, I Banks, & G MacGregor (eds), *Townships to farmsteads: rural settlement studies in Scotland, England and Wales,* BAR Brit Ser 293, Oxford, 20–30

Roberts, C, & Manchester, K, 1995 *The archaeology of disease* (2nd edn), Stroud

Rodwell, K A, 1988 *The prehistoric and Roman settlement at Kelvedon, Essex*, London

Rodwell, W J, 1966 The excavation of a 'Red Hill' on Canvey Island, *Trans Essex Archaeol Soc*, 2, 14–33

Rodwell, W.J, 1978 Relict landscapes in Essex, in H C Bowen & P J Fowler (eds), *Early land allotment*, BAR Brit Ser 48, Oxford, 89–98

Rodwell, W J, 1982 The production and distribution of tiles in the territory of the Trinovantes, *Essex Archaeol Hist*, 14, 15–76

Rodwell, W J, & Rodwell, K A, 1985 *Rivenhall: investigations of a villa, church, and village, 1950–1977*, CBA Res Rep 55, London

Rodwell, W J, & Rodwell, K A, 1993 *Rivenhall: investigations of a villa, church, and village, 1950–1977*, Vol 2, CBA Res Rep 80, London

Rogers, N S H, 1993 *Anglian and other finds from Fishergate*, The Archaeology of York 17/9, London

Rogerson, A, 1995, *A late Neolithic, Saxon and medieval site at Middle Harling, Norfolk*, East Anglian Archaeol, 74, Chelmsford

Rogerson, A, & Adams, N, 1978 A moated site at Hempstead, near Holt, *East Anglian Archaeol*, 8, 55–72

Rogerson, A, & Silvester, R J, 1986 Middle Saxon occupation at Hay Green, Terrington St Clement, *Norfolk Archaeol*, 39, 320–2

Rook, T, Walker, S, & Denston, C B, 1984 A Roman mausoleum and associated marble sarcophagus and burials from Welwyn, Hertfordshire, *Britannia*, 15, 143–225

Roskams, S, 1996 Urban transitions in early medieval Britain: the case of York, in Christie & Loseby 1996, 262–88

Roymans, N (ed), 1996, *From the sword to the plough: three studies on the earliest Romanisation of northern Gaul*, Amsterdam

Rudling, D R, 1990 Late Iron Age and Roman Billericay: excavations 1987, *Essex Archaeol Hist*, 21, 19–47

Ryan, N S, 1988 *Fourth century coin finds from Roman Britain: a computer analysis*, BAR Brit Ser 183, Oxford

Salter, M, 1984 Compilation of age of fusion data from 12 sources, unpub Natur Hist Museum report

Saller, R, 2001 The non-agricultural economy: superceding Finley and Hopkins?, *J Roman Archaeol*, 14, 580–4

Salzman, L F, 1952 *Building in England down to 1540. A documentary history*, Oxford

Saunders, P, 1986 *Social theory and the urban question* (2nd edn), London

Saunders, T S A, 1992 Marxism and archaeology: the origins of feudalism in early medieval England, unpub PhD thesis, Univ York

Schiffer, M B, 1976 *Behavioural archaeology*, New York

Schmid, E, 1972 *Atlas of animal bones*, Amsterdam, London and New York

Schofield, A J (ed), 1991 *Interpreting artefact scatters: contributions to ploughzone archaeology*, Oxford

Schofield, J A, 1984 *The building of London from the Conquest to the Great Fire*, London

Schofield, J A, 1987 Archaeology in the City of London: archive and publication, *Archaeol J*, 144, 424–33

Schofield. J A, 1995 *Medieval London houses*, New Haven

Schofield, J A, & Maloney, C (eds), 1998 *Archaeology in the City of London, 1907–91: a guide to records of excavations by the Museum of London*, Lavenham

Schofield, J A, & Vince, A, 1994 *Medieval towns*, Leicester

Schofield, J, Allen, P, & Taylor, C, 1990 Medieval buildings and property development in the area of Cheap-

side, *Trans London Middlesex Archaeol Soc*, 41, 39–238

Schour, I, & Massler, M, 1941 *Development of human dentition* (2nd edn), Chicago

Scott, E, 1993 *A gazetteer of Roman villas in Britain*, Leicester

Scott, S, 1994 Patterns of movement: architectural design and visual planning in the Romano-British villa, in G Locock (ed), *Meaningful architecture: social interpretations of buildings*, Worldwide Archaeol Series, Avebury, 86–98

Scull, C, 1993 Archaeology, early Anglo-Saxon society and the origins of Anglo-Saxon kingdoms, in W Filmer-Sankey (ed), *Anglo Saxon Stud Archaeol Hist*, 6, 65–82

Scull, C, 1997 Urban centres in pre-Viking England?, in J Hines (ed), *The Anglo-Saxons from the migration period to the eighth century: an ethnographical perspective*, Woodbridge, 269–310

Scull, C, 2001 Burials at *emporia* in England, in D Hill & R Cowie (eds), *Wics: the early medieval trading centres of northern Europe*, Sheffield, 67–74

Sealey, P A, 1995 New light on the salt industry and Red Hills of prehistoric and Roman Essex, *Essex Archaeol Hist* 26, 65–81

Serjeantson, D, & Waldron, T, (eds), 1989 *Diet and crafts in towns: the evidence of animal remains from the Roman to the post-medieval periods*, BAR Brit Ser 199, Oxford

Shepherd, J D (ed), 1998 *Archaeology in the City of London, 1946–72: a guide to the excavations by Professor W F Grimes held by the Museum of London*, Lavenham

Sheppard, E, (ed) forthcoming *Norwich Castle Mall excavations*

Shimmin, D, 1994 Excavations at Osborne Street, Colchester, *Essex Archaeol Hist*, 25, 46–59

Shimmin, D, & Carter, G, 1996 Excavations at Angel Yard, High Street, Colchester 1986 and 1989, *Essex Archaeol Hist*, 27, 35–83

Shipley, G, & Salmon, J, (eds), 1996 *Human landscapes in classical antiquity: environment and culture*, London & New York

Shipman, P, 1981 *Life history of a fossil: an introdution to taphonomy and paleoecology*, Cambridge, Mass

Shirley, E A M, 2000 *The construction of the Roman legionary fortress at Inchtuthil*, BAR Brit Ser 298, Oxford

Shotter, D C A, 1989 Roman coin finds in Cumbria, *Trans Cumberland Westmorland Antiq Archaeol Soc*, 89, 41–50

Shotter, D C A, 1990 Roman coins, in M J McCarthy & C M Brooks (eds), *A Roman, Anglian and medieval site at Blackfriars Street, Carlisle*, Kendal

Silvester, R J, 1988 *The Fenland project No 3: Norfolk survey, marshland and Nar Valley*, East Anglian Archaeol, 45

Silvester, R J, 1991 *The Fenland project No 4: The Wissey Embayment and the Fen Causeway, Norfolk*, East Anglian Archaeol, 52

Simmons, I G, 1996 *Changing the face of the earth. Cul-

ture, environment, history (2nd edn), Blackwell, Oxford

Simon, J L, 1981 *The ultimate resource*, Oxford

Sjoberg, G, 1960 *The pre-industrial city, past and present*, Free Press, New York

Skipper, K, 1989 Wood-pasture: the landscape of the Norfolk claylands in the early-modern period, unpub MA dissertation, Univ East Anglia

Slater, T R, 1980 The analysis of burgages in medieval towns: three case studies from the West Midlands, *West Midlands Archaeol*, 21, 52–65

Slater, T R, 1982 Urban genesis and medieval town plans in Warwickshire and Worcestershire, in Slater & Jarvis 1982, 173–202

Slater, T R, 1985 The urban hierarchy in medieval Staffordshire, *J Hist Geog*, 11.2, 115–37

Slater, T R, & Jarvis, P J, (eds), 1982 *Field and forest: an historical geography of Warwickshire and Worcestershire*, Norwich

Slofstra, J, 1983 An anthropological approach to the study of Romanisation processes, in R Brandt & J Slofstra (eds), *Roman and native in the Low Countries: spheres of interaction*, BAR Int Ser 184, Oxford, 71–104

Smith, C A, 1976 Exchange systems and the spatial distribution of elites: the organisation of stratification in agrarian societies, in C A Smith (ed), *Regional analysis*, 2, 309–74

Smith, J T, 1997 *Roman villas: a study in social structure*, London & New York, Routledge

Smoothy, M D, 1989 A Roman rural site at Rayne, Essex: excavations 1987, *Essex Archaeol Hist*, 20, 1–29

Snooks, G D, 1995 The dynamic role of the market in the Anglo-Norman economy and beyond, 1086–1300, in Britnell & Campbell 1995, 27–55

Soderstrom, O, 1993 Spectacle ecology, human ecology and crisis of urbanity, in D Steiner & M Nauser (eds), *Human ecology. Fragments of anti-fragmentary views of the world*, Routledge, London, 331–45

Southall, A, 1998 *The city in time and space*, Cambridge University Press

Southgate, D, Sanders, J, & Thin, S, 1990 The causes of land degradation in Africa and Latin America: population pressure, politics and property arrangements, *American J Agricultural Economics*, 72, 1259–63

Speth, J D, & Spielmann, K A, 1983 Energy source, protein metabolism and hunter-gatherer subsistence strategies, *J Anthropological Archaeol*, 2, 1–31

Spufford, M, 1974 *Contrasting communities: English villagers in the sixteenth and seventeenth centuries*, Cambridge

Steedman, K, 1994 Excavation of a Saxon site at Riby Crossroads, Lincolnshire, *Archaeol J*, 151, 212–306

Stirland, A, 1991 Diagnosis of occupationally related pathology: can it be done?, in D T Ortner & A C Aufterheide (eds), *Human palaeopathology: current synthesis and future options*, Smithsonian Institution Press, 40–7

Straker, V, 1987 Carbonised grain, in P Marsden, *The Roman forum site in London: discoveries before 1985*, London, 151–3

Stren, R, White R, & Whitney, J (eds), 1992 *Sustainable cities: urbanization and the environment in international perspective*, Oxford

Stuart-Macadam, P, 1991 Anaemia in Roman Britain: Poundbury Camp, in Bush & Zvelebil 1991, 101–14

Suchey, J M, Wisely, D V, & Katz, D, 1988 Evaluation of the Todd & McKern Stewart methods for aging the male os pubis', in K J Reichs (ed), *Forensic osteology*, Springfield, 33–67

Suffolk County Council Archaeology Service, 1996, *Annual Report 1995/6*, Suffolk

Sundick, R I, 1978 Human skeletal growth and age determination, *Homo*, 30, 297–333

Swan, V G, 1984 *The pottery kilns of Roman Britain*, RCHM Supp Ser, 5, London

Swift, E, 2000 *Regionality in dress accessories in the late Roman west*, Montagnac

Symonds, R, & Wade, S, 1999 *Roman pottery from excavations in Colchester, 1971–1988*, Colchester

Tatton-Brown, T, 1991 Medieval building stone at the Tower of London, *London Archaeol*, 6.13, 361–6

Taylor, C, 1972 The study of settlement patterns in pre-Saxon England' in P J Ucko, R Tringham, & G W Dimbleby (eds), *Man, settlement and urbanism*, London, 109–13

Taylor, J, 2001 Rural society in Roman Britain, in James & Millett 2001, 46–59

Thirsk, J (ed), 1967 *The agrarian history of England, Vol IV*, Cambridge

Thirsk, J, 1987 *Agricultural regions and agrarian history in England 1500–1750*, London

Thomas, C, (ed), 1983 *Research objectives in British archaeology*, London

Thomas, J, 1991 The hollow men? A reply to Steve Mithen, *Proc Prehist Soc*, 57–2, 15–20

Thomas, K D, 1993 Molecular biology and archaeology, *World Archaeol*, 25.1, 1–17

Tilley, C, 1990 Structuralism and beyond, in C Tilley (ed), *Reading material culture: structuralism, hermeneutics and post-structuralism*. Oxford, 3–85

Timby, J, 1988 The Middle Saxon pottery, in Andrews 1988, 73–124

Todd, M, 1970 The small towns of Roman Britain, *Britannia*, 1, 114–30

Todd, M, 1989a Villa and fundus, in Branigan & Miles 1989, 14–20

Todd, M (ed), 1989b *Research in Roman Britain: 1960–89*, Britannia monogr, 11, London

Tomber, R A, 1988 Multivariate statistics and assemblage comparison, in C L N Ruggles & S P Q Rahtz, *Computer and quantitative methods in archaeology 1987*, BAR Int Ser 393, Oxford, 29–38

Toynbee, J M C, 1971 *Death and burial in the Roman world*, Baltimore

Trotter, M, & Gleser, G C, 1952 Estimation of stature from long bones of American whites and negroes, *American J Physical Anthropol*, 10, 463–514

Trotter, M, & Gleser, G C, 1958 A re-evaluation of estimation of stature based on measurements of stature taken during life and long bones after death, *American J Physical Anthropol*, 16, 79–123

Trow, S D, 1990 By the northern shores of Ocean: some observations on acculturation process at the edge of the Roman world, in T F C Blagg & M Millett (eds), *The early Roman empire in the West*, Oxford, 103–18

Turner, B R G, 1999 *Excavations of an Iron Age settlement and Roman religious complex at Ivy Chimneys, Witham, Essex, 1978–83*, Chelmsford

Tyers, I, Hillam, J, & Groves, C, 1994 Trees and woodland in the Saxon period: the dendrochronological evidence, in Rackham 1994c, 12–22

Tyson, R, 2000 *Medieval glass vessels found in England c. AD 1200–1500*, CBA Res Rep 121, York

Ubelaker, D H, 1989 *Reconstruction of demographic profiles from ossuary skeletal samples (case study from Tidewater, Potomac)*, Smithsonian Contributions to Anthropology, 18, Washington DC

Uerpmann, H-P, 1973 Animal bone finds and economic archaeology: a critical study of the osteo-archaeological method, *World Archaeol*, 4, 307–22

van Andel, T H, & Runnel, C N, 1988 An essay on the 'emergence of civilisation' in the Aegean world, *Antiquity*, 62, 234–47

Van der Veen, M, 1992 *Crop husbandry regimes*, Sheffield Archaeol Monogr, 3, Sheffield

Verhulst, A, 1997 Medieval socio-economic historiography in Western Europe: towards an integrated approach, *J Medieval Hist*, 23 1, 89–101

Vince, A, 1989 The petrography of Saxon and early medieval pottery in the Thames valley, in J Henderson (ed), *Scientific analysis in archaeology and its interpretation*, Oxford Univ Comm Archaeol Monogr, 19, Oxford, 163–77

Vince, A, 1994 Saxon urban economies: an archaeological perspective, in Rackham 1994c, 108–19

Vita-Finzi, D, & Higgs E S, 1970 Prehistoric economy in the Mount Carmel area of Palestine: site catchment analysis, *Proc Prehist Soc*, 36, 1–37

Wacher, J, 1995 *The towns of Roman Britain* (2nd edn), London

Wackernagel, M, & Rees, W, 1996, *Our ecological footprint*, Canada

Wade, K, 1978 An early medieval settlement at Wicken Bonhunt, in Buckley 1978, 96–102

Wade, K, 1983 A model for Anglo-Saxon settlement expansion in the Witton area, in A Lawson (ed), *The archaeology of Witton, near North Walsham*, East Anglian Archaeol, 18, Chelmsford, 74–77

Wade, K, 1988 Ipswich, in Hodges & Hobley 1988, 93–100

Wade, K, 1997 Anglo-Saxon and medieval (rural), in Glazebrook 1997, 47–58

Wade-Martins, P, 1978 *Excavations in North Elmham Park, 1967–72*, East Anglian Archaeol, 9, Chelmsford

Wade-Martins, P, 1980 *Village sites in Launditch Hundred*, East Anglian Archaeol, 10, Dereham

Wade-Martins, S, & Williamson, T, 1999 *Roots of change: farming and the landscape in East Anglia* c. 1700–1870, Agric Hist Rev Supp Ser, 2, Exeter

Wager, S J, 1998, *Woods, wolds and groves: The woodlands of medieval Warwickshire*, BAR Brit Ser 269, Oxford

Wagstaff, M, 1991 The archaeological 'site' from a geographical perspective, in Schofield 1991, 9–10

Waldron, T, 1994, *Counting the dead. The epidemiology of skeletal populations*, Chichester

Wallace, C, & Turner-Walker, C, 1998 The Roman pottery, in Clarke 1998, 98–112

Wallace, P F, 1985 The archaeology of Viking Dublin, in H B Clark & A Simms (eds), *The comparative history of urban origins in non-Roman Europe*, BAR Int Ser 255.2

Wallace-Hadrill, A, 1991 Introduction, in Rich & Wallace-Hadrill 1991, ix ff

Wallis, S, 1988 On the outskirts of Roman Chelmsford: excavations at Lasts Garage 1987, *Essex Archaeol Hist*, 19, 40–6

Wallsgrove, S, 1992 *Kenilworth 1086–1756*, Kenilworth

Ward-Perkins, J B, 1984 *From classical antiquity to the Middle Ages. Urban public building in northern and central Italy AD 300–850*, London

Warner, P, 1996 *The origins of Suffolk*, Manchester

Warnock, P J, & Reinhard, K J, 1992 Methods for extracting pollen and parasite eggs from latrine soils, *J Archaeol Sci* 19, 261–4

Warwick, R, 1968 The skeletal remains, in L P Wenham, *The Romano-British cemetery at Trentholme Drive, York*, London

Watson, J P N, 1972 Fragmentation analysis of animal bone samples from archaeological sites, *Archaeometry* 14, 221–7

Watson, J P N, 1979 The estimation of the relative frequencies of mammalian species: Khirokitia 1972, *J Archaeol Sci*, 6, 127–37

WCED: World Commission on Environment and Development, 1987 *Our common future 'The Brundtland report'*, Oxford

Weber, M, 1958, *The city* (trans D Martindale & G Neuwirth), Glencoe, Ill

Webster, G, 1966 Fort and town in early Roman Britain, in J S Wacher (ed), *The civitas capitals of Roman Britain*, Leicester

Webster, G, 1978 *Boudica: the British revolt against Rome, AD 60*, London

Webster, G, 1980 *The Roman conquest of Britain*, London

Webster, G (ed), 1988 *Fortress into city. The consolidation of Roman Britain, first century AD*, London

Webster, G, & Backhouse, J, 1991 *The making of England: Anglo-Saxon art and culture, AD 600–900*, London

Wells, C, 1977 Disease of the maxillary sinus in antiquity, *Medical Biol Illus*, 27, 173–8

Wells, P S, 1986 Europe's first towns and entrepreneurs, *Archaeology*, 39. 6, 26–31

West Yorkshire Metropolitan County Council, 1981 *West Yorkshire: an archaeological survey to AD 1500* (ed M L Faull & S A Moorhouse), Leeds

West, S, 1985 *West Stow: the Anglo-Saxon village*, East Anglian Archaeol, 24, Ipswich

West, S, & Wade, K, 1983 The origin and development of

the Kingdom of East Anglia project: provisional research design, *Bull Sutton Hoo Res Comm*, 1, 18–20

White, R, & van Leusen, M, 1997 Aspects of Romanization in the Wroxeter hinterland, in Meadows *et al* 1996, 133–43

Whittaker, C R, 1990 The consumer city revisited; the vicus and the city, *J Roman Archaeol*, 3, 110–18

Whittaker, C R, 1995 Do theories of the ancient city matter?, in Cornell & Lomas 1995, 9–26

Whittaker, C R, 1997 Imperialism and culture: the Roman initiative, in Mattingly 1997, 143–64

Whittaker, D, 2000 Ageing from the dentition, in Cox & Mays 2000, 83–99

Wickenden, N P, 1986 Prehistoric settlement and the Romano-British small town at Heybridge, Essex, *Essex Archaeol Hist*, 17, 7–68

Wickenden, N P, 1988 *Excavations at Great Dunmow, Essex: A Romano-British small town in the Trinovantian civitas*, Essex County Council, Chelmsford

Wickenden, N P, 1992 *The temple and other sites in the north-eastern sector of Caesaromagus*, London

Wickham, C, 1984 The other transition: from the ancient world to feudalism, *Past and Present*, 103, 3–36

Wickham, C, 1988 Mark, Sherlock Holmes and late Roman commerce, *J Roman Stud*, 78 183–93

Wickham, C, 1994 *Land and power: studies in Italian and European social history, 400–1200*, London

Wild, C J, & Nichol, R K, 1983 Estimation of the original number of individuals from paired bone counts using estimators of the Krantz type, *J Field Archaeol*, 10, 337–44

Wilkinson, T J, 1998 Archaeology and Environment in South Essex. *Rescue Archaeology along the Gray's by-pass 1979/80*, East Anglian Archaeol, 42, Chelmsford

Williams, J H, 1971 Roman building materials in south-east England, *Britannia* 2, 166–95

Williams, J H, Shaw, M, & Denham, V, 1985 *Middle Saxon palaces at Northampton*, Northampton

Williamson, T, 1988 Settlement chronology and regional landscapes: the evidence from the claylands of East Anglia and Essex, in Hooke 1988b, 153–75

Williamson, T, 1993 *The origins of Norfolk*, Manchester

Williamson, T, 1995 Land use and landscape change in the Norfolk claylands c.1700–c.1870, *The Annual: Bull Norfolk Archaeol Hist Res Group*, 4, 44–58

Williamson, T, 1998 Questions of preservation and destruction, in Everson & Williamson 1998, 1–24

Willis, S, 1990 Mould-decorated south Gaulish colour-coated cups from Fingringhoe Wick, Essex, *J Roman Pottery Stud*, 3, 30–4

Willis, S, 1994 Roman imports into late Iron Age British societies: towards a critique of existing models, in S Cottam, D Dungworth, S Scott, & J Taylor (eds) *Proc Fourth Annual Theoretical Roman Archaeology Conference*, Oxford, 141–50

Willis, S, 1996 The Romanization of pottery assemblages in the east and north-east of England during the first century AD: a comparative analysis, *Britannia*, 27, 179–222

Willis, S, 1997 The English Heritage samian project. Report on the results of phase 1: the pilot survey', unpub Univ Durham report

Wilmott, T, 1982 Water supply in the Roman city of London, *London Archaeol*, 49, 234–42

Wilmott, T, 1983 Roman timber lined wells in the city of London: further excavations, *Trans London Middlesex Archaeol Soc*, 35, 5–11

Wilmott, T, 1996 Whitby Abbey, North Yorkshire: archaeological evaluation assessment report, unpub English Heritage report (CAS Project 490)

Wilson, B, 1994a Mortality patterns, animal husbandry and marketing in and around medieval and post-medieval Oxford, in Hall & Kenward 1994, 103–115

Wilson, B, 1994b Projects modelling the spatial patterning of bone: limited success in publication, in Luff & Rowley-Conwy 1994, 57–68

Wilson, B, 1996 *Spatial patterning among animal bones in settlement archaeology*, BAR Brit Ser 251, Oxford

Wilson, B, Grigson, C, & Payne, S (eds), 1982 *Ageing and sexing animal bones from archaeological sites*, BAR Brit Ser 109, Oxford

Wilson, D M, (ed), 1976 *The archaeology of Anglo-Saxon England*, Cambridge

Winder, J M, 1992 A study of the variation in oyster shells from archaeological sites and a discussion of oyster exploitation, unpub D Phil thesis, Univ Southampton

Winder, N, 1993 Using modern bone assemblages to estimate ancient populations, *Circaea*, 10.2 (for 1992), 63–8

Woodcock, J, Davey P, & Tomlinson P, forthcoming *The medieval pottery database*

Woolf, G, 1990 World systems analysis and the Roman Empire, *J Roman Archaeol*, 3, 44–58

Woolf, G, 1995 Romans as civilizers. The ideological preconditions of Romanization, in J Metzler, M Millett, N Roymans, & J Slofstra (eds), *Integration in the early Roman West. The role of culture and ideology*, Luxembourg, 9–18

Woolf, G, 1998 *Becoming Roman. The origins of provincial civilization in Gaul*, Cambridge

Wormald, P, 1978 Bede, 'Beowulf' and the conversion of the Anglo-Saxon aristocracy, in R T Farrell (ed), *Bede and Anglo-Saxon England*, BAR Brit Ser 46, Oxford, 32–95

Wrathmell, S, 1980 Village depopulation in the seventeenth and eighteenth centuries: examples from Northumberland, *Post-Medieval Archaeol*, 14, 113–126

Wymer, J J, and Brown, N, 1995 *North Shoebury: settlement and economy in south-east Essex 1500 BC–AD 1500*, East Anglian Archaeol, 75 Chelmsford

Young, C J, 1977 *Oxfordshire Roman pottery*, BAR Brit Ser 43, Oxford

Young, C J, (ed) 1980 *Guidelines for the processing and publication of Roman pottery from excavations*, DAMHB Occ Pap, 4, London

Index